NEW INDIANS,
OLD WARS

NEW INDIANS, OLD WARS

Elizabeth Cook-Lynn

UNIVERSITY OF ILLINOIS PRESS

Urbana and Chicago

Library of Congress Cataloging-in-Publication Data
Cook-Lynn, Elizabeth.
New Indians, old wars / Elizabeth Cook-Lynn.
p.   cm.
Includes bibliographical references.
ISBN-13: 978-0-252-03166-3 (cloth : alk. paper)
ISBN-10: 0-252-03166-0 (cloth : alk. paper)
1. Indians of North America—Historiography.
2. Indians, Treatment of—United States—History.
3. Indians of North America—Public opinion.
4. Public opinion—United States.
5. United States—Race relations.
6. United States—Politics and government.
I. Title.
E76.8.C66   2007
973.04'970072—dc22   2006100929

Keyapi: [they say this]

My grandfather's father was a scout. One time he opened a mound,
they say, and there was the skeleton of a human being. A deer
horn lay beside it. My grandfather's father always parted his hair
in the middle, and in 1876 he threw water on his horse at the
Little Big Horn River just when the battle started.

When Chou En-Lai said, "One of the delightful things about Americans is that they have absolutely no historical memory," (*Killing Hope*, William Blum), his ex post facto statement failed to take into account the history of the indigenous peoples of the continent who for a thousand years have kept their stories in their hearts. Aren't we Americans, too?

"The decimation of the native peoples in the Americas is like a haunting question which floats in the wind: Why did we allow this to happen?"

—NELSON MANDELA, 1996

CONTENTS

PREFACE

More than seven decades after the passage of the Indian Reorganization Act by the U.S. Congress, American Indians remain among the most rigidly colonized people in most democracies. The question of who will control the stories and the histories is secondary only to the question of who will control the land and the water, the gold and uranium, the coal and timber, and all of the vast resources owned by the people of the First Nations of America. They have few representatives in the governing bodies of the United States and are, as tribal nations, omitted from the many organizations of states throughout the globe. Because this is so, the act of writing by American Indians has become a survival technique of major importance in researching and analyzing the hard issues of the day. The First Nations of America are rather like Israel, a country that, according to writer Amos Oz, exists conditionally.[1] They exist not for the same reasons but, in many ways, with the same possibilities.

The irony of this comparison escapes no one, especially the Palestinians, for it is not the Israelis, they say, who are the indigenes; in fact, they are the intruders. It is not the Palestinians who are the colonizers, they say; only the tragic victims. In some respects, then, neither the Jews of Israel nor the Palestinians are the Indians of America because there is no question in America who invaded whose lands. Yet, after almost a century, American Indian nations (like the state of Israel and even the unlucky Palestinians) are not really accepted in the country of their origins.

New Indians, Old Wars, which started out as a conversation in Indian Studies, is a collection of writings about conflict and consensus. As a professor of Indian Studies and a citizen of the Sioux Nation, I've been worried for a long time about the arguments between American Indian nations and the United States over how to define the *sovereign* condition of what have been called the "nations-within-a-nation," clearly a concept of alliance seen nowhere else in the world. This collection tells much about how one can look at the dismal folly of an erosive governmental relationship because it concerns many facets of native life—the successes and meager victories as well as the haunting and terrible legacy of people of goodwill who fail as much as they succeed in seeking justice.

This collection of essays addresses the politics of writing and the conversations about how we are governed, subjects of essential importance to Indians, to lawyers and scholars, and to people in general all over the world. They are political writings that suggest that, in order to understand the perennial nature of Indian–white conflict in the United States, one must understand contemporary politics. My way of thinking about politics is everywhere in my writings and I am often confused about the nature of political thought because of what others have condemned about it.

Before I left the reservation to go to college, a German philosopher named Carl Schmitt was writing books about politics; he joined the Nazi Party, condemned liberalism, and said that all genuine political theories presuppose man to be evil.[2] He was a major precursor to some of the political figures of today who call themselves conservatives and on the Right, and he is probably controversial because he sees everything through the lens of European thought. Today, so many years later, I muse: If all political theories presuppose man to be evil, isn't that a little like Christianity? And isn't he suggesting, then, that Christianity may be at fault for the nasty political dialogue of today that has become a national disgrace? Is there no alternative to original sin?

There is, perhaps, no answer to this one, but because I've said publicly that "Indian Studies Is Politics" and because I make no bones about being a political writer, I want to make it clear that I don't agree when I hear the statement "I think humans are evil." What I mean is that we as indigenes want to direct the political discourse of the future for ourselves, rather than simply occupy space as nonpolitical entities. In my mind, political discourse is the most important conversation that Indians can have with one another, so I am always a bit disheartened when I hear opposing, derogatory statements.

At a 2004 meeting of the treaty councils in South Dakota, I heard Buzzy Antoine Black Feather, one of the respected Lakota representatives to the United Nations in Geneva, say this: "'Politics' is a dirty word in Lakota" and "we are not governed by political laws." What irony! He also said, in some sort of contradictory political thought: "We know about occupation, and we are not alone, and in the twenty-two years that I have been at the U.N. as an indigenous representative, I have found out that there are 350 million people in this world who are fighting governments worldwide." He was a brilliant native man, a man of broad experience, like many others among us. Politics, his experience tells all of us in spite of his rejoinder, is the crucial form, perhaps the only form, through which American Indians can preserve, protect, and restore the treaty environments that indigenous nations possess.

Writing in Indian Country is a sacred responsibility if the nations are to protect sovereignty. Many thinkers today believe that there is some kind of neutrality in the rules of the universe. In truth, neutrality has no agency in Indian–white relations or in the broader relations of the universe. When I wrote a collection of essays, *Why I Can't Read Wallace Stegner,*[3] I got a note from an Indian colleague from the University of Nebraska who said: "I like your writing, Liz, but the trouble is you make us choose sides."

Indeed! Indians must not withdraw unilaterally into some kind of colonial state, dependent on the Bureau of Indian Affairs or the Department of the Interior or any of the other schemes and structures of the occupational regime of America. Nor must they get to the stage in their relationship with the United States when they have no one to talk to—which is a distinct possibility unless centuries of colonization are confronted whenever and wherever they are centered. Indian Studies as an academic discipline has become the finding of the form in which writers and scholars have been able to enter into consensus as well as standoff.

All sorts of writers have written about politics and the law and they have, in many instances, seen their writings influence society and civilization both for good and evil. The same must be said about the literature and storytelling and poetry and scholarship of the First Nation natives of this country, which can move entire peoples toward expanding the powers of government and law in appropriate ways.

This text, *New Indians, Old Wars,* like an obscure chapbook of poems I wrote decades ago, is like the musings of the determined Badger, a character in Dakota Sioux storytelling, which suggest that talking, storytelling, and writing are, very simply, an effort to keep the plot moving.[4]

NEW INDIANS,
OLD WARS

INTRODUCTION

Conversations like those between Indians and their colleagues who have known, in the latter part of the twentieth century, that their sun is rising again began a long time ago. They have been long on ideas, strategies, and fiery debates. It is the hope now that these ideas and strategies and debates will move toward consensus, but no one can be sure. Consensus is not the same as reconciliation because justice—the most significant condition for reconciliation and justice for tribal nations and tribal peoples—so far at least, has been unachieved; thus, reconciliation amounts to merely a futile, empty gesture. The recent faux movement toward reconciliation stirred in some parts of Indian Country to reestablish, resolve, acquiesce; to reconcile one's self to defeat; to make compatible; or to settle is an unapproachable place at this time. On the other hand, after years of fighting back, consensus very simply means that to work toward a satisfying dialogue is the best that people of goodwill can do. "Consensus," as far as Indian tribal nations are concerned, means what Dr. Edward Valandra's recent book of the same name says it means: *not without our consent*.[1] It means fighting back, protesting, and finding solutions for that to which we can consent.

To agree that it is a sacred responsibility to write is to grasp with a sense of mission the clear knowledge of the crimes suffered by indigenous peoples in a colonized world, to listen, and to participate on one's own tribal terms in the intellectual life that emerges. This reality has pinpointed many questions: In indigenous societies, what has been the political responsibility of writers and artists? What about democracy and literature? Who frames the dialogues? What about politics and literature? Who is in charge of telling the stories, presenting the images? Of history? Of experience? Is the spiritual capital of the vast empires of the native peoples of this continent—rising as it does from the Plains, the borders, and all sections of this country—going to continue to echo throughout the history of one of the great democracies of any age? Is it going to be taken seriously? These topics are the stuff of Amerindianism, but they require the attention of the entire world these days.

The ideals of a democratic state were set in motion prior to the American Revolution when the social theorists of the time tried to say what the words "America" and "American" might come to mean. For the indigenous peoples of the continent, the policies of Americanization were to secure political freedom and liberty for the individual, ignoring and tearing down tribal and communal value systems. This meant destroying the native, indigenous past. It wasn't until the mid-eighteenth century that the original inhabitants were even considered humans with human rights, let alone Americans. And it was even later when they were considered by America to be tribal peoples with tribal histories and family names, people with the possibility of pulling themselves out of a colonial orbit that was oppressive and wrong.

Rather quickly after the American Revolution, in the view of nations on the rise, the new United States was to become the most important experiment in freedom and human rights the world had ever known. Americans of the Revolutionary period probably really believed in and cherished the notion that such ideals as individual freedom and human rights could form the basis of a just society. America was to see itself as an immigrant society and individuals came from all over the world (and still do) to participate in a version of capitalistic democracy almost unknown to the world until that time.

The native occupants who had lived on the continent for thousands of years were curiosities to the newcomers and very soon were considered enemies. However, it wasn't until the nineteenth century that the indigenous populations and their tribal ways were considered real impediments to the progress of the ideals of the newcomers, which were based on an unrelenting individualistic paradigm.

A long period of war and death was the consequence. It was realization of this consequence that spurred the critic Helen Hunt Jackson to write the classic *A Century of Dishonor* (1881),[2] the title of that work suggesting that something had gone very wrong and that she believed democracy had been forever corrupted. Were it not for the events of the twentieth century, when democracy had to be defended in Europe and other places in the world against totalitarian regimes of great power, the flaws in the development of an American immigrant society's attitude toward the indigenous population might have been calculated as a serious matter rather than as a mere nuisance with the potential for detracting from building a durable and lawful empire.

We are led to believe by most historians that democracy in Indian Country has always been a face-to-face matter, a smoking-of-the-sacred-pipe matter; in other words, tribal business in orality sustained through art and painting and exiled lives. Writing and reading about democracy in Indian Country, then, is a contradiction in terms, just like democracy is a contradiction when looked at from the vantage point of indigenism rather than from the point of view of an immigrant nation, which is what America calls itself. Unless one thinks about treaties and accords between Indian nations and the federal government of the United States of America, one will not make peace with what America has finally become in the twenty-first century: an efficient colonizer and determined assimilator known throughout the world for its power to persuade and conquer.

In this modern world, since writers have appeared on the scene in great numbers to proclaim themselves chroniclers, the keeping of records and the forming of the dialogues about history have become much admired activities in academia. On a person-to-person level, there has always been just talk, but in the book world, people are inspired to participate as literate folks who can record a bit of historical analysis of art, crimes, exaggerations, politics, or even the most mundane of events. They can claim with whatever intelligence and wit they can muster a place in the dialogue, and this has resulted in a great body of works by American Indian writers. Conversation and dialogue, analysis and definition, research and science are common and shared activities among humans of the modern world and that is what writing and telling the stories is all about. At the beginning of the twenty-first century, the First Lady of the United States, herself a librarian and, therefore, a keeper of records, was talking to news reporters in an effort to defend her decision to cancel a gathering of poets that had been set to take place at the White House in Washington, D.C. When the reporters asked if her decision to cancel was based on the awful probability that some of the poets might make critical statements in their works concerning the political actions taken by her husband's administration to go to war in Iraq (there was at that time the beginning of a "poets against the war" movement), she hedged. Her reluctant response seemed to suggest that, yes, the cancellation might have had something to do with that possibility and it was such "a pity" because, she said, "There is nothing political about American literature." It is painful for most critics, even if they are not unrelenting academic rabble-rousers like the writer of this text, to hear such a remarkable denial of the function of literature and literary studies. And history. And politics. Poetry, art, and literature and writing in general assist all of us in understanding and interpreting the world in all ways—politically, philosophically, and aesthetically.[3]

To suggest that the politics of literature and literary theory must be exempted from our discussion of the works of any writer is to censor the complex representations available to us from the vast imaginations and experiences and events called for by the human resources of our world. It is the claim of the writer of this collection of essays that not all writers create literature or art in order to agree with common thought, to seek truth and knowledge, to find answers or to persuade others to share their points of view, to reclaim history, to construct and deconstruct anything, or even to change the world. These are some of the reasons often given by writers for their works. Tom Wolfe gives the best explanation of all: "Only on the printed page can you really explain anything!"[4]

Some of us, on the other hand, write and create literature and art in order to see the world look back at us personally, politically, and collectively; to show us ourselves. This is often called the "looking-glass effect." For American Indians, the central subjects of this book, who have been examined and artfully described for five hundred years by others, this looking-glass rationale is an essential component of the creative process. To be sure, ever since Lewis and Clark met the Tetons (commonly called the Sioux) on the Missouri River in 1804 and described them as the "vilest miscreants of the human race," the suggestion has lingered that the sentiments of these adventurer-invaders and their published diaries have been given archival authority in contradistinction to the images of self that may have been reflected in the Teton mirrors. Surely the Sioux would not have described themselves as miscreants. This possibility also suggests that the epistemology of the white man's history made from such nonmirrored expressions as the Lewis and Clark diaries might appropriately be used as part of a strategy of dominance, for few would believe that vile miscreants (defined in Webster's as "deformed evildoers") could in any way participate in humanistic endeavors. History has shown these sentiments to be nothing if not political statements used to pass unjust laws directed toward indigenous peoples.

This distinction spoken of here of image making is an unfortunate reality of history and politics and literature and art. It is the reason to think that having images of self look back at us is probably the essential function of the contemporary Native American novel and novella (fiction), prose (narrative nonfiction), and poetry. These major genres have become the vehicles for much contemporary creative expression by natives in the twentieth century.

Because the genre of choice of most of the young writers of the Indian Renaissance period (from 1960–2000) has been the novel, and because it is probably the most popular of all kinds of current literary expressions, it is useful to begin this collection of essays with a discussion of the novel as literary form. I don't presume to know much of what John Locke or Jacques Derrida would have had to say about it, or Ian Watt, or even T. S. Eliot as I have had a very inferior formal education; but there is a dialogue in which almost any of us can engage if we care enough about the written word, the creative arts, and history.

To analyze this briefly, this collection begins with a discussion of the law as a feature of the structures and prisms through which tribal people must face what has happened to them as citizens and how the law impacts the narrative. In the face of such calumny as one finds in the law, the question becomes: What can mere narrative do? Examining the works of the most important native writers of the twentieth century, there emerges an important notion of what literature can do to find a synthesis between events and experiences. From there, art and pedagogy and politics provide a natural leap of faith.

Some of the academic essays in this collection seem unrelated to the title of the collection, and even unrelated to literary criticism, but wars and literatures, analyses and experiences are part of the circle so evident in Indian life. Many of these pieces have been revised and rewritten because they have appeared in print in some other venue. Some have been published as reviews, some as class lectures; others have appeared in newspapers and commentary pieces, and some have been in the form of addresses or speeches at conferences. Some of them are longer treatises meant to explore scholarship and pedagogy. All of them hold that it is the sacred responsibility of every human being to work toward establishing harmony and social justice on earth. Through long periods of suffocating colonization, American Indians have nurtured and deepened their feelings of survival and pride and have concentrated on how to find the basis for an organized life. This has sometimes meant poverty, torture, defeat, sacrifice, rage, inspiration, and wisdom as their First Nation status in a country fully dominated by others has remained fragile.

It is a great responsibility to be an Indian in America. One must do what one can to help the people. These essays attempt to tell something about that responsibility. I once published a little chapbook, *Then Badger Said This*. It took its title from old Dakota stories, which included such characters as rabbit, raccoon, spider, bullhead, meadowlark, Ikce, and, yes, badger. Many of those characters were traditional figures who gave the rules to live by: how to be a decent Dakotah. Badger, unfortunately, had no such influence. He simply went along. And he went along. And he went along. While going along, he was sometimes asked questions by others and he always had answers. Often he was right, but just as often, he was wrong. What he did, though, was—he kept the plot moving.

Without him, the story would have come to an abrupt end.

1

TO KEEP THE PLOT MOVING

A LEARNED PROFESSION

In the first decade of the twenty-first century, the atmosphere in the academy toward indigenous studies seems to be varied, often seemingly lackluster, coated with a veneer of Cartesian blandishment of logic and rationalism but very little passion, a far different scene from that of the decades of the 1960s and 1970s. That is either a good thing or a bad thing, depending on what you expect as you remember, observe, and record the stories, secrets, and scandals of the past. It is a good thing because it is time for the passionate rhetoric to be cooled and the general agreement of our past struggles for our place in the sun to be, by common consent, intellectually and verbally conveyed into positive ideas and consequences in all ways. This is one of the significant pathways to American Indian Studies as an academic discipline. It is a bad thing because the discipline risks losing its evocative dialogue so important to an almost legendary time known in the vernacular as "the sixties" when American Indians told a callous and greedy America that we are not vanished and our lands our not for sale or trade.

It is almost impossible in this early decade of the 2000s to get anyone in the mainstream to talk about the things that aging American Indian scholars like the writer of this text want to talk about as participants in those fabulous years of origin. The average American does not want to talk about how to improve tribal governments or the schools, as Indians of the past century have wanted. The average American does not want to talk anymore about ongoing and radical racism in America, only the end of racism, according to Dinesh D'Souza,[1] and nothing about the work of a contemporary Indian intellectual like Dr. David Wilkins, whose study of the U.S. Supreme Court and American Indians is perhaps the most important book of the past decade, which indicates that Indians are at great risk in U.S. law.[2] When those subjects are brought up, silence falls upon the room and the speaker is looked at as though he or she has some contagious disease or has just brought up the subject of herpes or some other unmentionable horror.

In 2004, a public event illustrated the point that what America wants to talk to Indians about, if they want to talk at all, is distant and irrelevant; thus, this event caught the eye of mainstream folks and the media. I bring it up here to illustrate that the real issues of finding solutions to a better life for contemporary Indians in the region known for its racist atmosphere were once again put on the back burner so that that the public could look away from the actual troubling matters of the people and, instead, address the latest sensation. In the early winter, people flocked to the federal courthouse to witness a contrived/staged murder trial in Rapid City, South Dakota, of a hapless Oglala, Arlo Looking Cloud, who had spent most of the past few decades on the streets of Denver, Colorado, and was now caught in a dragnet for old American Indian Movement (AIM) personages and troublemakers. The trial was about who killed Anna Mae Pictou-Aquash, a Micmac Indian from Canada who joined AIM in those fabulous years of the 1970s; Looking Cloud, some thirty years later, was charged with her murder, found guilty, and sentenced to life in prison. The issue of that trial was whether Pictou-Aquash was murdered by Looking Cloud at the behest of some unnamed and unnamable participants in the discredited American Indian Movement because it was thought she was an FBI informant.

The trial drew in all of the old suspects and bystanders. Participants and news organizations from around the region were in attendance, notebooks and cameras in hand. Among the witnesses was Darlene Nichols (formerly known as Kamook), the ex-wife of AIM generalissimo Dennis Banks, who testified for a substantial time recounting the fear in her friend Pictou-Aquash who, it was said, was terrified of AIM. The truth is, Pictou-Aquash was probably scared of the FBI, too, as we all were during that period. At the time I was a professor in Indian Studies at Eastern Washington University in Cheney, Washington, and was casually visited and rigorously interrogated by the FBI a couple of times because of my acquaintance with the issues and some of the people involved in the movement. It was a frightening time and we were all afraid, not of movement leaders, but of the federal government and what it could do to us in terms of U.S. law and justice. We trusted no one. The belated trial itself was an astonishing event, not because the U.S. prosecutors had prevailed throughout the thirty years of investigation and court procedures, but rather because no one expected that luminaries of the movement would be found testifying against themselves and for the prosecution years later.

In the intervening years, as we all know, life has a tendency to just go on. Dennis Banks's ex-wife, a major witness for the prosecution in the Looking Cloud murder case, has become for a brief time a casting director for a movie studio in Hollywood, which means that we can probably expect some third-rate movies at our theaters soon, as well as some poorly written books about the subject of justice in Indian Country. Indeed, there is a book published by the University of Oklahoma Press about Dennis Banks entitled *Ojibwa Warrior*, written by Dennis Banks and Richard Erdoes.[3] Does this sound familiar? It should. Erdoes, the European photographer who made a star of a half-breed teenager named Mary Moore (aka Mary Crow Dog), who bore a child during the 1974 seventy-one-day siege or takeover at Wounded Knee, South Dakota. In the heat of the battle, she was portrayed as a brave-hearted woman bearing a child in the midst of a warrior cult during a mythic time. At that same moment, without any press notices of any kind, matrons on the Lakota/Dakota homelands were objecting to her celebrity, saying, "No. No. Mary Moore is NOT a role model for our young daughters. . . . She is like the young girls caught up in the concubinage of women expressed by the male leadership of the movement, and we do not want our daughters to think this is the model for traditional Lakota womanhood." In spite of those objections, Erdoes's work on Mary Moore became a classic in feminist studies. In many cases, it was the only book on Indian affairs read in women's studies enclaves for decades and it is still on the shelves of bookstores everywhere.

It is safe to predict that Erdoes's work on Dennis Banks will also be taught as history in many of the comparative academic venues because there is a deeply sympathetic portrait of the writer and the subject. In all honesty, it is a good thing to remember the stars of the period for their unique qualities. People like Banks were at the forefront of a political revolution that, in the views of many, including this writer, changed forever the Indian world from despair to a profound understanding of Indian political affairs and history. Banks is an essential figure and deserves better.

Yes, there is something quaint about this attempt at as-told-to life story. The awfulness of Erdoes's prose demeans everyone involved. Here is an example of the banality of the narrative, stated, apparently, in the words of Banks himself: "Machiko and I had been together for two years when she became pregnant. It was inevitable. After our little baby girl was born I felt wonderful. We decided to get married in the old Japanese way and went to a Shinto Priest. Machiko looked so beautiful in her wedding kimono. We drank to our mutual happiness from tiny cups of sake."[4]

There is little that one can say in a straightforward way about finding any speck of the analytical intelligence one might ordinarily expect from Banks in the retelling of events of this important historical era. It is almost as if Erdoes has deliberately and mercilessly satirized the life and times of an Indian leader who deserves to be taken seriously. For what reasons this seeming satiric abuse and trivialization occurs, one can only surmise. Perhaps it is the genre itself that requires the theological flavor. These kinds of histories always have about them a giving-back quality, and outsiders like Erdoes seem more anxious about spiritual commitment and pacifism than they do about the political realities that face the *takini* Indian nations, the barely surviving.

To get a clear and concise reading of those moments in 1973–74, there are several texts. One of the outstanding is *Wounded Knee II,* written by Rolland Dewing, who claims he used 25,000 pages from FBI files as source material; however, even that text fails to examine the federal Indian policy of the period, namely the relocation/termination laws promulgated by the U.S. Congress in 1954 along with the destruction of hundreds of thousands of acres of tribal lands for hydropower dams put in the Missouri River, which caused massive flooding and dislocation. These events, among others, were the essential causes for the uprising in the part of the country I come from.[5]

The killing of Anna Mae Pictou-Aquash happened more than thirty years ago! The AIM occupation in South Dakota happened in 1973. Poems have been written. Books. Scholarly papers. Films. This narration has become essential to the American story because it is a civil rights matter, a national obsession. Americans go about the globe crying about civil rights, yet refuse to return treaty rights and lands stolen from tribal nations and refuse to lift the stigma of colonial oppression in native enclaves and the law. The irony is that the treaty rights matters indicative of the same conflict belong in the courts and in our dialogues as much as murder does, but as long as we continue to focus on civil rights and sensation, we can ignore treaty matters. To take up treaty rights would require an honest look at colonial law, not just criminal law, as it affects the indigenes.

It is worth noting that the record of history is almost barren of authentically novel responses to novel circumstances; at least that is what a favorite historian of mine, Richard Drinnon, says in his remarkable book *Facing West: The Metaphysics of Indian-Hating and Empire-Building.*[6] Without analyzing the reasons, then, for historical impoverishment as well as for the outpourings concerning these old AIM cases (the decades-old civil rights case of Leonard Peltier comes to mind), one might ask, What has been the consequence of this civil rights focus for education and politics in Indian affairs? What does all of this have to do with the development of the discipline of Indian Studies as a strategy of hope for native nationalism? It is my contention that it has very little to do with Indian Studies; in fact, it is irrelevant to the discourse needed in Indian Studies, which is described by many important scholars as an ethno-empowerment model of education and a strategy for problem solving in Indian affairs.

This irrelevance is in direct proportion to the concentration of civil rights focus. As we follow American historians and their static, fixed view of American practices concerning their precious myths, we are still asking who killed Billy the Kid and what ever happened to Jimmy Hoffa. Murder, though, is a civil matter and it is a criminal matter and it is a civil rights matter—what it is *not* is a treaty rights matter! This is not to suggest that civil rights matters are not important. But those matters are not essential to the function of Indian Studies. What we in Indigenous Studies must recognize in American history is that Manifest Destiny began on the eastern seaboard and it has been carried around the world as a colonial fantasy and it must be revised, if not defeated. Questions irrelevant to our cause have been the centerpiece of all of our histories for far too long.

The dissatisfaction I have felt over this kind of trivialization of events caused me in 1997 to publish an essay in the *Wicazo Sa Review* titled "Who Stole Native American Studies?"[7] in which I discussed a number of issues that have been troubling all of us since the beginning of the development of the discipline: the issues of irrelevance, tokenism, marginalization, domination, and co-optation; the attempt to discredit tribal scholars and their work; the new historicism based in multiculturalism and diversity; and how the disciplinary work in Native Studies has been neglected and what must be done about it.

Today, as the new century begins, we are still complaining about many of the same issues and are asking the same questions. As just one example that illustrates the ubiquitousness of this complaint, Dr. Jack Utter, a former visiting professor of federal Indian law history at Northern Arizona University and Prescott College and consultant to the Navajo Nation's water code administration and natural resources management, has revised and enlarged his earlier text, *American Indians: Answers to Today's Questions.*[8] He asks, literally, the same questions asked in his previous publication and, as a matter of historical fact, the questions that America has promulgated for the past 200 years as a way to obfuscate survival mechanisms and solutions: What defines an Indian tribe? Who is an Indian? Who is Native American? What is sovereignty?

Are we going to continue to ask what sovereignty is and never get around to finding ways to actually use the concept to better our lives and defend our lands?

We are still asking questions that have little relevance if land reform, economics, defense of treaty agreements, and survival as nation-to-nation entities are the salient directives of the discipline. What is the present inquiry about, then? Is it Dennis Banks? Is it AIM trials and sensation? Is it writing third-rate novels and staging film festivals in Utah? Is it telling personal stories of historical grief? I don't think so. Rather, it is a question of finding ways for forming decent governments; it is the development of appropriate health systems and economic systems for native populations; it is what Dr. Wilkins has told us about removing the "masks of justice" concerning land thefts and ridding the U.S. Congress of its claimed notion that it holds plenary power over Indian nations. Instead of tackling all of that important work, we are still asking ourselves, Who is an Indian? Every scholar in the discipline should consider this an outrage.

Who is an Indian? was not the essential question that we started with several decades ago, because we knew then who was an Indian and that the thrust of Indian Studies was the forming of an educational strategy to defend tribal nationhood, native lands, and native rights. We knew thirty years ago that as a discipline, this body of knowledge and inquiry possessed by American Indians for thousands of years on this continent had to be (1) internally organized (this means that native scholars must direct the disciplinary work); (2) it must be normatively regulated (this means that the native directors come to some agreement [consensus?] about the principles and methodologies); and (3) that this knowledge has to be consensually communicated (this means that a core curriculum must be taught to undergraduates as the gateway to further consensus as native peoples direct research and writing toward specific ends so that tribal nations can throw off colonialism and further their contributions to the knowledge base of the world).

What is very important to acknowledge here is that since we began decades ago, there has been the development of competing epistemologies as a way to diminish the power of Indian Studies, its faculties, and its research. That fact may have been a major focus of my "Who Stole Native American Studies" essay. The undue influence of multiculturalism, for example, or diversity, feminism, minority higher education, postmodernism, or cultural studies has led Indian Studies to accept the notion that it can be all things to all people in academia and society, and that an Americanization of the colonial thrust of history is to be sustained.

We in Indian Studies have let this theft of our academic objectives happen. To get specific, the Indian Studies faculty members of the past several decades, along with self-serving administrators, have allowed the competing epistemologies to flourish and even dominate. It is essential to understand the risk involved in this reality, for no epistemology such as an emerging one like American Indian Studies can be nurtured unless the teaching and administrative forces of a university or school form its body of knowledge into a learned profession with power and privilege. A learned profession is the goal. Our Indian Studies faculty members know that this has not happened for us and it has not happened for our profession. Why? Because we have allowed our power to be subsumed by and fed into other related disciplines. Our profession is in danger of being dismissed as irrelevant and co-opted by the more long-established forces of privilege in university enclaves. Perhaps the same can be said about any intellectual endeavor in America when you look at the influence of MTV or Viacom or Clear Channel but the truth is, our faculties in Indian Studies continue to be small, weak, and without the prestige of even our local tribal politicians who have risen to power through SEATA and gambling casinos.

In most cases at state universities around the country, we have only a few faculty members with appointments in the discipline of Indian Studies. Most are still appointed in related disciplines because that is where they see power and privilege. The implication for our work in light of this reality must be taken up as a major concern.

Have we developed departmental status? The answer is largely no, if we are talking about the mainstream rather than the exception. The truth is, we are still programs. We are still embedded in the departments of related disciplines and we have seen in the past decades what happens when there is no departmental status for faculty members and, therefore, no defense of tenure for those faculty members. When the embedded faculty member leaves his or her position in the related discipline, no one teaches the classes he or she has developed in Indian Studies and the program dies a natural death of attrition. This has happened in countless instances.

In spite of these obstacles and in answer to the questions of what we have accomplished as faculties and how we have contributed to our professional lives, our students, and our disciplines, there is quite a lot of good news.

We have developed minors and majors at universities across the country, although, unfortunately, because of the influences of related disciplines, many of these curricular models are still goodness-of-fit or old-wine-in-new-bottles efforts. What that means is that many of the courses offered in our discipline are simply not distinguishable from the offerings in other departments and there is the charge of redundancy. Yet many of the new and exciting offerings, especially at those universities with large Indian student bodies, are innovative and useful. In most cases, enrollments are increasing. Indeed, in my recent teaching stints I have noticed an enthusiasm, almost a clamoring among young students for many of our offerings, even some of the undergraduate courses such as Introduction to the Discipline, or Federal Indian Policy, or Contemporary Indian Issues. These are popular courses at the undergraduate level and every graduate student who intends to teach had better learn how to teach these courses effectively. In addition to course development, faculty members have contributed as scholars to the discipline with substantial publications. This is the good news and it is our challenge to go forward with that work.

There are other matters that are examples of how such good news can be overshadowed. The question of a sustained and tribally based curriculum is critical and it is still one of the neglected matters of the discipline. It is not unusual, for example, for American Indian curricular offerings to be pirated from history, anthropology, or the social sciences. Here is an unnamed but ubiquitous example. Thirteen courses are offered at a southern university I am familiar with and a student can earn a major or minor in Indian Studies by starting with these offerings; unfortunately, the curriculum model does not include federal Indian policy, does not offer a U.S.–Indian treaty course, does not start with an introduction to the discipline, and does not require or even offer a Native language course. In addition, it does not offer a course in law and society, economics and tribal government, or native thought and philosophy—all of which are essential courses in a classical model of the discipline. These are the sins of omission and they are evident everywhere in academia.

What is offered to students at this university is this: Southwestern Indian Histories from 1200 to 1880; an encounter course with little or no recognition of recent native scholarship; a course that belongs in an American history curriculum; a 300-level Native American literature course that offers well-documented European views of Native Americans and the fiction of Native American novelists Sherman Alexie and Leslie Silko; a course called American Indian Societies, which is an anthropology course about lifeways and customs; a contact-zone course called Comparative Readings in Chicano and Native American Heritages, which is an immigrant history of immigrant groups that have no real similarity to the indigenous tribal groups in the United States, a course which is loath to even mention the essential core concepts of sovereignty or indigenousness, let alone explicate the significance of those concepts. There is a diversity course that teaches the works of Louise Erdrich, Michael Dorris, James Welch, and James Fenimore Cooper along with the speeches of famous Indian chiefs of the eighteenth and nineteenth centuries. Finally, there is an archaeology course that spans the time period 10,000 B.C. to European contact time that suggests that the Kennewick Man, thousands of years old and found on the banks of the Columbia River in the twentieth century, looks more like Patrick Stewart (Captain Jean-Luc Picard) of the television show *Star Trek: The Next Generation* than any native personage.[9]

These offerings are entirely inadequate. They should not be labeled Indian Studies but, rather, American Studies. Worst of all, this inadequacy can be laid squarely at the doorstep of faculty members. What may be called "inadequacy" is really the sin of commission in curricular development wrongly labeled Indian Studies. This course work, rather than representing the academic discipline of Indian Studies, is more realistically just a rearranging of courses from other disciplines, described earlier as old wine in new bottles. This failure is a serious matter because educators from around the globe will stand by the idea that a robust and appropriate curriculum is the single greatest predictor of success for students as well as for the communities they presume to serve. The second greatest predictor is in the guidance from an effective, well-prepared, and expert faculty. With appropriate curricular models, Indian Studies can become the most important tool, other than the study of law, for tribal nations in their efforts to become strong, independent, and sovereign participants in the modern world.

Two additional subjects cannot be omitted from this discussion. First, the appropriate graduate school experience is vital to the training of professionals in our discipline. Since the U.S. Congress officially embraced Native American self-determination as a policy in 1975, it has been suggested by scholars that an independent intellectual foundation for native Studies was to be the focus.[10] It clearly outlines the movement from related disciplines and long-standing European epistemologies into indigenous theory and thought. The epistemological status of Indigenous Studies is a thorny problem for those harboring the colonial mentality so pervasive in much of the First World. The reasons for that are numerous and complex, not the least of which is the problem of origins. The epistemological ground on this matter has been explained by one of the major native scholars in the discipline, Professor Vine Deloria Jr.,[11] and these explanations should be our focus, transcending the power/play models of discourse struggling for primacy in most university settings, which the Kennewick Man controversy implies. This means that appropriate strategies for developing think tanks and advanced studies paradigms are crucial for the discipline to establish boundaries and direct meaningful research in the coming years. Graduate schools are responsible for many of the problems we face in academic preparation and successful professional lives because of their assimilative nature. To do graduate work in any of the major universities of this country, one must be a conformist to a large degree, but to know this is to resist it in whatever ways seekers of advanced degrees can muster.

Secondly, many universities, and particularly inchoate disciplines like Indian Studies, spend entirely too much time catering to students. We worry that they will evaluate us in a bad light, that our deans and provosts will deny us tenure on the basis of those evaluations, and that our enrollments will decrease; thus, we let their evaluations drive curricular development and pedagogy. Do not misunderstand the point here. I am not saying that meeting the needs of our students is not critical to good outcomes. I am not saying that the problems native students face aren't enormous: poor academic training, worries about tuition, part-time-ism, being the first in their families to attend college, transferring from two-year institutions, cultural-difference needs, labels and stereotypes—obstacles of all kinds. But the reality is that such comments can be made about many student groups in American colleges, particularly minority students.

However, Indians are not minorities and should not accept that description. Indians are not ethnics in American societies and should not be treated as such. They are indigenous peoples with lands and resources and treaties and histories different from any other population in the United States. They should be understood as constitutionally sovereign and treaty-protected populations. Thus, the question of the academy's Indian Studies future is not just about meeting the needs of our students. It is not just about enrollments and recruiting native professors.

Indian Studies is about government and politics and sovereignty for Indian nations. It is about rights based on the extraconstitutionality of a government-to-government relationship with the U.S. federal government unlike any other in the United States. Sovereignty, as we all know, has been denied Indian nations for 200 years, and that denial remains the ultimate political racism at the core of this democratic nation's beginnings. To deny sovereignty to Indian nations is the ultimate denial of justice in this country; our discipline, Indian Studies, is on the front lines of that reality. Our students must be taught to accept that knowledge and responsibility.

Finally, Indian Studies is also about opportunity. Only with the passage of affirmative action strategies promulgated in the past three decades have American Indians been welcomed into the academy. Even that is ironic because, in the beginning, affirmative action had to do with blacks, not Indians. It is sometimes accepted that affirmative action as a social policy was encouraged as early as the 1860s and 1870s by the Reconstruction Congress after the Civil War to assist former slaves adapting to American society. A hundred years later, the Civil Rights Act of 1964 was passed as a way to diminish racial segregation and discrimination against blacks in this country. Thus, it began as a race policy and emerged as a political policy for all minority populations in the United States. Even so, for the reasons articulated in the above paragraphs, it did little to alleviate the stress in Indian populations, neither black nor minority as it concerns the right to self-government and sovereignty over its native population.

When that problem was looked at carefully, the Indian Civil Rights Act was passed by the U.S. Congress and hailed by many Indian individuals, but it did little except restrict Indian tribal governments.[12] David E. Wilkins and K. Tsianina Lomawaima[13] suggest that the civil rights legislation was enacted in order to fend off what is known as state jurisdiction and intrusion in law and order issues but, in practical terms, the states continue to believe that they retain "governmental interest" over lands within their borders and the act, some say, is not explicit enough. And so the controversies concerning sovereignty continue.

Today, there are those who still rail against affirmative action as a national racist policy. Recently, Linda Chavez, an important spokesperson for Hispanics, the largest minority group in the United States and a group that is sometimes put into the same category as American Indian students, said in an article in the *Chronicle of Higher Education* that the biggest problem confronting Hispanic students in higher education today is that many of them have been admitted through the double standard of affirmative action.[14] She says, also, that too many Latino faculty members are marginalizing the curriculum with bilingual and bicultural issues, a charge often heard by native professors when they wish to defend sovereignty and indigenousness as historical principles and native languages as essential to the development of the cultural parameter of the discipline.

Even the new fictional work *Love* by the 1993 Nobel Prize winner and prestigious black novelist Toni Morrison sits on the fence concerning the efficacy of affirmative action (though the word does not appear in the text because the work is about class, not politics).[15] Ultimately, it is about two black women separated because one is poor and the other is upper class and they come together in the end. It tacitly suggests the controversy about affirmative action and implies that what might be called "full citizenship" cannot be achieved through such mechanisms as affirmative action. Morrison gives no real answers to that dilemma because her interest is in full citizenship and class antagonisms rather than indigenous rights.

Talking about citizenship and class, about gaining rights and liberties, and about getting a "piece of the pie" is what the National Association for the Advancement of Colored People (NAACP) is all about but, conversely, that is not what the National Congress of American Indians (NCAI) is all about, as one of its early directors, Vine Deloria Jr., would tell you. The NCAI is about title to land, the return of stolen lands, treaties, war, dispossession, law and legislative policy, sovereignty, and indigenousness. Affirmative action has played an enormously important role in putting native intellectuals in seats of academic and political power, so that the direction of the dialogue can be moved away from seeking "full" citizenship for Indians, assimilation, and democracy in the usual context. Rather, its role is to defend the notion of landlordship, the indigenous presence in America, dual-citizenship, tribalism, and nation-to-nation status. The defense of resources and lands is a major issue for American Indians. The concept of indigenousness is a difference that is crucial for the immigrant nation of America to understand if history is to have a moral and progressive place in academia.

These examples, only a couple of the many that lead to the present controversies, illustrate the fact that some minority issues are in direct conflict with what we need to do and strive for in Indian Studies. I dare say that most of the intellectuals of the Indian world would not be in their positions in the academy were it not for the affirmative action policies of the federal government in the past three decades. Oddly enough, Indian informants were welcomed as early as the eighteenth and nineteenth century into academic enclaves by disciplines such as anthropology, but few Native American scholars, professors, and credentialed intellectuals in a variety of disciplines and particularly in Indian Studies were institutionalized until well into the twentieth century.

Because of these real and recent controversies, Indians must not give in to the ultraconservative notion that affirmative action policies have been a problem to us, a detriment, that they have damaged us, as is stated over and over again by a black conservative judge who now sits on the Supreme Court bench as he joins countless other minority intellectuals loathe to admit the necessity of this far-reaching principle for equality in education and law. These policies of affirmative action have been a driving force in the progress Indians have made in education in the past thirty years. The future of native intellectualism depends on the defense of those policies. Even the reservation-based community colleges owe their very existence to those policies.

In spite of that assistance through federal principles, some educators in Indian Country find it heartbreaking to see how little progress education has made toward improving the political strength and nation-to-nation status of our tribes because, as the twenty-first century begins, tribal nations are still at risk and still in the clutches of colonial masters through the claimed plenary power notions of the U.S. Congress. Although there are successes, aging Indian scholars who began this journey thirty years ago expected much more.

As we look toward the future, Norbert Hill, executive director of the American Indian Graduate Center in Albuquerque, New Mexico, tells us that that, on average, fewer than one in five Indians who enroll in college earn a bachelor's degree and even fewer Indian scholars will make it through the academic pipeline to earn Ph.D.'s in any year.[16] Many of these graduates eschew Indian Studies, saying things like: Well, yes, I am teaching in Indian Studies but, you see, I am really an anthropologist, or a scientist, or historian. Those who say that have been taught the unfortunate truth about where power and influence lies in the academy. This is clearly the thrust of graduate programs and administrative entities.

To keep the focus on the beginnings of the discipline when emphasizing that the two major concepts of sovereignty and indigenousness were at the forefront of curricular development, universities must put aside usual hiring practices to attract and keep native faculty. They must be innovative and informed about the work that has been done by native scholars in the past two or three decades. Research initiatives must focus on the work and Studies that will sustain the nation-to-nation status of tribes and their sovereign governments. Massive fellowships and funding mechanisms must be directed toward tribal populations.

The reality is that antagonists to Indian Studies as an academic discipline are still out there. At the beginning of this new century, scientists are still fighting over the bones of indigenous peoples.[17] In 1996, a fossil named the Kennewick Man was found on the shores of the Columbia River in Washington State and the Umatillas, Yakimas, Colvilles, Nez Perce and others immediately knew him as their relative. Yet their claim has been in the courts for years and the bones reside in the Burke Museum at the University of Washington in Seattle. This is the consequence of an appeal by the persistent nonindigenous scientists who disagree fundamentally with indigenous peoples concerning origins. These antagonists say that because human remains must bear some relationship to present existing tribes, and since, they say, such a finding is impossible to demonstrate because there is no recorded history, the Indian claim is invalid in the courts.

It is the function of Indian Studies to provide the evidence in this case as well as all the others that indigenousness as a concept is something more than mere fantasy, that it can be defended intellectually as well as culturally. The continuing mantra of these ubiquitous antagonists who say that indigenous theory concerning origins is not "scientific" and, therefore, indefensible can be examined through the works of native scholars and tribal intellectuals, the disciplinary work of Indian Studies, the oral traditions of the tribes, and other aboriginal records.

· · ·

COLLABORATION OR CONFLICT?

The question of resistance to the coercive Americanization of native populations is a huge part of the curricular development of Indian Studies, as it is in other instances, as well. Hannah Arendt, for example, speaks to this resistance as it concerns the condition of Jewish populations. African scholars like Wole Soyinka and Homi K. Bhabha and Palestinian writer Edward Said have persistently argued that there is no future for the indigene in colonialism. Linda Tuhiwai Smith (Ngati Awa and Ngati Porou), in her book *Decolonizing Methodologies,* has been a major influence in resistance studies in all fields.[18]

In Indian Studies, the works of tribal scholars have surveyed the consequences of history with great skill and incisive analysis and have come to the conclusion that decolonization should be the focus for future studies and writings. In literary studies, however—a body of work that has had a huge impact on the discipline of Indian Studies—there is, perhaps, no body of scholarship (other than political science) more fraught with ambiguity, and that includes the recent literatures produced by Indians. The literatures of the Third World and the literatures of the American indigenous peoples have always been described by critics as either primitive or militant, which means that issues of collaboration and conflict, law and art, and aesthetics and meaning are primary issues. Although the grip of the American legal system on the lives of American Indians has been researched and is an object lesson in the brilliant reconstruction of Indian lives after what is often wrongly called "conquest," there is also the notion that the peoples who have been under the domination of colonizing nations are now in the process of enormous change. Much of the curricular development in Indian Studies focuses on that change.

This means that much writing about American Indians (and the Third World in general) reads like a war saga, a drama of tragic intensity, a fascinating maneuver that gains power by degrees over some period of time resulting in stereotyping and misinformation. This is true even though most Indian nations in America never went to war at all and many other nations won more wars than they ever lost during the nineteenth century. The reality of colonial propaganda masquerading as history as it concerns all of this brings up a major question in Indian Country, and it affects writers as much as it does politicians or people in the street: Should the colonized simply collaborate with the laws of their masters, make the best of it, sign peace treaties, and watch the lands and lives of indigenous populations be overtaken? Should colonization will out? Or should the colonized fight back? This is as much a literary question as it is a political question. If the colonized choose the latter, how shall resistance be most effective? If they do not choose to fight back, what are the consequences?

We may assume that, in the beginning, almost all writing has asked these questions, having been concerned about politics and the law and power. Certainly that is true of classical writing—the Bible, the Koran, and other great books about justice vis-à-vis the philosophy and religion of the world. In a major instance, Greek drama as genre is about politics and the law and politics and justice, assisting readers in understanding the roots of conquest, terror, retribution, war, democracy, colonialism, and all of the human activities to take to the world stage from time to time: *Antigone, Oedipus Rex,* the *Iliad*; the Greek chorus going up and down the aisle chanting the appropriate interpretation of Greek law that everyone now recognizes as Euro-American law based in biblical tenets. Finally, there are the works of William Shakespeare and the Victorians, all giving substance to the cultural and philosophic matters of Europe.

Even today, novels like *The Bonfire of the Vanities* or Richard Wright's *Native Son* are works concerning the law.[19] I certainly consider my meager work, even my fictional works and poems, a common literary reaction to the law. In 1998 I published a book of poems with the title *I Remember the Fallen Trees*,[20] a reference to the mid-century sacrifice for hydropower of an entire timberland in the Dakotas to technology and political hegemony; my first novella, *From the River's Edge*, was about the flooding of hundreds of thousands of acres of treaty-protected land in the Dakotas for hydropower by the U.S. government without the consent of the governed.[21] My work is about the struggle of the Sioux Nation to survive its colonizers, the U.S. government and the law and American justice. It is Tragedy in much the same manner as the works of the Greek theater and of Dostoyevsky, Melville, Kafka, and Camus. It is all Tragedy. It would seem, then, that the tragic consequences of politics and the law is essential subject matter for art and creativity. So, as far as literary types are concerned, the law has a lot to answer for.

While this may look like a reasonable accounting of the role of literature, the definition of "Tragedy" in the classical sense must be understood as apolitical if we mean to suggest that politics is a system of power rather than a dialogue about how we are governed. Law, not politics, as far as the Greeks were concerned, had to supercede all other possibilities for human potential, yet their literatures crossed a variety of realistic thresholds rather ambiguously. As Aristotle saw it, Tragedy realistically embodied the inevitable fall of a noble character because of his or her inherent flaw of character, and, naturally, Tragedy in the classical sense told us over and over again of the superior role of the gods (i.e., fate), whose function in the narrative was essential to the unraveling of the chaos brought about by human activity. To take human events out of the realm of human activity and give it to the gods was an easy way out of any dilemma (moral or otherwise)—if one refused to introduce politics as a conditioner in human lives. Destiny rules. The apolitical nature of Aristotle's definition of Tragedy, because of its dependence on the gods, has always troubled me (and falls into disuse, perhaps, in today's non-Christian societies). When the roles of the bureaucracies of the American government and of the colonizing powers of the real world intervene in Indian stories, the sense of tragedy and the definition of Tragedy in literature must be broadened. It is no longer Tragedy with a capital *T*, describing the noble intent of democratizers of goodwill, but rather just an inevitable and sad and sorry and political story put in place by men, not gods.

It becomes apparent, then, that Tragedy is not all there is to it. As one examines specific cases, one sees that American Indians and their tribal nations exist outside the U.S. Constitution and the democracy that has been deemed so precious by Americans, which means that Indian efforts at examining treaty relationships are regarded as mere nuisances in many cases by those in power. What the experience of the past 200 years of Indian history has suggested is this: the attempts of the federal government, with whom Indian nations have signed solemn pledges, to establish a concept called "trust" have been a notorious failure; it has been for generations and it continues to be. "Trust," for those unfamiliar with Indian law, is a legal concept through which a protectorate (like the United States) deals with a lesser or more fragile and weaker nation; that is, a tribe of people. To be sure, "trust" seems a facile concept in a modern world based on the hegemonic notion that there are superior nations and there are inferior ones when, in fact, a nation is a nation with constituted authorities of its own.

Nine out of ten Indian history books don't even mention the word "trust," but it is nonetheless a concept that argues colonization as a moral endeavor. It arises out of the notion that the American Indian is a ward of the U.S. government and his lands must be held in trust by the federal government. How this concept arose out of the treaty-making period (when a nation-to-nation relationship was assumed very early on) is one of the Alice-in-Wonderland facets of Indian history and law. The Indian commissioner of every decade assumed (and still does) that as soon as the Indian was deemed competent, he could be given full control of his property.

Whatever one thinks of the concept, it exists.

While some may argue that much of this dilemma has been attended to and corrected through recent legislation and state governmental action, specifically through something called state/tribal compacts and various agreements, as well as through the establishment of coalitions, reconciliation movements, and various other law and social remedies, quite the opposite is true. The following examples suggest that little changed in the decades of the previous century.

Recently in the northern Plains, legislation has been promulgated that is called "land transfer legislation," which was put forth in the U.S. Congress by state elected officials. Former Senator Tom Daschle (D-SD) and the discredited Representative William Janklow (R-SD) put in front of the public what is called the South Dakota Land Transfer and Wildlife Habitat Mitigation Act of 1997. The public is told this is a good law concerning the Sioux homelands and the Missouri River, but it is really a law designed to diminish tribal sovereign status, to claim land for the state of South Dakota and to claim non-Indian jurisdiction concerning hunting and fishing and tourism. Looking at that legislation carefully (put together by very clever lawyers and politicians, even tribal ones), it is easy to see that this is another landgrab by the state and that it will benefit no tribe along the Missouri River on a long-range basis.

It is wrong. It is wrong law and wrong history yet it is touted as a measure (as the representative and the senator say) to put to rest all jurisdictional questions over water and hunting and fishing and tourism. It will put to rest all jurisdictional questions concerning the river, says a quotation from area newspapers like the *Rapid City Journal* and the Sioux Falls *Argus Leader*. That is a false claim. More important than such a false claim, however, is the fact that tribes do not need this legislation to protect the Fort Laramie Treaty of 1868, to be specific. These rights are both implicit and explicit: tribes have the right to use, administer, control, and exercise their property rights independent from state control and interference.

One need not take the word of a mere observer to know that this is true. Instead, the works of Felix Cohen, the modern "Father of Indian Law," tell all that one needs to know about the sovereign rights of Indian nations. One can also listen to *The Elders Speak* and *My Relatives Say,* stories of the victims available on tape since 2001, told by Mary Louise Defender, a Dakota Sioux who lives in Shields, North Dakota, as well as explore the works of scholars like Michael L. Lawson, who wrote the first scholarly examination of the violation of the river in modern times in his book *Dammed Indians,* published in 1982.[22]

The mitigation in law put forth by South Dakota legislators and the reaction to it by Indian people is just one recent example that suggests that law and the narrative are tied together. Stories have been told for several decades, told by the people of the reserved lands of the Missouri River tribes concerning the river, and they all tell of the wrongness of law, the homelessness, and poverty. It is not appropriate, perhaps, to describe this legislation as immoral law, because we are told over and over again that morality has little to do with the law, that the concept of moral wrongness has no agency in the law, that there is no way to address morality in the law, and that morality has to do with religion, not justice.

Just for the sake of argument, however, let us say here that there is a moral wrongness suggested in the narrative, that there really exists the concept of wrongness in Indian law. Indians know that such a thing is real. It was wrong, Indians will tell you, to force their children BY LAW into federal and Christian boarding schools as early as the 1840s—prisons, really—located hundreds of miles from their homes. It was wrong to force the General Allotment Act of 1887 on communal societies, BY LAW draining the assets of the nations and causing the loss of hundreds of thousands of acres of land as well as poverty and disease. It was wrong to massacre unarmed Minneconjou Lakota men and women and children at Wounded Knee and give the murderers medals of honor, a massacre that is a symbol for many hundreds of such massacres of native people throughout the country during the war and genocidal period.

If we accept the concept of moral wrongness in Indian law, we are forced to confront the task of justification. *The task of justification.* That is what Indian law is all about. That is what the writing of American history has been about for far too long. God knows that wrong law toward Indians has been justified not only in history, not only at Wounded Knee, but in the courtrooms of this country as well. It must be acknowledged that the United States makes and enforces laws all the time that are prima facie undesirable. It is obvious that these laws are undesirable because they involve the curtailment of some of the most fundamental of human values, such as freedom, self-determination as a people, economic well-being, and spiritual wellness.

How, then, are these laws justified? They are justified in two ways.

First, law is justified through the principle of a certain mode of reasoning. Ever since the Greeks put Socrates to death for speaking his mind, ever since they fought a twenty-seven-year war with Sparta and made slaves of them and put to death their male children, they justified wrongness in law by saying: "But we are called a democracy; our life is refined; the law secures equal justice to all alike because we are a democracy; the fruits of a whole earth flow in upon us." This thinking justifies colonization. It justifies massacre. It justifies the curtailment of human values for others.

Second, it is demonstrated that the employment of this reasoning is superior to other kinds of reasoning. It is said that democracy is not perfect, but it is better than any alternative; democratic ideals are not just in self-interest; rather, they are in the interest of civilization. In these ways, the moral wrongness of the law is justified. At one time it was not morally wrong in this country for one person to own another person (a black person, of course) for profit. This was justified in law. When it could no longer be justified, it became illegal. Not without argument, of course; legal argument and war. But a certain reasoning to right a wrong became superior in the argument and overruled other kinds of arguments—economic ones, for example. American Indian societies are the most strictly colonized enclaves in this country or in many other democratic societies. Law has said that enforced colonization of Indians is just. Thus, the legacy of colonization is everywhere in Indian law and history. It is the basis for the mitigation act just mentioned, the flooding of 550 square miles of treaty-protected lands for hydropower along the Missouri River in 1950 and 1960; it is the basis for the 1877 theft of the

Black Hills decided and held by the U.S. Congress for a hundred years to be a taking rather than a theft. Finally, a century later, the Supreme Court of the land described the loss as a rank theft and ruled that compensation (not the return of stolen land) was the remedy, a remedy that has been rendered unacceptable to the people of the Sioux Nation who want to talk of land reform and return. There are literally thousands of cases of the wrongness of Indian law that justify colonization and colonial practice on Indian lands and in Indian enclaves across the country.

In the final analysis, writers, poets, journalists, and scholars don't need to be told that the most obvious wrongness in Indian law and the ubiquitous failure of the trust responsibility toward Indian nations is the misuse of political authority. And, again, the question of the function of narrative in the face of such political misuse, such political indifference, such deliberate historical criminal behavior arises. What can narrative do? The answer is that narrative is the only refuge, the only place where one can raise one's spirits and teach the children; it is in the constant storytelling passed from mouth to mouth, from book to book that real power toward progress and freedom is made. Political authority, it must be said over and over, is not only in the offices one holds. It is not only in the elective process that political authority exists—sorry, you believers in the governing systems of the world. Truth is, political authority can be claimed. And it can be claimed through writing and scholarship no matter how obscure and out of the mainstream it is. It is an unfortunate reality that it can also be claimed no matter how corrupt it is.

In the long run, writing, as a political act, is perhaps the most risky but surely the most sacred responsibility of them all. It is the grass dancing that precedes all activities out on the prairie; it is preparing the ground before the *wacipi* begins.

WHAT ABOUT LITERARY CANON?

A Basis for Judgment, Standard, Criterion

Situating Amerindian literary studies within colonialism and the law has always been a challenge. Some have suggested that the new critical idiom is not useful in those places where postcolonialism is still contested in a myriad of ways both political and social, in places where tribal peoples have been literally stunted because of the goodness-of-fit model, those places where the new Amerindian novelists, writers, and poets, in between a rock and a hard place, are no longer committed to First Nation status. The dismantling of colonial rule has not happened on the homelands, it is said; only in the imaginative writing of nontribal spokespersons.

What is difficult to remember, as tribal scholars go about attempting to situate literary studies into a contemporary American Indian Studies curriculum or even in the Western literary paradigm, is that there is a precolonial canon of tribalism, largely forgotten and accessible mainly in the imagination. There is, according to such Old World critics and forgotten poets as T. S. Eliot, the notion that every literature has its standards and those standards are based on the literature behind it. This is probably as true for contemporary Native American literatures as it is for any body of literatures.

What Is a Classic?

When Eliot wrote his essential piece entitled "What Is a Classic?" he was talking about the Western literary tradition, of course, and he made sure that everyone understood that all literature has precursors and that the precursors emerged from the Western literary tradition, because the Western tradition dominated all literary studies everywhere.[23] Eliot wrote and published his useful theory just after the close of the World War II and, although his intent was to talk of the superiority of Western literatures, his theoretical approach to the function of literature can find its way into discussions concerning all bodies of literature.

It was a time of great upheaval, a result of the experiences that two world wars had wrought, when Eliot wrote this theory and it was a time of new beginnings when, even as the French existentialists were saying god is dead, the influence of Latin and Greek literatures, though ebbing slowly away, was still of some significance in literary studies in general ways. One is reminded of the great upheaval in American Indian lives and subsequent studies just after the failure of the mid-twentieth-century federal policy: the federal laws of termination and relocation. This was the subject of the work of a major twentieth-century Dakota Sioux scholar named Vine Deloria Jr., when he was writing his seminal nonfiction books *God Is Red* and *Custer Died for Your Sins*. The history he spoke of performed the same function in Indian lives that the world wars performed for Europe, as a great literary movement often referred to as the American Indian literary renaissance began. During the period Deloria spoke of, native populations were decimated by poverty and disease, tribal nations and their lands were diminished, thousands of Indians were relocated to the cities, and racist laws were enacted in order to get rid of huge populations of Indians and their treaty rights so that their lands and resources could be subsumed by the needy mainstream Americans.

Not all literary theories rise out of social upheavals, but many of them do. The theory that classics in literature are those that embody precursors was an inevitable mode of thinking; the result is that now it is an acceptable notion among critics that what was said in Eliot's essay—that is, that a classic is not possible without a literature behind it—has claimed its place in modern eclectic literary studies. The notion of what embodies a classic in literature promulgated by Eliot and his colleagues is an important theory that has been too long neglected in the study of Native American literatures.

As one looks at the development of the notion of literary canon, it is clear that Eliot's theory concerning the classic in literary studies can still be sustained. The Eliot theory has been taught in all literary enclaves for generations. It still suggests that the Western literary tradition is primary, of course, and that the ancient literatures and languages of Greek and Latin, as precursors, were unsurpassed because of the subsequent works of such notables, certainly, as Shakespeare, Marlowe, Milton, Spencer, Pope, Chaucer, Dante, Molière, and Montaigne. Eliot used these writers and their works as evidence for his theory. There is very little argument these days about the fact that Eliot was an elitist, one of many, who defended the western literary tradition as superior to any other, yet the subsequent and perhaps unexpected professorial response to all of this called for the broadening of the canon, not the restriction of it. Whatever one's position is on the notable creators of Western literatures, their claimed primacy should not mean that even if one no longer teaches the works themselves because of taste or manners or fad, the theory is to be abandoned as well as the works. It is like throwing the baby out with the bathwater. It should mean, instead, that the notion that standards and ideas can be developed by scholars and writers for the "classic" may be utilized in other unlike bodies of thought and creativity.

If that notion can be sustained, and I believe it can, the role of indigenous mythology and native ideology, which is often called the oral traditions of the tribes, must be understood in theory as the "literature behind" the modern works of Indian writers such as Momaday, Young Bear, Silko, and other notables of the great American Indian literary renaissance of the twentieth century. This can be explicit even in the use of the English language as the language of expression, as well as translation. The role of mythology and Indian ideology in the creative imagination is crucial to understanding the work of today's tribal writers.

Thus, a good place to begin in student learning is to read a translation and view a film version of the Popul Vuh. A good film was made available by the University of California, Los Angeles, in the early 1970s entitled *Popul Vuh: The Creation Myth of the Maya.*[24] The first reading assignment must be one of the several available translations of that work essential as the "literature behind" the contemporary novels and poems called Amerindian literatures. The reason for its essentialness is that the Popul Vuh examines the central monomyth of the Americas, just as the Bible is the central monomyth of the Western canon and the Koran is the central myth of Middle Eastern works. Present-day Indians of Guatemala are the possessors of the surviving narrative and, although it is recorded in the Quiche language, many good translations are available. The creators of this literature are descendants of the Maya people, who developed a remarkable indigenous civilization in South America, a world described in the Popul Vuh as the monomyth of the Americas.

What this means is that the symbols, themes, ideas, literatures, and subsequent ideologies of the monomyth permeate all of the indigenous mythologies of the continent. These are non-Christian mythologies that inform the native populations that their origins occurred on this continent. This is the essential and substantial ideology that must be taught in contradistinction to the Christian ideology imposed by the colonizers. For the Mayas, the belief is that they emerged in the North and South American geography as human beings, first men and then women, created from a paste made of corn, the plant most venerated by their forefathers, connecting origin and development throughout the Americas to the hundreds of other native cultural ideologies in this arena. As the biblical Adam and Eve story permeates all Western literatures, so must the people's voice narrative of this continent permeate Native American literatures.

These beliefs form the basic emergence narratives and are the beginnings of all native literatures and thoughts and ideas on this continent in theory and praxis and they precede the Christian intrusion into the continent; they are the "literatures behind it." In the mythic sense, then, in what is now Guatemala, the indigenous peoples there are created and their migrations across the specific lands of the continent occurs. This kind of mythic narrative concerning the universe informs all indigenous peoples on this continent and is an essential introductory background for reading and understanding the works of those who claim to be tribal writers in the same way that the Bible is the background for studying the works of Dylan Thomas, Shakespeare, Wallace Stegner, Dante Alighieri, and all the rest. Because of the failure to acknowledge this theoretical base for the study of Amerindian or indigenous literatures, the native peoples of the Americas, like those of Africa and later of Australia and other indigenous enclaves, are said to be without history and are designated as savage, their works forever in the margin.

To be sure, a variety of theories concerning the emergence of important literatures may be utilized in the study of native thought and creativity. What is a theory, after all, but a system of assumptions, accepted principles, and rules of procedure devised to analyze, predict, and explain? It seems to be an important move forward in the teaching and studying of native literatures, that models having lasting worth are being recognized. Classics are, perhaps, to be distinguished from the popular by suggesting that they are standard and authoritative rather than new and experimental. This isn't an elitist stance; rather, it is a cultural imperative in understanding the function of literature in any society.

Whatever Happened to D'Arcy McNickle?

When D'Arcy McNickle, a Salishan Indian writer born and raised in Montana, wrote *The Surrounded* in 1936, he wrote about real people and real events, the struggle of Indian governments, the politics of Americanization, and assimilation. His second novel, *Wind from an Enemy Sky,* another classic, was published posthumously. Although McNickle may not have thought of himself primarily as a fictionist, his early imaginative work was the beginning representation by a modern Indian Studies and literary master, yet it is almost forgotten in literary studies today. McNickle also wrote the classic scholarly work *The Indian Tribes of the United States: Ethnic and Cultural Survival,* a study that was published by Oxford University Press under the auspices of the Institute of Race Relations in London as early as 1962 and, unlike his fictional work, is often still used in those rare Indian Studies courses worth examination.[25]

Another classic novelistic work by Osage intellectual John Joseph Mathews, *Sundown,* fictionalized some of the same real-life dilemmas as the McNickle novel *The Surrounded,* and is just as likely to be ignored in today's literary Studies. Only in American literary Studies can a writer of novels be ignored because he is also a scholar, analyst, and researcher and is politically inclined. The truth is, the characters in these early Native American novels developed the benign and chaotic themes and ideas of tribal life, roots, and geography so appropriate to modern times. There is nothing irrational about this kind of imagination, nothing impressionistic; just real people living real lives.[26] Things have changed in fiction and art and now it may be the time to ask some questions about that change and its consequences. Although Native

American literary study in fiction is a broad field, the contemporary novel seems to be the most visible genre used in schools and universities. Any attempt at assessment of this flourishing art will probably be inadequate but the few observations in this essay may add spark to the current dialogue, which seems to have stagnated into endless discussions of spiderwebs and mixed bloods and fractured lives on the rez.

I would like to argue that the clear message in the most visible of the new American Indian novels, those works written in the past decade or so, is that it is important to escape roots and legacies and geographies even while imagining them in ironic and sophisticated ways. This seems to be the path to literary notice these days. One reads endlessly about chaotic families, or the magic realism of native characters doing out-of-this-world things. One reads about the deficit lives of urban Indians on the streets of America, or the anguish of living lives of despair on the homelands told by characters who can't wait to escape. Stories develop wildly but characters do not develop beyond that yearning. While there is evidence that this may be true of the novel in general, the flourishing message that one must escape one's roots is particularly noteworthy to those scholars interested in contemporary native literatures.

James Wood, a remarkable British critic whose work appears regularly in such literary magazines as the *London Review of Books,* published a piece not too long ago in which he observed this trend in worldwide novel writing and asserted that the need to escape roots in fiction is much more important than the reality one came to expect when one read the novels of thirty years ago. The vision most novelists of today have, Wood asserts, is that real lives either aren't interesting enough or relevant enough for publishers to prepare them for public consumption, and editors, he says, seem to go along with the trend toward magic realism, surrealism, or any of the other techniques in vogue at the time. Keep in mind he isn't talking about the works of those American novelists of substance from the 1970s like E. L. Doctorow, whose interest in and use of history in novels like *The Book of Daniel* was profound. Rather, he is discussing those writers more prominent in the past two decades.[27] Wood's complaint is that many novelists now write works that suggest realism and roots and identity, while lamented, won't matter now or in the future because they can't, they mustn't, that roots are just too long and tortuous. Characters in the new novels, Wood says, look forward to when roots won't matter anymore because they are just buried too damn deep. His comparative examples are the novels of Salman Rushdie, Thomas Pynchon, Don DeLillo, and David Foster Wallace, among others. You may disagree about the choices here but it is his suggestion that these are the writers of what may be called the big contemporary novel. Obvious omissions are many, among them Saul Bellow (1915–2005) and Philip Roth (b. 1933); although Wood does not mention this as cause, this whole dilemma could be a condition of generational forces more than anything else, in which case it is simply an inevitable and irksome literary period from which we will probably move away sooner rather than later.

Wood's point, though, that novels have abandoned storytelling techniques in favor of magic realism and spectacle is as important to native writers as it is to any other writer. Perhaps more so since the storytelling tradition is nothing if not sacred in native life. Wood is afraid that novels have simply become perpetual motion, caricature, and hysterical magic realism and he examines several features of character and plot as evidence: always the great rock musician appears who, when born, began immediately to play air guitar in his crib (Rushdie); a talking dog, a mechanical duck, a giant octagonal cheese, and two clocks having a conversation (Pynchon); a man named Sister Edgar who is obsessed with germs and who may be a reincarnation of J. Edgar Hoover and a conceptual artist painting retired B-52 bombers in the New Mexico desert (DeLillo); and a terrorist group named Wheelchair Assassins devoted to the liberation of Quebec and a film so compelling that anyone who sees it dies (Foster Wallace). Other examples Wood cites feature a Jewish scientist who is genetically engineering a mouse; a group of Jehovah's Witnesses who thinks the world is ending (I would guess they have always thought that); and twins, one in Bangladesh and one in London, who both break their noses at the same time.

Wood asks what it all means in terms of the function of literature in a society and its contribution to civilization—not a trivial question for our times. It is hard to say what it all means but what one may assume is that the conventions of realism are not only being distorted or abolished as one expects in magic realism but, as Wood contends, they are being exhausted and overworked. These writers are simply trying too hard, Wood asserts. It is not a question of objecting to this because of a lack of verisimilitude, which is the usual charge against botched realism, he broods; it is that this kind of writing cannot be faulted because it lacks reality but, rather, because it is evasive of reality. Its purpose is to evade reality, Wood asserts, its purpose is to escape roots and real humanity and real character development, but he doesn't say why.

Reasons for that evasion seem more accessible in Native American literary examples. We know why the rock musician comes to the Spokane Indian

Reservation in Washington State in the Sherman Alexie work *Reservation Blues,* an enormously popular fiction with both native and nonnative readers.[28] It is to vitalize, to give life to a dead, staid, dull culture that no longer has any relevance, to place new roots in the soil of a caricatured place where the roots of reality are buried so deep they are dead.

Other examples seem more ambiguous regarding roots and identity. In Gordon Henry's novel *The Light People,* a character speaks only in haiku and some drunks try to repatriate a severed leg that has been frozen and is now floating down the river. In Louise Erdrich's writing we have come to expect characters full of strangeness. One female character, I think it is Fleur in *Tracks,* goes about with a severed finger in her apron pocket but, again, we don't know why. When I taught a largely non-Indian class in Native American literatures at the University of California, Davis, a few years ago, some students were convinced it was some kind of traditional Ojibway practice of medicine women. In *Bearheart* by Gerald Vizenor there is all manner of curious behavior and events that we can expect because the novel is set in a post–nuclear war period, the point being that in this new world order there can be not only no roots, there can be no morals or ethics either. In Momaday's new work, Set goes mad and is recovered through Bear spirit. Young Bear says: "I once envisioned my mind as a burly porcupine magnificent in its body armor protected by long fire-hardened spikes."[29]

Speaking of porcupines (veering off a bit from the subject at hand), in reading James Welch's final novel *The Heartsong of Charging Elk,*[30] one finds the starving Oglalas out on the Stronghold eating porcupine soup, which would in reality be something like eating their own horses or each other, an activity they would consider so offensive as to be indecent. In reality, Oglalas never ate porcupine. He was called Pahin and even when they wanted to rip off his quills and hair for their own accoutrements, they never killed him, let alone made a meal of him. This complaint, however, is one concerning verisimilitude and probably does not belong in this discussion.

There may be other points to be made but the fact that Charging Elk becomes Francois and never goes home again is probably the most salient point to be made concerning the message about the need to escape roots. Welch, we are told, researched a real-life character, even traveling to France to find him in history, an author's technique that is meant to give this message and its interpretation authenticity.

Even if such an event of relocation occurred (and it no doubt did), one might conclude from this reading that the message in Welch's fictionalized story is that Charging Elk embodies the "vanishing" theory so well known in Indian history. He is obliterated as an Oglala. Admittedly, such things may have happened in real life, although several historical realities are evaded in the story: for example, the fact that most of the Oglalas who participated in the Buffalo Bill extravaganzas during this historical period of genocide that encompasses this story did return to their homelands, Sitting Bull of the Hunkpati being the most famous Indian among those who returned home to lead the people in continued nation building and protest. This means that the Charging Elk story is probably in no way representative of the nineteenth-century Oglala experience because so few Indians really had this experience and even fewer of them exiled themselves forever to a foreign land.

The story, then, in itself, fictionalizes a bizarre and wondrous experience, a spectacle rising out of the Buffalo Bill extravaganza, which was even then based in propaganda and the imagination rather than in history. It must not be assumed by those who write and publish or by those who read the works that this rare and strange experience can be taken to be an important historical event when placed in the context of the new world history being experienced by Indian people all over the continent. The odd thing about this novel is that it is thought to be historical fiction, historical realism. It is not when looked at from the position that there were probably far more important events taking place for the thousands of Lakotas living on the northern Plains of that era. In all likelihood, many political and historical realities of reservation life, native life, of that time were far more significant. In 1877 the Black Hills were stolen by the U.S. government; in 1883 Crow Dog shot Spotted Tail and the Major Crimes Act was passed two years later, and everything changed from that time on; in December of 1890, Sitting Bull was shot by the U.S. colonial police force; and Red Cloud negotiated the 1868 Fort Laramie Treaty after successfully fighting the Powder River Wars. Although some of this is implied in the Welch story, there is little real encapsulation of the history of the brutalization of the American Indian in this genocidal period that one might expect. It is, therefore, a disappointing read for those who have come to think that art can contribute to social criticism, which is surely what D'Arcy McNickle must have been thinking as he wrote fiction several decades ago, and which is what modern literary critic Wood discusses.

Returning to the point that Wood makes, Charging Elk does escape his roots. At the conclusion of the story, still curiously bewildered by the turns his life has taken, Charging Elk is content in his marriage to a French woman, his roots dead and unlamented. He has escaped the reality of being an Oglala in the modern world and he, among the few, has had an unusual experience of displacement, which is what, perhaps, makes him a subject for fiction. As a fictionalized character he seems confused and unresolved. He doesn't seem to grasp much about history, except he knows of the proclaimed defeat of his people. The curious bewilderment displayed by this character seems to give substance to the idea that this is a clear case of sacrificing a character to the message that his people are doomed.

Wood goes on even further to say that the evasion of reality while borrowing from reality itself is a cover-up. It covers up, he contends, the notion that roots matter in this modern world or that they are even accessible. In the case of the American Indian novel of the past decade, the question of what authors are covering up or evading is curiously unexamined. It is true that native writers of today are several generations removed from war or brutal colonization or enforced assimilation or even the memory of exile. It is true that the present scene is 200 years distant from treaty signing, Wounded Knee, the Powder River Wars, the removal of the tribes, the Long Walk, and the theft of a continent and is equally distant from old languages and values and customs stemming from a long ago way of life. But wasn't that true also of D'Arcy McNickle and his companion writers? Is it this distance, getting ever more removed, that makes the cover-up or evasion so tempting to the current crop of fiction writers?

Explanations may be far-reaching into forgotten historical experiences that produce and exhibit a personal rather than a tribal self-imposed hysteria of the imagination expected from writers several generations removed from history. Therefore, this kind of expatriation, perhaps even experienced by the American writers of immigrant stories and histories talked about by Wood, may be still another ancillary explanation useful in native literary studies. By law and national U.S. policy, indigenous peoples all over the country as well as those in other countries developed through colonial practice have been removed from their specific geographical homelands. Because of the nonvoluntary nature of this displacement, so-called Third World writers (which in my view could describe American Indian writers) may have an explanation different from that of Wood, the British critic.

Their explanation might be more in keeping with that of Wole Soyinka, for example, a Nigerian writer now living in the United States, who suggests that the condition of the writer in exile (or one removed from specific tribal geographies) is that of the telephone person, in touch with all the world but with no world to call his own. It is a compelling metaphor. Assuming for a moment that the American Indian writer can be seen as an exile, the world he or she re-creates in the imagination can certainly be a world without roots. While on the telephone, a singularly isolating instrument of technology, one can give credibility to all manner of rumor, exaggeration, lies, and traumas.[31]

If exile is a real cause for the hysterical nature of the magically realistic stories being told, which way will the Native American novel go and what is its future? Will it continue to be the spectacle it has become in the past decade, a sprouting of bizarre and deformed imaginings that make tragedy and anguish irrelevant or, worse, a silly joke, or will it approach characters and make them human in an intelligent balance of family, sex, war, history, life, memory of the past, and vitality? Real humanity in characterization is what is at stake here.

To arrive at exile as a writer, however, according to Soyinka at least, is a matter of choice. One must say, "I have arrived at Exile," and go on from there into taking whatever role is useful to reinterpretation. If the loss is too anguishing, the surreal imagination is a way out. If cultural longing is overwhelming, suicide and the end of character becomes the function of plot. If we take literature seriously, though, we must know that as histories and writers are defeated in this way, the pages of human recall become empty, and this is dangerous for the whole world.

Wood goes on to suggest that the need to escape human memory and roots is something that can be sacrificed to magic and the marketplace if the responsibility of literature is only for the sake of the popular embrace of conflicts to reality that should not be there in the first place. A literature that succeeds on the threshold of reality but accepts the surreal in order to keep in touch, however distantly, with the chaotic world that is moving on with or without either the reader or the writer has its own risks.

The chasm between the works of Montana Salishan writer and historian D'Arcy McNickle and the newest of the American Indian novelists may widen. Thus, the question of what the need to escape roots means and what the current novelists are evading in the new fiction may boil down to the private expression of themes and ideas of permanent exile. The radical conscience and the stunning renaissance of the mid-twentieth century will be over and I, for one, will no longer consider the creation of Native American literary art a cause for rejoicing.

INTRODUCTION TO CLASSICISM IN NEW
AMERICAN INDIAN LITERATURES

The story *Remnants of the First Earth* by Ray A. Young Bear begins in 1960 along the Iowa River. Because the setting is both mythic and realistic, it is a useful work for introducing the notion of classicism in contemporary American Indian literatures.[32]

When professors began to teach Native American literatures in the 1960s as one of the major course offerings in the academic discipline of Indian Studies, Ray A. Young Bear was just beginning his academic writing career. It was easy then to lecture and discuss and advance any kind of literary notion, no matter how out of the way one's preferences were, because there really wasn't a common body of fiction or novels yet written by American Indians nor was there a substantial body of useful criticism. So they began with the Pulitzer Prize–winning *House Made of Dawn* by N. Scott Momaday and talked out of two sides of their mouths. They (1) examined stories and legends of the southwest Indians and Kiowas and (2) studied such Euro-literary techniques as stream of consciousness and imagery in the modernist tradition of novel writing.

Dr. Larry Evers, who was at the time a professor in the English Department at the University of Arizona in Tucson, eventually wrote several pieces of essential criticism on Momaday's work and on other short fictions and these became the guidebooks of choice used to help everyone in English departments struggling with the massive and difficult matters taken up in the novel concerning native history and culture. Evers presented a crucial paper, "Ways of Telling a Historical Event," at the Rocky Mountain Modern Language Association annual meeting in Santa Fe, New Mexico, in 1976 and at the Modern Language Association seminar on Native American literature in Flagstaff, Arizona, becoming an essential scholar in the study of the works of tribal writers of the Southwest.[33] For the most part, that criticism centered on the theme of violence and the death of the white intruder, but other works by Evers have concentrated on the oral traditions of Southwest cultures. Those are the spectacular beginnings that followed Momaday's precursor, the classic yet modern emergence narrative titled *The Way to Rainy Mountain*.[34] Evers' essay on Momaday's *House Made of Dawn*,[35] entitled "Words and Place: A Reading of *House Made of Dawn*," made it possible almost single-handedly for critics and teachers to access the novel in appropriate ways.[36] These works by Evers, who later did groundbreaking work in translation, became the earliest essential criticism and have been influential ever since.

From there, professors and scholars went to poetry by James Welch, Duane Niatum, and Ray Young Bear and the short stories of Simon Ortiz, Leslie Marmon Silko, and many lesser-known writers. There was little notion of canon then, and there was nothing to compare anything to except early American fiction writing like Faulkner's southern regional oeuvre and, certainly, there was no such thing as theory. Then, Louise Erdrich and Leslie Silko came along, which not only allowed but also encouraged the emergence of studies in comparisons and contrasts with such Americanists as Faulkner.

Since that time, teaching Native American literatures as the invention of the twentieth century has been opened up by the enormous body of work produced by American Indian writers. Thus, the teaching and writing about the works has become an undertaking of great possibilities and illuminating discovery. For the most part, contemporary American Indian fiction has concerned itself with places and people largely forgotten by the mainstream. Place, as demonstrated in Momaday's *House Made of Dawn,* is the dominant finding of form that produces a variety of characters almost unknown to America, not only Abel and Tosamah but also Nanapush and Lulu, Lame Bull and Cecelia Capture, Ted Facepaint and Archilde, and even Aurelia Blue.

To read and teach Young Bear's autobiographical novel *Remnants of the First Earth,* one must first read his *Black Eagle Child: The Facepaint Narratives,* where it all begins—the characters, the themes, and the setting.[37] Because several questions that encompass all of the major novels of the twentieth century by American Indian writers come to mind, it is most curious that we don't know much about where Indian writers come from and how they are assessed in their own literary terms. What does the average American really know about Indian writers and how is it known? What do we know of the traditional literatures of natives to this continent and how do we know them? What is the role of the oral traditions so ubiquitous in the study of writers like Momaday and Young Bear and others in the past decades? Most important, if the contemporary literatures of native writers is to be a major focus of study, why is a novel like *House Made of Dawn* considered a classic and given a Pulitzer Prize while the novel *Remnants of the First Earth,* Ray Young Bear's first full-length fiction, remains obscure and rather more useful as a study in traditional ethics than as a mainstream literary work?

These are among the questions posed by modernists and postmodernists of the period just before 1980 and just after 1990. This was the so-called fallen time in American literary study, when writers who it is said had inherited a body of inaccessible and disagreeable fiction began to notice the dismalness of current life and express it in their stories; people who followed, perhaps,

Ezra Pound or Philip Roth. Indeed, Robert Rebein, in his study *Hicks, Tribes and Dirty Realists: American Fiction after Postmodernism,*[38] suggests that any one of the writers taken up in most college courses these days might easily be forgotten and out of print thirty years from now, probably because of the disagreeableness of their visions, which many say is the reflection of modernity itself. None, then, one supposes, will emerge as classics if Rebein is correct in his assumptions.

Rebein, who may not be considered a major critical voice but one who rises from his very substantial classroom experience, does not take up the Young Bear work or N. Scott Momaday's work except to mention that Momaday has won literary acclaim. But he does take up such diverse works as those of Ray Carver, Cormac McCarthy, Don DeLillo, Louise Erdrich, Dorothy Allison, Barbara Kingsolver, E. Annie Proulx, Chris Offutt, James Welch, Christine Quintasket, Leslie Silko, and even Sherman Alexie. His brief discussions concerning Indian writers is not authoritative because his focus is on what he calls "dirty realism, minimalism, and the new west novel" as a whole rather than the more tribally oriented works of native writers like Young Bear, whom he does not even mention.[39] Nonetheless, the Rebein criticism illuminates some thoughts concerning the question of what we realistically know of contemporary Indian writers and where that knowledge comes from as well as the more theoretical questions for those who are considered modern writers: what is a classic, and what comes after postmodernism?

Rebein muses: "Does not postmodernism itself connote a kind of finality, the end of things not the least of which would be the end of innocence with regard to language and mimesis? Does not the term refer to a period of time we are still, demonstrably, in? And, anyway, doesn't a denial of the dominion of postmodernism amount to a de facto admission of artistic and cultural conservatism? Are we not speaking here of a kind of regression, aesthetically speaking?" His discussion of literatures produced by American Indian writers is included in this end-of-things musing about aesthetics and philosophy, but he takes up very little politically and fails to even mention classicism.[40]

Rebein, as one of many critics who knows modernism, argues that there is a renewed appreciation of the importance of the concept of place and expansion of our traditional ideas of authorship for all current writers, but he admits that American Indians are at once the most displaced of all twentieth-century persons and those to whom the concept of place is perhaps most vitally important.[41] This may be a stereotype that arises out of the eastern tribal experience; if one looks at a current map of the large western tribes today, they are essentially where twentieth-century cartographers like D'Arcy

McNickle suggests they always were, at least in broad terms. This is certainly true of the setting, myths, and characters written about by Young Bear, the most undisplaced Middle Plains writer of them all. He is a writer aware and knowledgeable of the "literature behind it," which is a feature of setting and culture and, therefore, an exemplar of those of the classical literati.

Young Bear was born in the Midwest in the middle of the twentieth century and is a first-language and bilingual native speaker of the Mesquawkie language (Sac and Fox). His birthright is an essential tribal family and his place is the geography of indigenousness notable for its many centuries of development in this geography, his tribe presently residing in what is now Iowa. In spite of all that (or perhaps because of that background), he is considered to be a fiction writer and a modernist by critics and readers, as are most of the contemporary American Indian writers of the so-called renaissance that emerged subsequent to the publication of Momaday's *House Made of Dawn* in the 1960s.

There is much to be said, however, concerning the controversial place Young Bear occupies among twentieth-century native literati, which may illuminate the reasons that he is not included in a work like *Hicks, Tribes and Dirty Realists*. In some ways, it may not be surprising that most modernist and postmodernist critics have said little or nothing about Young Bear's work. It is probably not just a function of who publishes who, or that university presses published early Young Bear work while the commercial house of HarperCollins published Erdrich. It may be, more appropriately, a function of the differences between humanist and antihumanist critics, the former concerning themselves with what can be described as mainstream reality and mainstream life, the latter perhaps functioning without the literature behind it. This suggests a pan-Indian literary canon rather than a tribal one.

Because we can assume that the narrative of realism has been largely abandoned by the newest American writers (except, as Rebein describes it, as "dirty realism"), modernism and postmodernism have come about because the world has been drastically altered and there are no more certainties. Many literary movements have come about for these same reasons: for example, the rise of existentialism, particularly in Europe just after the two world wars; stream of consciousness during the Freudian period; and magic realism in South America.

That being the case, it has always been a curious fact that existentialism, a literary movement of vast influence, has rarely been used to describe the works of native American writers who, surely, suffered as much catastrophe as those nations of middle Europe in the 1930s and 1940s. There is no doubt that the so-called Indian world has changed drastically during what is considered modern times—that is, the twentieth century—and Young Bear has been witness to it all, his work contextualizing a compelling tribal past from about 1950 to the present. To connect his classical fiction to modernism and postmodernism instead of existentialism or stream of consciousness or magic realism may be because European world wars were not the cause of the catastrophic change in the Indian world; rather, ongoing invasion and persistent colonial policies perpetuated by the U.S. government on tribal sovereign communities were the causes of massive upheaval in Indian lives.

The protagonist of Black Eagle Child, Edgar Bearchild, is married to a tribal woman with her own name, Selene Buffalo Husband. There is the suggestion here that by remaining in the community of his birth rather than relocating or, worse yet, mirroring the whites who surround his village, those folks notable, he says, for having burned their bridges to the past, his characters will be true to their people's stories and their modern lives. This determination has been called by critic Albert E. Stone, wrongly, I think, a "distinctive and thoroughly American artifact."[42] "Artifact," as I understand the term, refers to any object made by humans with a view to subsequent use, a contrivance to take the place of something original. Is that what the Young Bear story exemplifies? I am not so sure because that would imply that he, too, burns bridges and is, therefore, not an original. Of all the tribal writers one reads, Young Bear is the least likely to burn his bridges to the past. Therefore, using caution before we apply that term is probably wise.

Taking this work out of the context of the American literary canon into which Stone places it because of the colonial nature of the canon, Ray Young Bear's voice is neither distinctively American nor is it a substitute for something original. It is tribal and ceremonial and it may be the only work of its kind at this moment. Critic Craig Womack has not taken up Young Bear's work but has made useful arguments in his text on literary studies for a tribal nation–based model of criticism that suggests the distinctiveness of critical traditions of distinct Indian nations. Womack's work is, perhaps, the most important anticolonial literary criticism work so far from native scholars.[43] Young Bear's work connects with America only tangentially as an inevitable journey that ends through the "scattering of cigarette tobacco on the floor and through the ever-circling stories to remind its native readers every day how imperative it is to realign our destiny, to salvage these cherished but immutable islands of ourselves that tumble aimlessly among the blinding stars."[44] How anticolonialistic and, therefore, antipostmodern are those ideas and themes? How classical?

This concluding imagery directed toward destiny and the stars is essential to understanding Young Bear's point; that is, that a direct connection to the origin stories of Plains Indians places all of the events of a tribal history in the context of ancestral experience, much of which has little or nothing to do with the matters of ongoing current events. He places this direct connection in the hands of those who recognize mythology to contend that they were once the star people; because they are, they remain connected to and placed in a specific geography through tribal creation stories. The sense of place, then, is much more essential than mere borderlands or the new West, where an entire group of Western types—the cowboys and gold miners and roughriders and Leatherstockings—reside. What remains admirable about the Young Bear oeuvre is its liberating antithetical directionlessness as it confronts modernist literary theory. There is nothing about the concrete universal so ubiquitous in modernism or postmodernism that bothers him or his work, and this means that critics must of necessity look at the "literature that precedes it."

2

AN ASIDE:
HOW DO WE KNOW ABOUT
LITERARY INDIANS?

WHY CALL YE?

In his writing and speaking of how modern America has come to know of his people, the Sac and Fox of eastern Iowa (or the Mesquawkie, as they call themselves), Young Bear has been critical of the scholarship that has been available concerning the imaginative tribal voice he has known intimately. The so-called Americanism that has pervaded most of the tribal literatures over the last few centuries has been handled largely through nontribal translators. *Fox Texts* by William Jones is one such example; Fred McTaggart, another collector of Indian lore, wrote *Wolf That I Am* in 1976. Young Bear satirizes those texts by writing his rejoinder *Wolf That I Iz.* He has continued to take a pejorative look at the work of such intruding scholars in his prose and poetry, often through the use of satire and irony. This in spite of the fact that Jones was said to be a half-Mesquawkie native speaker and bilingual, as is Young Bear.[1]

A brief overview of the works of the nineteenth century indicates that readers have learned about Indians not only from William Jones and Fred McTaggart but also from such luminaries as Longfellow, Henry Rowe Schoolcraft, the Jesuits, George Catlin, Frank Cushing, Ruth Bunzel, Franz Boas, Henry David Thoreau, John Neihardt, Natalie Curtis, and other prodigious writers of books and scholarly works. Thus, the history of literary studies in Native America has largely been that of an exogenous study that has been taken up, recorded, translated, and analyzed by Euro-American scholars. This methodology has been defended as unbiased by those outside of the culture and experience, a theoretical defense that is often derided by native scholars.

It is useful to say just a few things about this period of access that produced the above-mentioned scholars and their works. Colonizing nations of the West, and particularly the United States, invented the disciplines of anthropology and ethnology, from which we get the earliest studies of native peoples. Frank Cushing was a nineteenth-century anthropologist who did scholarly work on the Zuni peoples of the Southwest. Some go so far as to say that Cushing invented anthropology and that there was not really such a discipline until he came along.

Cushing called himself the first war-chief of the Zuni, was photographed in Zuni dress (which he said was traditional but simply has a look of bizarre tackiness), was supported by and was the envy of many anthropologists of his day, and said, mostly in way of critical analysis, that Zuni oral narratives resembled Victorian prose. Here is an example of one of his translations:

> Why call ye,
> small worms of the waters,
> ... why call ye the words of my name?[2]

I am unfamiliar with the original work from which Cushing translated this, but it is safe to say that the Zuni would hardly recognize themselves in this kind of translation and aesthetic. To even the most uncritical reader, the poem sounds corrupted and derivative. Nonetheless, it may be argued that the American public might be able to respond in positive ways because of the comparative approach to translation, the examination of how things are alike. If we are determined to see how Victorian prose is like Zuni expression, anything is possible.

Henry Rowe Schoolcraft (1793–1864) did much work on the Ojibwa, as did Henry David Thoreau and Longfellow, whose verse narrative *The Song of Hiawatha* became an essential text in early American literatures and filled the need of a nonnative public that was longing for some connection to the land and its original inhabitants. This was a very long piece of what Longfellow defined and described as "Indian poetry" and it was made quickly into pageantry, becoming quite popular with the masses.

These pageants are still performed at historical places in Minnesota and other eastern Plains cities and towns for local consumption and the tourist trade. Longfellow, who is studied in every classroom in America, said the Indians are full of poetry; I am not certain how he knew this because he did not have a clear grasp of native languages, and he invented and corrupted

Indian "serenades" that were useful for entertaining white readers of prose and poetry who were filled with the desire to more fully understand the romantic nature of Indians.

A serenade, as you may know, is an honorific musical performance, especially one given for a male's lover or sweetheart! Longfellow's invented rhythms are known to all of us who have gone to the movies over the years: BUM, bum, bum, bum, BUM, bum, bum, bum, BUM, bum, bum, bum. These beats permeated the imagined literature, movies, and songs about Indians in the nineteenth century.

Longfellow noticed not only rhythms, creating what he thought were aesthetically pleasing sounds for nontribal audiences, but also what he named and defined as "structural parallelisms," such as the following:

> the skunk appears in the blue of the sky
> the owl appears in the blue of the sky
> the salamander appears in the blue of the sky
> the grandmother appears in the blue of the sky

This half-singing, half-reciting parallelism in verse appealed to American tastes of the time and, perhaps, still does. Some contemporaries are today writing poetry much like this. Many Indian writers who have little access to tribal language rhythms find this parallelism and sound appealing. One can even find this parallelism in the work of Kiowa poet N. Scott Momaday, which might reflect the notion that all American writers have been heavily influenced by early translators of largely contrived Indian works.

Later in the nineteenth century, Franz Boas emerged as a major influence; Ruth Bunzel, just one of his hundreds of followers, did a quite a lot of work in translating the ritual poetry of native peoples. Bunzel compared Indian ritual poetry favorably to the scripture and literature shaped by Judeo-Christian works. All Indian ritual poetry, she said, could be understood and valued and appreciated—if one understood that it was shaped just like scripture and literature and biblical studies.

Natalie Curtis, also influenced by Boas, was a musician by training and got interested first in native songs and later in culture and lifestyle. She did work in Hopi-land and published some Hopi translations as early as 1904, and in 1907 she published *The Indians' Book*,[3] which has become a handbook for the study of Indian art and is still in publication and can be bought at almost any bookstore. Curtis's work is exceedingly popular with mainstream scholars of many disciplines. You may not be able to find any book written by Young Bear in a bookstore near you, but you will be able to find *The Indians' Book*.

Oddly, Curtis worried about Christianity in the Hopi schools; thus, she had more of a consciousness than most of what might happen as intrusions into cultural realms occurred. She wanted the Hopi untouched by white hands, yet, ironically, exempted herself from that intrusiveness.

A later entrant into this literary milieu was John Neihardt, a poet and Nebraska professor who wrote *Black Elk Speaks* and a large number of poems that he said resembled the poetics of Plains Indians, namely the Lakota Sioux. *Black Elk Speaks* is an ethnographic biography, a generic subspecies of the classic scholarly work done in anthropology and ethnology. This genre is an outgrowth of fieldwork done by people who consider themselves to be scientists because they use the scientific method and tools such as tape recorders and linguistic knowledge and theories. Most of these people were not fluent in native languages but they claimed a linguistic facility that transferred one language into another—if not for the purpose of appreciation, at least for the purpose of explication.

In fact, we also know about Indians by going back to the boarding-school era of indigenous writing as a briefer and probably less accessible and less acceptable companion to the scholarly anthropological era of exogenous writing. A number of novels and short stories written by the captives and graduates of church and government boarding schools early in the nineteenth century treated many of the themes thought to be important during those times: personal stories that lacked political or legal analysis.

As early as 1891, Sophia Alice Callahan wrote *Wynema,* Simon Pokagon wrote *Queen of the Woods* in 1899, Christine Quintasket (Mourning Dove) wrote *Cogewea, the Half-Blood* in 1927, John Joseph Mathews wrote *Sundown* in 1934, and D'Arcy McNickle wrote *The Surrounded* in 1936.[4] In 1919, a Sisseton-Wahpeton named Amos One Road, while he was a theology student in New York, began a manuscript with Alanson Skinner, a white curator and anthropologist, recording tales, customs, and folklore of the Sisseton Sioux people. It was finally edited by Laura L. Anderson and published in 2003 as *Being Dakota.*[5] In the same era as One Road's work, Ella Deloria wrote *Dakota Texts* under the guidance of Franz Boas.[6] Many of these works were ignored for decades by literary establishments until white academics, professors of literature, and researchers discovered them and made them available through academic presses. A bibliographic work, *American Indian Literatures* by A. LaVonne Ruoff, a scholar associated with the Association for the Study of American Indian Literatures (ASAIL), has put much of this in perspective.[7]

Some think that these early boarding school and missionary-educated writers, who were largely concerned with assimilation and border crossings, brought about the renaissance that, in turn, produced the fictional works we are studying today—writers such as James Welch, Leslie Marmon Silko, Sherman Alexie, Louise Erdrich, and N. Scott Momaday. Others think that the new renaissance works are the result of affirmative action policies starting in and during the politically charged climate of the 1960s.

Still others think that the new renaissance works are more the function of MFA programs than they are of genuine artistic merit or tradition. Indeed, Robert Rebein suggests the possibility of overriding influence of MFA programs as well as other political influences after postmodernism. He suggests a rather dismissive note on the part of literary scholars concerning much of this current work when he says: "at their best, these books represent a whole new line in American literature, something fresh and exciting to read, talk about, and include in an ever-expanding literary canon. At their worst, which is only to say their most suspect, they are the result of an affirmative action wave in publishing and academic circles that since the early 1970s has been ever on the lookout for authors from minority backgrounds. While many have praised Momaday's novel, often lavishly, others see its success as more a reflection of the political climate circa 1969 than of clear artistic merit."[8]

Some critics of the western literary scene have suggested that this writing is the result of the New West Renaissance, which had as its major interest the sense of place; and they, therefore, pose the possibility that Erdrich and Welch are not distinctly engaged in cultures or histories that are very much different from those explored by Barbara Kingsolver, John Nichols, Gretel Erlich, Ivan Doig, or, for that matter, Faulkner; that there is an assimilation of the imagination and craft that can be identified as Americanism, particularly the New West. Perhaps one of the reasons for the rather dismissive note of some of these critics is that, by and large, few literary critics are equipped to undertake the role played by tribal literary canons in their assessment of these imaginative works because they have never studied tribal literatures and languages. They can only say what the works amount to as "minority" literatures in terms of an all-inclusive American literary canon. It is my suggestion that this may be one important method used so that the works of new American Indian writers can be cast into inferior literary spectra where early classicists have said their works can more appropriately be assessed, not out of any malicious intent but because of the dominance of American works and, also, because of the argument concerning "oral" literatures as being inferior to "written" literatures. Early critics believed that "oral" literatures are not to be referred to as literary works but, rather, folk literatures.

More insightfully and less dismissively, a well-known critic and editor from New York, Ted Solotaroff, published a seminal essay entitled "Writing in the Cold" in 1985.[9] He said: "I don't think one can understand the literary situation today without dealing with the one genuine revolutionary development in American letters during the second half of the century, the rise of the creative writing programs." At a time when more American Indians than ever before were enrolled in college programs, most of the writers we study today in the literatures of Native America courses rise out of the creative writing developments at universities or, put in the broader related context, out of academe. The question of what this means in terms of the development of the literary voice of the contemporary American Indian is something that must be taken up by critics and students alike.

One of the reasons for calling for this examination is to verify the tribal literary sources of contemporary works, a way to validate the vast body of literatures and languages and histories of tribal peoples. This would be serious and difficult work, since many of the source materials we speak of are thought to be inaccessible except through scientific rather than literary scholarship. Solotaroff's sentiments, if taken seriously, can move what we say about contemporary American literary study out of the doldrums of anthropology and put it into the context of what we call now creative writing. This makes the observations by the more staid critics among us less relevant, perhaps; critics like Bernd C. Peyer, for example, who says: "The history of American Indian literature can be roughly divided into three phases that correlate with major historical trends shaping colonial and federal Indian policy."[10]

These are the Peyer phases:

> First, the Salvationist period from early seventeenth century to the beginning of the Civil War, those educated by missionaries and, with few exceptions, trained by them to serve as ministers of the gospel. Their pietistic writings consequently reflect their own acceptance of Protestant ideals and their sincere belief in the need for all Indians to adapt to the dominant society in order to survive. In most cases, however, these authors also made rational and critical assessments of contemporary Indian–White relations and expressed their own notions for improving their people's situation. This still characterizes much of the contemporary Indian literatures which means that much of it has its roots in the lives and the writings of the Indian missionary-writers.

The next period, according to Peyer, is the transitional period from the Civil War to the 1930s, and the final period, the modern period, encompasses a great number of transcultural individuals with unique life histories and remarkable contributions to the growing genre.

The categories created by Peyer assess the historical flow of native expressiveness but cannot be thought to be "literary" studies because languages and oral predecessors are rarely considered. The transcultural period is a popular period and has produced popular genres such as life stories, which follow American reading tastes. In this period there is, generally, some focus on political or even ideological topics but the emphasis is on people who think that power is in personality. Much of it is derivative and all about "me" (in accordance with American tastes), but that does not make it a lesser body of work, just a nonliterary oeuvre.

This being the case, Indians like La Malinche (Dona Marina), Hernan Cortes's ally in the conquest of Mexico, who glorify the mixture of cultures, the crossbreeding of cultures, and the role of the intermediary, are probably the foremost standard-bearers of the early native voice. Malinche was a slave of Aztec rulers, given to the Mayas and then passed on to the Spanish conquistadores, a kind of early Sacajawea. In the case of Sacajawea, it is said that she married Frenchman Toussaint Charbonneau and, some historians say, died in childbirth. The discussion about whether Sacajawea was Hidatsa or whether she was not is currently the question thought to be of historical significance. Rarely is it said that she, like Malinche, was a useful tool for colonizers, the controversial bearer of the colonizer's children, and very likely thought by some Indian activists to be a treasonous figure. After all, she was assisting in what activists call the "invasion" of sovereign lands.

After the 1620 landing of the Pilgrims in Massachusetts, many Indians played these roles from various tribes of the continent, such as Micmac, Wanape, Huron, Wampanoag, Capawake, tribes that are not any longer (if they ever were) a part of the treaty-tribal paradigm of the modern Western political struggle, many of them passed away into a very fragmented history. Everyone in America now reads of these historical figures, natives such as the famous Squanto who proved to be invaluable to the American/English survival and subsequent conquest but whose tribal nation has disappeared from the globe. The names of others are less notable and have only recently become part of the dialogue concerning the early native voice: Samson Occom (Mohegan), William Apess (Pequot), Elias Boudinot (Cherokee), and George Copway (Ojibway). The essential traits of the writings of these early periods seem to me to be the expression of the clear inevitability of assimilation and forlorn abandonment by these writers and scholars and historical figures of their native communities as continuing nationalistic paradigms, although there is some argument concerning this assessment.

WHY NOT POSTMODERNISM?

In terms of a modern revolutionary development that is talked about in literature rising out of academe at the passing of the twentieth century, classicism is seldom a part of the explication. Yet several theories are useful and several terms should be introduced as a way to analyze the present dilemmas. The term "postmodernism" is most often used to describe the writing of the last decades of the twentieth century and probably should be applied to almost all of the novels written by modern English-speaking American Indians.

A good place to begin the study of American Indian postmodernism is with the novels of Leslie Silko. Her novels and other similar ones written by Indians do not express faith in America, its democratic system, or its prosperous future. This is one of the major traits of postmodern American Indian fiction distinguishing it from early assimilationist writings. In Silko, as in postmodernist writing in general, there is little reference to the "literatures behind it" and no assertion of America's grand potential that one finds in the novels of early writers; some critics say that is because John Wayne has replaced Abraham Lincoln as the representative man for many American audiences. The world has changed irrevocably in response to modern events: the Vietnam War, the Nixon Watergate scandal, the rise of the religious right, preemptive bombings, 9/11, and all the rest.

The resigned pessimism that characterizes postmodernism is said by critics to be a major trend in the writings of most American writers, not just American Indian writers. Almost all of the so-called minority writers of this period, certainly all of the American Indian writers, accuse America of massive crimes against humanity—that is, blacks and slavery, American indigenes and genocide, Chicano/Chicana immigration and border discrimination, even ecocide—thus, these postmodern writers generally are filled with disgust, are unrelenting in their accusations, and seem to be absolutely unforgiving. They do not take part in the pride of America or the hope for the future of America that has characterized writers of different eras and cultures. This differs, too, from what went on in the sixties when it was thought that America was unachieved and there was an accompanying sense of hope for appropriate change. On the contrary, a writer like Silko suggests that white America has not changed its stance toward natives and she wants us to know that America will, therefore, suffer God's wrath. She is intent upon retribu-tion, which means that America must pay for its crimes; something must be given up in payment—if not death, at least punishment.

INSTEAD, PRAGMATISM

Philosophically speaking, these postmodern works tell us that it is simply absurd to think that America can redeem itself, so in terms of literary critical analysis, it might be useful to think of these writers not as hateful propagan-dists but rather as pragmatists. They don't want the contemplation of one's soul asking what is right, but instead want to ask what is useful. Defined more fully, pragmatism is a nearly forgotten and discredited theoretical guide to philosophical thought in the studies of American literary works. These works, rather than just miring themselves in pessimism, often want to ask what is possible in the real world and what is useful, and sometimes they want to speculate about how solutions can be sought in the face of near hopelessness; sometimes even solutions are not required.

To get to that point, they must force readers to stop focusing on the failed hope that America can become enlightened on its way to greatness. They have simply and irrevocably abandoned that notion. Silko is filled with disgust and, therefore, is doing something in contrast to even disillusioned writers like Upton Sinclair and Mark Twain, who, in spite of the realistic stories they wrote, continued to believe in the future of America. The opposing notions exemplified by Silko give postmodernism a way to revolt against the formal-ism of the fiction of past eras.

Not only that, Silko's literary disillusionment gives substance to the practi-cal decolonization work being done by native scholars such as Linda Tuhi-wai Smith and Taiaiake Alfred and others who speak of the imperialism of Western nations as predatory and disastrous not only to indigenous life but to any kind of life on this planet. This is dangerous talk because Smith, in particular, believes that imperialism is an inescapable yet "integral part of Europe's economic expansion" and, therefore, is the precursor to and an integral part of America's capitalistic democracy that Silko despises and says must be destroyed.[11]

Although there is probably little doubt that Young Bear shares these po-litical views concerning the assessments of the power of America, there are several traits that set his work apart from modernity and postmodernism and even from the writers discussed here. Why not label it "pragmatism," which can still be defined, one supposes, as the theory that the meaning of a proposition or course of action lies in its observable consequences, and that the sum of these consequences constitutes its meaning. This is a theory promulgated by many and summarized by scholars such as Charles S. Peirce and William James who reference it in the *American Heritage Dictionary* of the English language.

Unlike Silko, Young Bear does not center his characters and his stories on disgust for America so much as he centers it on a humorous kind of self-mockery, a taunting contempt for America that stems from tribal experiences that are entirely political rather than literary. His response to these experiences is to disclaim in whatever ways he can the earnestness of those who really have a vested interest in America and its future. He lives, after all, in that lily-white state of Iowa, a place largely unfamiliar with the concept of diversity, where the state fair displays a life-sized cow made entirely of butter, and where serious-minded evangelicals inhabiting churches on every block look daily toward their own redemption. He finds the phoniness that is at the heart of America's darkness and has fun with it. This may be a tradition in contemporary Indian life that predates modernism, a survival technique used in the face of relentless and devastating domination—a political stance rather than an aesthetic one.

Richard Rorty, in his book *Philosophy and Social Hope,*[12] says, "Pragmatism was reasonably shocking seventy years ago but in the ensuing decades it has gradually been absorbed into American common sense. Nowadays, Allan Bloom and Michael Moore seem to be the only people who still think Pragmatism is dangerous to the moral health of our society." In addition, Rorty references Allan Bloom's *The Closing of the American Mind* and Michael Moore's "A Natural Law Theory of Interpretation."[13] All of this would seem a natural trend toward storytelling and fiction writing to an indigenous writer like Young Bear because he, like many natives on this continent, has probably always been suspicious of the so-called scientific method on which law (embedded in politics) is supposedly based. Solutions to such outrageous perfidy probably do not come readily to native minds struggling in the throes of binding colonialism, and they are rarely a part of the plot structure in ancient or modern tribal fiction plot making. Plot, as it is understood in Western literary theory, implies solution, but for colonized peoples, it often implies that the story begins and then it simply goes on.

This leads us to another trait that sets Young Bear apart. It is his reliance on the flawed political and legal experience that is his tribal experience and his dependence on the rise of that old structural realism (maybe even legal realism) so well known in the novels of the early part of the century. What happens in Young Bear's stories is not fantasy, not magic, not metaphysics, not mixed-blood angst, but a realism framed within a tribal belief system and tribal experience that might seem absurd to outsiders.

Even when (in his second novel) One Most Afraid waits by the Iowa River bridge for her lover and is clubbed until she is lifeless, we are told that the perpetrator of this crime rises out of a phenomenon described in the English language as witchcraft. This is not fantasy, nor is it magic. Instead, it is a real phenomenon in many native cultures that has to be taken seriously; that is to say, it can be accounted for in language and myth and history and tribal experience. Thus, the men who probably did the killing are transformed into three owls whose function is to bring knowledge or information to the community and, therefore, no suspect will ever be sought, nor will any suspect be apprehended or brought to justice in the American courts. To distinguish all of this as pragmatic thinking and legal realism is to contextualize this work in its tribal roots. This may be a political interpretation rather than a literary one, yet it seems plausible because there are some things in native life that are simply glossed over, forgotten, or denied by those outside of the tribal attitude. This kind of behavior and event, Young Bear tells us, is not only possible for the Mesquawkie in their relationship with the elements of the natural world; it is expected and can be predicted. These figures move away from the crime scene and its investigation into a space for self-knowledge and cultural revitalization.

This means that for Young Bear the writer, a return to the notion that one must deal with facts or actual occurrences with an emphasis on their practical outcomes guides his story and his characters. In early American theoretical choices for literary critical thought, this was called "pragmatism," noticeable primarily in the studies of American literary authors like Hawthorne of "Young Goodman Brown," and it was essential to the tribal culture that is so important to Young Bear. Oddly, then, and perhaps inexplicably, the knowledge of this death of One Most Afraid and what one personally makes of it as a tribal person and what stories are eventually told about it is what unites the community in its practical and active meaning. While Rorty talks of the banality of pragmatism and suggests that pragmatism is bankrupt in its application to law,[14] native peoples do not agree. Those who confront an aggressive system of law that is basically colonial in its treatment of them can find meaning in the pragmatic approach to the implacability of this flawed legal reasoning that inexplicably keeps them in a condition of domination and suppression.

In order to understand the function of such stories and the function of a tribal writer like Young Bear in Indian communities who share much of the reality of the natural world he examines (as well as the failure to solve hard questions of law in tribal life), it might be said that there is a rejection of Western theory concerning life and death. It may be that just as such a tribal writer rejects the notions of enlightenment and epiphany that Western readers and Christians have come to expect of Western literatures, they continue to find meaning in the natural world that surrounds them and they create literatures that give precedence to the natural world; thus, most significantly, tribal life simply goes on as before, according to Young Bear, and he finds joy in that.

Pragmatists like Young Bear seem to be interested in the study of historical phenomena and real events with the focus on practical outcomes. The practical outcome for Young Bear is not retribution or justice, those Christian concepts sought by Silko; it is, instead, the reassertion of the power of what he calls "first-named systems." Observable consequence is what he tells us about in story after story. An ignorance on the part of readers who know little of Indian myth and tradition and a lack of knowledge concerning the function of ritual life and animal spirits is no excuse for America to be dismissive of the work that tribal writers like Young Bear are attempting in the modern American book culture.

The third literary trait that sets Young Bear apart from the depressive tone and expression of malicious hatred toward an oppressive white culture that one finds in Silko's work and that of other postmodernists is the marvelous element of self-mockery in his narrative. (Tony Bearchild and Edgar Bearchild are used as fictional selves of the author: alter egos. Even Ted Facepaint is another side of the self, a second self, an intimate or inseparable friend, a constant companion.) In order to achieve this, Young Bear devises many hilarious and unlikely supporting characters described as stemming from his tribal community:

> Luciano Bearchild, my first cousin who wore black pinstriped, hand-tailored suits, white silk scarves, Italian shoes, and perforated fingerless gloves used to say, Ah, bo-shit, neighbor! to our futures. He would acquiesce to change by tightening his bow tie and shuffling across the concrete floor like James Brown. In addition to dancing like the famous black entertainer, he was addicted to soul music. He made uncultivated Indians like me cultivated.[15]

To know more about First Cousin is to be drawn into a spellbinding, weird, complicated world of the Mesquawkie that makes you laugh aloud. There is little regression here, no anger or angst, and certainly very little nostalgia concerning inevitable change, only the forward thrust into whatever zany combination the white man and the Indian can make of each other's worlds. Assimilation here is not a problem of isolation and alcoholism, anger and resentment and tragedy, as one sees in Sherman Alexie's *Reservation Blues,* one of the most relentless of tragedies in modern Indian life stories. Instead, the seeming contradictions of assimilation and acculturation are foregone conclusions and do not interfere in any substantial way with the sense of belonging that in contemporary Indian politics is defined as the sovereign condition of nationalism. There are no lost causes in Young Bear's marvelous cultural-based stories, no marginality, no homelessness. The tribal nation is still, for Young Bear, the primary forum for collective self-knowledge and moral law, even as the white man's law is inadequate.

Not everyone speaks the tribal language like First Cousin Luciano (with what approaches archaic perfection), yet they do speak the language and, like Junior Pipestem, they know how to do a Charlie Chaplin routine, and on any log cabin door there is a huge color poster of Rommel, the Desert Fox. On any day, Luciano could sing you to the Black Eagle Child Afterlife, and the next day attend a Navajo Indian anthro lecture at Grinnell College, a twenty-minute drive south to a foreign country.

No problem.

In the process of describing this Mesquawkie tribal world, there are no anxious and unhappy and unfulfilled border figures, no identity-seeking figures here like Archilde in D'Arcy McNickle's *The Surrounded* or Yellow Calf in James Welch's *The Indian Lawyer* or the dozens of characters created by Erdrich who are the literary descendants of entire peoples who have been evicted from sacred homelands en masse and from that time on mourn the loss of sacred ground. Instead, Ted Facepaint and Rose Grassleggings and Selene Buffalo Husband and all of the Black Eagle children embody their own lives in the new times because they know the past (albeit imperfectly) and the tribal language and the religion of the ancestors and the homelands. They have accepted the absurdity of the Well Off Man Church with comedic surety, and the English language and the Why Cheer High School with the aplomb of their relative, Coyote.

The characters that seem to be Young Bear's alter egos—Ted Facepaint, for one—were introduced to Young Bear readers as early as 1992 in his first creative nonfiction, *Black Eagle Child.* They live together at the settlement, go everywhere, and get separated and reunited throughout life's journey:

> There must be nomadic-prone genes in Indian blood, mentally, and cellu-
> lar composition, for Ted Facepaint and I went the same way together—out
> from Tama Country to the eclectic West Coast. This wasn't the plan. It

was sheer coincidence that Ted somehow got his diploma and promptly heeded the advice of a teacher to pursue education instead of house building. Ever since the Arbie's Feeds fiasco, we had lost touch but were able to send word of our plans through friends. Ted was enrolled at the College of the Desert Cactus near Palm Springs which as I was apprised was about an hour's drive due east along the San Gabriel Mountains somewhere past the smog. Unlike most Indians who chose Haskell Indian College in Kansas or the Institute of American Indian Arts in New Mexico, we went to the western edge of the North American Continent. Going as far away as possible from the rest seemed the most logical choice.[16]

These choices, evident as difference throughout the narrative, are what make the Young Bear saga in fictional autobiography so unique and realistic and instructive, although as early as 1880, we have stories of tribal adventurers from the northern Plains finding themselves studying in Pennsylvania, at Carlyle and Dartmouth, and at theological seminaries and other unlikely places. These early encounters, however tribally specific, are serious stories of how to make it in the white man's world. Not so in Young Bear's work. Indeed, journeying together as cotenants in their tribal story, by 1975 Facepaint and Edgar have dropped out of school and have admitted the folly of their ways. Ted hitchhikes back to Iowa and Edgar goes on to poetry readings, two separate but conjoined entities of false tribal hopes and unmet potential. These were the last of their "feral years," says Facepaint by way of explanation, and they continue in their inseparable selves, like Indian Huckleberry Finns, toward maturity and bicultural knowledge, if not the success expected of them.

Moving away from the feral years, the stories simply go on. Relatives abound here and the connections aren't always easy to get straight. For example, Carson Two Red Foot is a brother to Bent Tree. Their father is John Two Red Foot who leaves them for One Most Afraid, the older sister of Dorothy Black Heron, who is murdered in real life. One Most Afraid had waited by the Iowa River bridge for her lover, it was said, and for sure she was clubbed lifeless; it is an unsolved killing that haunts the relatives and the tribal community to this day. Is this real? What does one make of the suggestion that the overlapping of the two worlds so inseparable in the Mesquawkie imagination makes such an event mere occurrence rather than an issue of *Crime and Punishment*?

When the suspected killers are transformed into three owls, the average American reader is thrust reluctantly out of the narrative as surely as the readers of William Faulkner's short story "Dry September" are thrust out of McLendon's car at the last minute along with the accused black man, and all the while violence is undermined by the seductive nature of storytelling. The reader is not obliged to witness the killings or the killers, but only must concentrate on what such outrage means.

If race relations is the subject matter in Young Bear's and Faulkner's narrative, the use of violence, they tell us, is not the way to understand its nature. This is an episode in an ongoing struggle to find a way to tacitly acknowledge the larger sociological attitudes of a community, and the reader must pay attention to the consequences, not the magic or the violence. The Young Bear story is only a story about human nature, after all.

Even though there is much history of inevitable and wrenching change that is endemic in contemporary Indian life, as we all know, *Remnants of the First Earth* is that rare Native American fiction that unexpectedly removes the Indian story from the usual canon of the West and Midwest. The Western story operates on many thematic levels, one of the most significant being that of nature versus man. But, nature *is* man here in these Young Bear stories, not versus man. *Remnants* ignores the conflicts and borders that are so pervasive in the New West writing, the struggle between a land ethic and development, for example, or the theme of the landscape as both threatening and threatened, which portrays many of the characters of the West that we read about and see in the movies as struggling in a world that shows the overbearing and tragic consequence of an ineffectual god. It's not that the struggle isn't there in Young Bear, it's not that the characters aren't aware of it, it is just that god is a given and he is not seen as meddling, nor is he vengeful. God has nothing to do with it and happenings aren't considered to be plot-conflict mechanisms that require a solution. The best that can be expected, then, is that life will go on.

For the past decades, readers of contemporary Indian novels have also enjoyed the border figures drawn both from culture and blood, ever since Momaday's classic novel *House Made of Dawn* described the character of Abel as "caught between two cultures." Indeed, this idea has become so ubiquitous that the Indian characters are often mistaken for their Anglo counterparts in the West. They are isolated loners grieving for the land, homeless ones seeking identity. Readers have endured the fictional themes of the dryness and starkness of the West and the destruction of the rivers for so many decades that there seems to be no difference between the Indian novel and the novel about the West. Thematically, in Western literatures, the universe is unhealthy for human beings, who are in the process of destroying it every day of their lives. It is the sin-and-redemption pattern of the Bible, perhaps.

Young Bear has a different take. Regardless of the many assaults upon the people and the land and the rivers, it is the Mesquawkie view that the supernaturals who reside in the landscape and the waterscape and with the people will continue to thrive because they have no alternative and they ultimately will bring meaning to human lives; that is quite simply their function. The characters Young Bear develops, because they are not minority figures, border figures, or mixed-blood figures, possess a reference to self and place for which there is very little ambiguity. No one here is waiting for God and no one is waiting for America to redeem itself and very few really believe that there are solutions for which individual man and his presence, alone, is responsible. The straightforwardness of other possibilities differentiates this fiction from the irony of Vizenor, for example, the pessimism of Erdrich, the satire of Alexie, or any of the other fictional devices that are used to illuminate but often, instead, obscure.

The realism of Young Bear, which fails to advertise the stereotypes so fruitful to other fictions, renders this fiction less popular with mass audiences and less accessible to readers than the fiction of other novelists of twentieth-century Native American literati. Because the characters (who are tribal) and themes (which rarely omit the presence of the supernatural life of the universe) are so out of the mainstream, scholars have not studied or written about Young Bear's fiction as prolifically as they have about the fiction of Silko, Erdrich, Alexie, or even Momaday.

Some critics have suggested that the self-referential and tribal content of the Young Bear works seems too ambiguous for many mainstream readers so they turn to irony as an explanation for what cannot be grasped as real. Irony is different from ambiguity not only because irony has an edge and generally proceeds as an overt attempt at deception but also because there is little attempt in irony to atone for the lack of some kind of solution to an altogether awful political situation known to colonized peoples. Yet irony is often the same as ambiguity because its function is to make unclear which characters in the story will gather the rewards of complicity and it is left up to the reader, therefore, to set the boundaries. Young Bear takes no responsibility for that. Indeed, he seems a bit flippant about it. It is the community itself, he suggests, that enables irony to happen, and if you get it, that's all right, but if you don't, that's all right, too. That may mean for the reader that there is a certain amount of exclusion and/or sharing that might be assumed.

In addition, readers and critics are confused over the generic definition of Young Bear's fiction and when the generic description cannot be specific, the interpretation cannot take on certainty, which is what readers and critics crave. Boundaries, again, fail to materialize. Can these prose works be called novels? Of course they can, because they do what novels are expected to do: they don't just present themes, they present a worldview. Is this kind of thing called "metafiction"; that is, does it stem from an imagination that is beyond fiction, involving change or transcendence? Frankly, I have never understood the term "metafiction," although it is coming more and more into the vocabulary of literary criticism to take on a variety of meanings. Metafiction is to storytelling what film is to drama, perhaps. In any case, *Remnants of the Earth* is not easy to define. It is neither memoir nor travelogue, though the characters travel through life and landscape. It is not fiction because so many of the events really happened, and it is not anthropology although Young Bear tells you more about culture than any of the scientists who have roamed about the northern Plains for decades.

Can Young Bear's stories be called "creative nonfiction," another term gathering generic nonspecificity? "Life story"? "Ethnographic biography"? Literary critics have been quite imaginative in coining terms to explore the diversity of experimental fiction in the past two decades, but there still seems an unquieting juncture that seems unbridgeable between experimental fiction, in which the writer simply attempts to be clever, and tribal fiction, which only wants to tell the story real-ly. If, as Young Bear suggests, an insect is a musician, which is what his tribal language defines it to be, isn't this a real thing rather than a magical or transcendent thing?

Young Bear's prose life opens with memories of early struggles in the white man's world as the focus, both in *Black Eagle Child* and in *Remnants of the First Earth*. Learning English at Weeping Willow Day School, dropping out of Why Cheer High School, keeping close to the heart the fascinating tribal histories of the Settlement and its politics told by his grandmother and his relatives, hearing about the Great Flood of the Iowa River and the murders and love affairs of his friends and relatives and neighbors—all of these stories are couched in cultural terms. They are expected to somehow reflect how it is that humans live with those the white man calls supernaturals who possess the rivers and the lands of the tribe. And, more basically, how it is that humans protect the natural tribal way of life learned and possessed over too many generations to count.

The intellectual-cultural politics taken on by American Indian writers like Young Bear in the twentieth century is crucial, yet it is often the last thing that a critic wants to hold discourse on as he or she goes about examining the development of Native American literatures. A literary critic much prefers aesthetics. Often critics and readers are afraid of the accusation of being unscholarly, or the accusation of participating in political activism, or, worse, that intellectual-cultural politics as a function of criticism may throw off the unbiased nature of what we claim we do as scholarly investigators. In addition to that worry, politics in academia has often meant turf wars, the lowest common denominator of how to define the word "criticism."

Nonetheless, Young Bear in his work seems to have made an actual political commitment. That commitment is to tribalism, nationalism, and anti-Americanism. This doesn't make him a traitor to America, but it does make him anathema to being a persuasive part of the American literary canon. This is not deconstructionism, because it does not argue toward any center, any boundaries. Readers often expect that the voices gathered in *Remnants of the First Earth* will employ the strategies of resistance, much like the ironic and cynical and romantic voices of other recent writers of the American Indian novel who work toward the dead and repetitious center. This expectation rises out of a whole body of novelistic work of the past three decades that has as its central core a politicized irony (i.e., deception). Yet Young Bear's work, on the contrary, does not embody this ubiquitous culture of resistance because it does not emerge from a place of powerlessness.

After all is said and done, according to Young Bear, the culture of the Mesquawkie, the language and the land, the spirits of place, the relationship of ancestors and the past—all are zones of empowerment, not places of tragedy for the children of the Black Eagle community and the first earth. Authority resides in the protagonist voices of Black Eagle Child and Ted Facepaint because they are never disappointed in the stories they translate, nor are we, the readers and critics.

I am reminded that I once knew a Spokane Indian man who lived near the Columbia River who used to gossip with me about people we knew. He knew them better than I did since he had lived there all his life and I was a comparative newcomer. Since the old man had spoken the Spokane language from childhood and I didn't, and since I knew the Dakota language and he didn't, we talked to each other in our common tongue, English. He often told my husband about the Bear Stories of the Northwest region around the Cascade Mountains, but he refused to tell them to me because women are not supposed to hear them. Because of these restrictions and others, we were reduced to gossip, me with my minimal observations and he in his fractured English that reminded me of so many of the Dakota speakers I had known in my childhood. It was only later, after I grew up and went off to study in far-off realms, that I began to understand the fractured English of first-language native speakers in term of syntax and other torturous literary and grammatical terms.

One day the old man and I were gossiping about a particularly annoying woman of the tribe whom we both knew, and we discussed the various egregious traits of this woman we disliked: her greedy nature, her silliness about men, what a bad cook she was. Then, in a serious moment, he said to me: "Hey, you know, Liz, what I really don't like is . . . is . . . people who go behind the bush and beat around!"

Yeah, I thought, smiling, how about that for imagery? The absurdity of the imagery escapes no one, but the point he makes about intentional or unintentional obfuscation is no exaggeration if one takes a look at the rhetoric one is confronted by in the newest literary criticism texts, which are becoming more and more dense and indecipherable.

The critic's task is not to try to obscure or diminish the possibility of human thought; it is to find a frame of reference. Much of the time this description by the old man is what I think we are doing when we try to develop critical strategies in American Indian literatures acceptable to the academy—we are going behind the bush and beating around.

In the final analysis, though, Young Bear is a writer of narratives, not criticism, and a man who commands the English language like any scholar of rhetoric and composition. Although he is often accused of ambiguity, he makes no bones about what it means to be Mesquawkie. He does not go behind the bush and beat around. Rather, he uses the literatures of the past generations of Mesquawkie to tell us what we need to know about the present, which, very simply, is that the spirits of the Mesquawkie world still surround us. He provides the space necessary for the imagination to thrive. That is the definition of classicism to tribal writers.

While thoughts of politics in *Remnants of the First Earth* are realistic and a good beginning, thoughts and questions concerning the role of mythology and ideology in the classic creative imagination may provide a better beginning because such musings help us to find ways to build on what it is that indigenous writers know. It is helpful to start by watching the UCLA version of the Popul Vuh, which is useful for directing early discussions of fiction. In this film we are told that the present-day indigenes of Guatemala are descendants of the Maya people who developed a remarkable civilization in South America, a world described in the Popul Vuh as the monomyth of the Americas. At the risk of sounding repetitive, it is important to repeat what this means in terms of literature; that is, that the symbols, themes, ideas, genres, and subsequent ideologies of this monomyth permeate all of the tribal mythologies of the continent. These are non-Christian mythologies that inform the native populations who believe their origins occurred on this continent. For the Maya, the belief is that they emerged as human beings, first men and then women, created from a paste made of corn, the plant most venerated by their ancestors.

Thus, their "emergence narrative" is the beginning of all literatures and thoughts and beliefs, even contemporary fiction and poetry. In the mythic sense, then, in what is now Guatemala, the indigenous peoples there are created and their migration across specific continental lands occurs. It suggests that the literary theory of origin thrusts itself toward the north from the south, a theory in direct conflict with the scientific theory of origin, which moves from north to south and is referred to as the Bering Strait theory. This theory has been challenged by Vine Deloria Jr. in all of his work starting with *God Is Red*.[17] Accepting the fact that literary theories concerning indigenous origins on this continent may differ significantly from the scientific theories of disciplines such as anthropology or archaeology may seem strange to most readers and scholars because we have been taught that we must trust science. Yet we must somehow learn to orient ourselves to the vast and powerful mysteries that indigenous mythology and knowledge provides. The kind of mythic narrative available in the Popul Vuh concerning the universe informs all indigenous peoples on this continent and it should be introduced as a background to reading and understanding the works of those who claim to be tribal writers.

A classic contemporary "emergence narrative" that is most often studied in survey courses is *The Way to Rainy Mountain* by N. Scott Momaday[18] and there is considerable effort on the part of scholars to explicate that work. Young Bear, in his oeuvre, provides a similar way of construing origin and can be suggested as "emergence narrative" development.

Because the setting of Young Bear's work is both mythic and realistic, the story begins in 1960 along the Iowa River. "The settlement" is a place in central Iowa purchased by the Sac and Fox Indians during the war and reservation period and occupied since then by Fox Indians who call themselves Mesquawkie. They challenged French occupation (rather than the usual English and other European occupiers met by other Plains tribes) and it is a legacy of the Fox (or Mesquawkie Indians) to have maintained their identity in the face of colonial France in the 1700s. They occupied central Wisconsin, opposed firearms and the fur trade, often refused to put up with their aggressive Sioux neighbors simply by avoiding them, and finally allied themselves with the Sac.

They share many ideas with their neighboring peoples in attempting to answer how it is that humans emerged on this continent. Young Bear's people are related to the Kickapoos, Santee Dakotahs, Osages, Potawatomis, Menominees, and Winnebagos and are said to speak an Algonquin language, although their language is unique to themselves. Creation is an ambiguous affair. Some say the Mesquawkie were created by Wisaka from blood-red clay and the creator was aided by his Grandmother. Spirits of the dead went to a place where Younger Brother (killed in a battle for supremacy by other supernaturals in another world) had prepared a place for them during mythic times, so Death was always known. How similar this is to the underworld struggle told in the Popul Vuh and the creation stories of all Plains peoples.

Young Bear speaks of Well Known Twin Brother in his fiction and says, "According to our Creation Myth, after the War of the Supernatural Beings obliterated the Earth, Me si kwi-Ne ni wa, Ice Deity, had agreed to put away the icy storms in a sacred mat. In the form of water his words were blended with a dark red herbal dye and drawn out as a picture. This was then rolled up, tied together with sinew in elaborate star patterns, and set aside for the Black Eagle Child people as evidence of their tenuous earthly standing. In it was a symbol of trust. As long as Ice Deity's pictures were kept warm and dry by its earthlodge keepers, they would never know the wrath of earth-splintering hail and bolts of cottonwood-seeking lightening."[19] Interplay between the supernaturals (both good and evil) forms an intricate part of the cosmology, just as in the primogenitor, the Popul Vuh. Spirits occupy the earth alongside the Mesquawkie (Fox) and they shape the lives of the people even today. Fire (and thus knowledge) was provided by the Thunderers who are ever-present as are witches who flourish causing sickness and disharmony. Witches can cause crop failure (the Mesquawkie raise corn as a tradition of most native peoples), can steal souls, and they are very active at night, usually. They sometimes assume the form of animals and often are seen passing through the forest as a ball of blue-green light.

The two main characters who impact what we call the contemporary narrative voice are Ted Facepaint and Edgar Bearchild. These characters might be alter egos of the author, Facepaint representing all the things the author loves yet fears, and Bearchild representing the author, the storyteller, the keeper of myth and legend. Facepaint is the "other self" of Bearchild and Bearchild is the "other self" of the author. Thus, the "narrative voice" is multilayered.

If it is true, as Argentinian scholar Jorge Borges says, that "myth is at the beginning of Literature and also at the end," we may speculate about specific examples from the Young Bear fiction that bear out that idea. In other words, it is important to ask two questions: What is "mythic" in this story? and How does this story blur the boundaries between history and legend? Defining "mythology" as something "other-worldly that happens," and "legend" as a story about a specific geography and time, it is useful to speculate about why Bearchild seems disappointed in his own family's history. "Old Bear fizzled," we are told, and this is inextricably connected to the murder that occurs before the turn of the century, the so-called legendary murder. Legendary murder, after all, can be departed from, argued about, and discovered, while mythology leads it to be a taken-for-granted phenomenon.

Young Bear's work combines mythic sensibility and knowledge with specific history, land and myth, personal anecdote, poetry, and a mostly fictional life story called autobiography. It affirms what we call the "oral traditions" and, very specifically, the oral stories of the Mesquawkie. Young Bear does not romanticize or glorify his characters, which makes it hard for those of us unfamiliar with this worldview to see these people he tells us about as "transmitters of culture." Because "the Emergence" embodies one of the most sacred of belief systems and widely held collection of ideas among all indigenous tribal peoples, and because it all remains connected to the home of the dead as well as the living on this continent, Young Bear's tellings and fictionalizations seem necessarily ambiguous. He does what he can to help us forget, yet remember—which is what is expected of all tribal storytellers.

WARRIORS, STILL?

1991

This was the year I stood with hundreds of horrified university students in front of television sets on the campus of the University of California at Davis and watched U.S. bombs fall on Iraq. Afterward, I wrote "America's Iraq Attack and Back to the Indian Wars!" Sometime later, I published this essay in a journal I was editing and this is what I wrote more than a decade ago:

> It is often said of war these days, by Americans of good intention that there are good wars, moral ones, and important ones, that there are wars which are fought for the great ideals. The other wars are bad, immoral, obscene. Traditionally, American Indians, and the Sioux in particular, who also justified war as a sacred business, know the arguments well. Whatever the justification, American Indians fought in the most recent war, Desert Storm, in great numbers just as they have served valiantly in all of this nation's military actions.
>
> The 1991 U.S./United Nations war in the Persian Gulf against Saddam Hussein, we have been asked to believe, was one of the good wars, moral and important. Thus, it was also asked of us as American citizens that we support our troops. Because of this latter request, which we can trace to former President R. M. Nixon's attempt to dispense with any kind of public debate in the waning hours of the Vietnam struggle, a debate which many of us in the 60s and 70s thought to be necessary to a democracy both fragile and corrupt, most of us have come to fear being called traitors to our national causes, whatever they may be; and, so, we often preface our remarks with some kind of personal history. Here's mine:
>
> I am a Dakota Sioux woman on the far side of 50 born and raised on the Crow Creek Indian Reservation. I was married there and all of my

children were born in the land of the Sioux. My only son, chu(n)skay, is now in the naval reserve; my elder brother spent 20 years in the U.S. Navy through World War II and Korea, and he never made it home alive. My father served as a private in the U.S. Army in 1916 almost a decade before he was made a citizen of what he always called an enemy nation which had signed treaties with his people and then tried so hard (and still does) to co-opt the nationhood through legislation. I was married for many years to a Minneconjou from Eagle Butte, South Dakota, who, as a teen-aged Infantryman in WWII (drafted out of the Holy Rosary Mission School at Pine Ridge) won two Bronze Stars carrying a machine gun around Germany. I am married now to a Spokane Indian who is a former Marine. One of my great-grandfathers from Crow Creek was named Bowed Head Ihanktowan and it is in the family records that he fought at the Little Big Horn with Sitting Bull and Gall.

I come, therefore, from a nation of warriors who defended this land long before any white man set foot on this continent in wars that were not wars of annihilation nor were they wars of conquest. It was only after they fought the white man that they came to know of those kinds of wars; thus, they, too, have been drawn into the debate concerning good war versus bad.

Though we as a part of the great American public are still uninformed concerning many of the details of that war, I have reached the sad conclusion that the Saudis and the Kuwaitis made a grave mistake when they invited the United States into their war, this most recent conflict which they were forced into with their Arab brothers in the middle East, a place which is many lifetimes away from mine.

Perhaps they did it because they did not have access to the appropriate Native American history. Few people do, no matter what part of the globe they inhabit. Had they done their homework in that history, they would have known that in offering such an invitation to the United States, they would never again be free of its aggression for they've now given it the chance for which it has been lying in wait: the chance to make its honorable (and sacred?) claim to the Arab oil fields. Nor will the Arabs now ever achieve parity with Israel, for that beleaguered country has now revealed its true status as a U.S. colony and the United States can now moralize its biased stance toward that country and against the Arabs as never before. Had they done their homework on the experience of the American Indigenes, the Saudis and Kuwaitis would have known that they now, at the close of the 20th century, have made it possible for tiny Israel, only a few decades old, to join its giant defender in redirecting and reshaping all of the ancient Arabian destinies. For Arab kingdoms as old as those in the Gulf this may turn out to be their worst nightmare.

Many of the tribes of the Indigenes throughout the Americas, I will not name them here, made the same kinds of historical mistakes and we have become unable to live our own lives. We continue to lose our resources and riches stolen from us by our greedy benefactor, the very thieves who have given us the reputation in history of being beggars.

In the same way that his ancestors 200 years ago said war with the Indigenes was really not about some obscure tribes in the wilderness, President George H. W. Bush has always said that the recent Gulf War was not about just one small country, Kuwait. This Gulf War, he says, was about great ideas, a new world order in which many nations will come together to achieve the goals of mankind. The colonized everywhere in the world, including American Indian Nations who defend themselves on a daily basis against the powerful bureaucrats and legislators in Washington, D.C., as well as in the states in which they reside, know that there is nothing new about this world order of which he speaks. For them, it is a replay of the Old Indian Wars, after which a forceful predator may impose, confine, and cripple.

The people who believe in [the first] President Bush's new order, those Arab leaders who believe that United States intervention in their conflict is an acceptable price to pay perhaps do not know that Bush [the senior] uses the same argument for a new world order which justified the killing of Lakota women and children at Wounded Knee, South Dakota, a hundred years ago almost to the day that bombs began falling in the land of the Tigris and Euphrates, that place where civilization, we are told, began. He uses the argument, i.e., that the United States engages in good wars, which won the Medal of Honor for U.S. Cavalrymen who shot down defenseless Minneconjou women and children under a flag of truce one December day in 1890.

The uninformed Kuwaitis and Saudis should understand the paradoxical nature of history: that the United States which now uses the failed and tarnished argument for this war, i.e., that the strong must defend the weak in a good war, refuses to return the sacred lands in the Black Hills stolen from the Sioux in much the same manner that it has allowed the State of Israel to steal and occupy Arab lands. It is the way of history that the strong always take from the weak and get away with it. Moreover, they must remember that as rich nations spend their gold on armaments, one American child in three will not live long enough to vote in this, the greatest experiment in democracy the word has ever known. That fact, alone, should given them important clues concerning the United States' intent and responsibility.

All of the nations of the past, one supposes, as one contemplates history, rose to empire as hard fighters, pagans, and adventurers. But none has been so successful as has the inchoate United States of America in convincing the world, and itself, of its own moral destiny, making believe that it has the right to colonize the resources of the world simply because it is good, pretending that it can impose world order on others who are bad by paying off its collaborators, declaring that it can decide who will be eligible to stake its claim and who will not.

As all of this happens, the world should remember that millions of the Indigenes have absolutely no voice in the United Nations which was so skillfully manipulated by pro-Western forces in the recent Gulf crisis and few rights in developing their own lives. The reason, we suppose, is because they are the invisible and vanishing tribes of which Frederick Jackson Turner spoke; they are the third-rate enemies of the West, the un-christianized, and the un-technologized cultures of the human species and they, therefore, deserve exclusion.

In spite of the fact that the Indigenes have heard all of the discouraging debates for centuries concerning justice in the world of nations, they continue to struggle for their so-called minority rights. The Sioux people have always known, just as the Palestinians and countless other disenfranchised peoples throughout the world have known, that colonists do not attend to the very International Law of their own making in the matter of acquiring territory and exploiting resources. None the less, the forever optimistic leaders of such people continue the struggle. In 1920, the Sioux lands claim was initiated as quickly as access to the U.S. Courts was achieved. Presto! Sixty years later (in the mere lifetime of my father, that private first-class who in 1916 served in the U.S. Army in defense of the land though he was neither U.S. citizen nor patriot) the Supreme court confirmed the Sioux claim. Yes, said the Highest Court in the land, the United States Government took your lands illegally and it will, therefore, pay you x-millions of dollars. As you might have suspected, the Sioux since 1980 have refused to accept the pay-off.

Such a refusal on the part of the Indigenes does not mean that the United States of America will stop its confiscation and occupation of Indian lands. But the Sioux know, as do the colonized of the world, that the face of immorality and the face of the powerful colonizer are one and the same.

As the Israelis refuse to return the West Bank and Gaza to its rightful owners, so do Americans refuse to return lands in the Black Hills to the Sioux. It is one of the great ironies of the modern world that these two thieves went to war (though one, indeed, is an undeclared adversary) to force another thief, Saddam Hussein, into doing what neither of them will.

The Indian Wars continue.[1]

We know so much more now about the Babylon adventure engaged in by America than we did on that day of bombing in 1991. The decade-later invasion by the administration of the heir, George W. Bush, in 2001, sometimes referred to as "Bush 43" to distinguish him from his father, is the more frightful because we know so much more about the players. George W. Bush became the forty-third president of the United States, and his father George Herbert Walker Bush was the forty-first president, whose own father was a Republican politician from Connecticut. Each generation of the Bush male progeny was interested in the oil that other countries possessed. There is continuity, then, concerning the obsession with the Iraqi leader, Saddam Hussein, an obsession that took on the greed and envy so well known to the antihistorical leaders who sometimes rule America and have always looked at the possessions of others with desire and acquisition in mind. Who knows this better than American Indians?

The American public had little notion in 1991 with the first bombing that the son would become the president of the United States to carry on this awful war because at that time he was merely the governor of oil-rich Texas, known for his interest in baseball and his born-again Christian redemption. "Dubya," as they called him in his home state, the son of a very rich oil man who ran the CIA for many years, became president of the United States as a result of one vote in the Supreme Court; some say he rose to power in order to continue the system geared for waging a U.S. war in the Middle East. And also to avenge an assassination attempt on his father by the dictator of Iraq. It seems now to some to have been a deliberate strategy by powerful colonizers and avengers.

There were other things that the American public was unaware of, though, that perhaps we should have been. We know now, for example, as we didn't know then, that the general who led the first Gulf War in 1991 (Norman Schwarzkopf Jr.) is the son of another historical figure and friend of the Bush family, the flamboyant American soldier General H. Norman Schwarzkopf, for whom "Stormin' Norman" is named. In 1942, the senior Schwarzkopf was the head of a military mission in the Middle East performing imperialist duties for the U.S. capitalists in propping up the power base for the corrupt

Shah of Iran. It took the better part of a decade for the people of Iran to overthrow this oil-rich shah who had collaborated with the oil-rich Texans and others. It would seem, therefore, that the roots of this present war in the Middle East are very deep, indeed. American imperialists have had their eyes on the Middle East in a serious way for most of the twentieth century. It would seem, also, that American citizens (and, certainly, American Indians) are the last to know what their colonial governors are up to in remote places around the world.

We now know so much more about the subsequent occupation of Iraq by Americans than we did then, but much of its intention is still a hidden history, very much like the genocidal history of the colonization of the American Indian on this continent has been hidden from public view. We know now that when Hussein, the leader of Iraq, complained in the 1980s that Iraq's neighbor Kuwait was exceeding its oil-production quotas set up by OPEC to please its American investors, driving oil prices down, he signed his own death warrant. Kuwaitis, like the unlucky Shah of Iran, were among the most avid of OPEC leaders doing the bidding of America, so when they refused to defend the Arabian provision concerning OPEC's authority over its own oil production, they were invaded by Saddam, who claimed that Kuwait has always been a part, a province, of what is now Iraq, never mind the meddling of the British government after World War II. The most recent colonizer of Kuwait, the United States, would naturally be expected come to its rescue. And it did. Bush senior said at the time of the invasion, "This will not stand." The war for Middle East oil continued.

The American public, notorious for its lack of historical sense, knows now as it didn't know then that Kuwait had at one time been the province Basra in what is now Iraq until it was granted independence by another colonizer, the British, as late as 1961. This Alice-in-Wonderland reality of recent history in a land as old as any in the world might have been looked on with hostility by border nations as the temerity of Americans sanctioned their interference in purely economic terms. But the world and those border nations could do little in response to the actions of the powerful United States, the only elephant in the jungle since the demise of the Soviet Union.

Priorities in the Middle East in the twenty-first century as America occupies lands for oil are far different from what they were in 1877 in the new American West when the Black Hills of Dakota Territory were occupied for gold in the northern Plains of America. This means that strategic and high-tech bombing might have been the only alternative in handling the Kuwaiti situation, whereas legislation and political malfeasance may have been the only consideration a hundred years ago in the American West. Both methods have the same source: unchecked political power.

The abuse of political authority in the American West during the settlement years could be persuasive in promoting and legalizing thefts because the Great American public benefited from each of the thefts just as it benefits from the oil wars in the Middle East. Victims, too, can be depended upon to make mistakes that invite further injustices. There are always mistakes made by the victims in history that assist in enforcing the tragedies. The mistake Iraq made was to acquiesce to colonial concerns when it was admitted to the Arab League in 1963 for the sake of being structured as a nation in the eyes of the world. The same mistake was made by Sioux Indians and the Sioux Nation, the most powerful Indian nation on the Plains in the 1800s, when it acquiesced to the Red Cloud notion of making a treaty nation that would consign itself to reservation status, a colonial paradigm of enormous controversy.

In each case, the idea of recognition from powerful nations throughout the world was a tempting rationale. This suggestion, however, simply blames the victim when, in fact, there have been few alternatives for the unprepared as they face the massing of hegemonic power by more fortunate national movements. Many historians will tell you that there have been no alternatives to the kind of aggressive colonial tactics of the First World. Continuous war, death, and disease is the historical substance of colonial aggression and imperialistic nation building.

Basic infrastructures here in New World America have not been in place for long, certainly not as long as when Europe was developing what the Roman historian Tacitus had called "imperial mentality," the driving force for many of the earliest colonial dynasties. That ancient thinking helped England (America's precursor) look longingly at unoccupied places like Ireland and, later, India, America, the Southern Hemisphere, and Africa. But the "imperial mentality" spoken of by the earliest scholars has been the legacy of the newly formed democracy in the New World. All that was required in 1877 in the new America was a congressional act, the Black Hills Act of 1877, and—whoosh—7.7 million acres of treaty-protected Sioux Indian lands came under the title of the United States of America, where it has been exploited, given over to settlers, and held in trust ever since. Nearly twenty years of sporadic warfare followed that theft, then poverty and submission, and finally enforced assimilation and bare survival.

The unfeeling coarseness of America has rarely been exposed because the mainstream refuses to look at the Indian–white history of the early centuries, but the foreign policy of violence and expansionism has never been lost on American Indian experiences and lives. The elites who have shaped America and continue to do so receive scant attention from the media for their defects; and those who wish to reveal them are rebuffed in countless ways. Few who look carefully at the colonial history of America can believe in American democracy as envisioned by Manifest Destiny because when we want to come to terms with the past, we want to be sure that imperial acquisitions and imperial impulses do not dominate the present.

Television viewers at Christmastime in 2003 watched the capture of Saddam Hussein and America exulted. Indians who watched the footage of U.S. Army physicians looking for lice in the dirty and disheveled hair of Saddam Hussein were reminded of Indian Health Service (HIS) doctors on Indian reservations who combed through the hair of Indian children at boarding schools with kerosene in their combs and a pair of scissors in their hands. The image of such degradation and humiliation is never erased from one's memory and it will never be erased from the memories of modern Iraqis. The Guantanamo kennels are filled with people denied legal and human rights and no one even knows their names, reminiscent of the concentration camps filled with citizens of indigenous nations who have remained anonymous for 200 years. A former U.S. president told us fortuitously that there is no history that matters except the history we do not know. But that was after he dropped the atomic bombs on civilian Asian populations, incinerating millions of innocents.

"Imperialism" is the key word here, a national policy of territorial acquisition through the establishment of economic and political domination of other nations. If there is one policy behind the scenes that links the Iraq experience in the twenty-first century to the Lakota/Dakota Sioux experience of the nineteenth, it is the policy of imperialistic dominance. Trampling on the sovereignty of other nations for most of its several centuries of nationhood has been the legacy of the American Republic's power. This is a history that American mainstream thinking ignores as it goes to war around the globe.

The spokespeople for the Bush administrations in 1990 and 2000 have proclaimed this: We don't want their land . . . no, we don't want their oil . . . no, we want them to be democratic and free. Who among us who knows our histories as natives to the land now called America can find comfort in these protestations? Because of the centuries of colonization at the hands of America, we know the opposite is true: America *does* want the oil of Arabia at the turn of the century, just as it wanted the gold and the land of the Sioux a hundred years ago. In fact, America wants the land and resources of other nations, if not in theory, at least in title for economic gain. This is the way of capitalistic democracies, is it not?

How different, then, is such protestation and denial and rationale of contemporary sources from Chief Justice John Marshall's Supreme Court decision in 1832 when he said:

> However extravagant the pretension of converting the discovery of an inhabited country into conquest may appear; if the principle has been converted in the first instance, and afterward sustained; if a country has been acquired and held under it; if the property of the great mass of the community originates in it, it becomes the law of the land, and cannot be questioned. So, too, with the concomitant principle, that the Indian inhabitants are to be considered merely as occupants, to be protected, indeed, while in peace, in the possession of their lands, but to be deemed incapable of transferring the absolute title to others.[2]

Looking carefully at this legal history is to realize that "protection" of the Iraqi citizens from Hussein and leading them to democracy is mere ruse. To the aggressive colonizer, it has always been about land and resources. It is about occupation in Iraq in 1990 and 2003, as it was about occupation in western America in 1890 and, ultimately, genocide. Some historians want to say that many of the Marshall decisions of the 1830s appeared to safeguard Indian lands from greedy developers in the capitalistic mode, but when the gold fields in the west, like the oil fields in the Middle East, shone in the eyes of the invading beholder, nothing could stop the invasion, occupation, theft, and ultimate colonization. This seems to be the nature of capitalistic democracies based in imperialism.

When the bombs fell on Iraq, first in 1990, and later in 2002, the unfortunate question, Do nations repeat their mistakes? rang in my ears. Today, as I look at the destruction of the cities of Iraq and the murder of thousands, I am reminded that continental armies of the nineteenth century left carrion remains for hundreds of miles across the Great Plains in 1870 and 1880 for many of the same reasons that Babylon lay in ruins a hundred years later: resources, a good society, liberty, and democracy; but, most important of all, for retaliation and revenge. After all, didn't they kill all those pioneers and settlers for no good reason? And, after all, didn't they kill all those innocents in the Twin Towers? Didn't they try to assassinate our oil president, George H. W. Bush? Retaliation as cause often gives war and death a realistic cast in favor of those who claim to be righteous, as those who defeated the murderous Seventh Cavalry (invaders of foreign sovereign lands) found out years later at Wounded Knee. Yet revenge, we are often reminded by biblical folk, only makes everyone blind.

We are told that America's wars are fought by good people against bad people. But history tells us that the massive humiliation of old and traditional indigenous peoples by an invading, colonizing people, ends most often in the defeat of any hope for a democratic world that would uplift not only the Christians, but also the largely non-Christian and indigenous peoples of the globe. These historical dilemmas were never more clear to me than when I stood on that clear January day in 1991 in the company of a crowd of stunned college students on the Davis campus and watched the U.S. military bomb thousands of targets in Iraq and demand the return of Kuwaiti oil to its wealthy sheiks and the corporate heads of the U.S. economy defended by George Bush Sr. Helpless, the students and I stood as if rooted to the floor until the sun disappeared from the smiling California sky; thousands of human beings died that day and so did my hope that America's terrible history concerning the indigenes would not be repeated.

I walked slowly back to my apartment, saying to no one in particular: America will pay for this! The people of the Arabian world will never forgive this! Nor should they. That weekend, thousands of people were in the streets of San Francisco protesting the bombing but those images were flashed for only an instant on CNN and protesters were quickly repulsed. Nothing was said about what had changed in that part of the country and the emergence of the most hostile hatred toward Americans of any century. Now we are told that they hate us because they hate progress, freedom, choice, culture, and music. Such obvious falsehoods and exaggerations are unconvincing to those who have studied America's indigenous history.

Thinking now of the horror of the September 11 events in New York City and Washington, the constant minute-by-minute replaying, hour after hour, of the scenes of panic and death lasting for days and continuing even while I wrote this, I realize there is little hope that the world can move away from the current terrible moments to speak of American Indian history. The terrible Indian history is too far away to consider. The momentous demolishing of the Twin Towers in New York City a decade after the first raid makes it impossible for the newest victims of war to take into account the Indian wars that may be at the heart of America's present dilemma. Yet nothing happens on the world stage without context and the old Indian wars are the backdrop for most of the modern events of horror. The United States refuses to discuss its own century of genocide, its own theft of the sacred Black Hills, and its own crimes against humanity. It refuses to acknowledge that there is no capitalistic nation in the world that is innocent. Instead, it uses the failed and tarnished argument that the strong must fight good wars. Everyone suffers for this lie.

At the time of the first Gulf War, I wrote in my notes: "As the Israelis refuse to return the West Bank and Gaza to its rightful owners, so, too, do Americans (told by their own Supreme Court in 1980 that they were thieves) refuse to return the lands of the Black Hills to its rightful owners who are only savages, after all, in the wilderness. Thus, the democratizers and the capitalists and the Christians have settled down in the Black Hills, the sacred lands of the Sioux and there is little to be done about it except to keep its grief in the hearts of the people. One of the great ironies of the modern world is that American thieves go to war against another thief, Saddam Hussein, to force him to do what they will not."

Their motives have been, again, hidden from those of us who ignore history. In truth, the United States had supported Hussein as an ally for decades even after they knew of his gassing of the Kurds. In the end, though, he, too, is given up and more tired proverbs about doing the right thing are disguised as history. The democratizers and capitalists will now settle down in the Middle East. There is much to be said about modern warfare, but as I listen to G. W. Bush, who claimed the U.S. presidency at the beginning of the twenty-first century, say that America will persevere in a dangerous world, I am reminded that General William Tecumseh Sherman, who led the war against the Sioux, said much the same thing: "We must act with vindictive earnestness against the Sioux," he said, "even to their extermination, men, women, and children."[3] Wars based in such determined aggression are never done and, for the rest of our lives, those of us who mourn the loss of sacred ground will feel a constant burden because we are the First Americans, people with large and poignant dreams.

· · ·

REMEMBERING THE SPIRIT AND THE LAND
IN THE TIME OF SITTING BULL—EVERY PEOPLE HAS A RIVER

From Appomattox to Wounded Knee
the same white men went about
celebrating their own jury's verdict:
    occupy Manila, recapture Geronimo
    invade Cuba,
    speaking words of pious
    real estate agents: *we fill*
    them with good ideas
    so we can take their lands.

Imagine for a moment
the bandit nation holding its breath
in quiet ravines above Grand River
committing justifiable homicide,
killing Indians as it would kill
snakes or coyotes or prairie chickens
Imagine the sun driving the horizon shelf
out of sight again
and again
above dirty water
dark water until
it ran crimson over the makeshift bridge
Imagine the dangers even then
a layer of dust would settle
like the sunset curving the earth
in a gesture called the sign of the cross
to make a place for the magic words of pious
poets: *we cover the scars of a new nation*
  staining the glass windows of a moveable river current
  with the promises of Paradise.
He saw the flash of a bullet
in the dusk as he walked
not a hundred yards from the Grand River
Imagine there was always the Army
as the empire expanded. There was
always the Army looking into the
impervious shine of the Grand River
reflecting itself in the pious words
of Majors and Generals: *they shall see*
  that there is malice enough in our hearts.
Imagine Indians
hunted like wild beasts along the
sun-drenched river beds
smoke on every horizon
the wounded lying in the bushes
unable to run
or regret
oha(n)h　　　you've got the picture.[4]

・ ・ ・

WAR

So many Indian narratives and poems are about war . . . so many wars, too many; especially now, because this time, young men and women go to war in the midst of lies and deceptions; this time, then, the aim of the most powerful nation in the world might not be on the right target, and Indians, who fight in these wars in great numbers, continue to try to tell the stories of their bravery. The language of this colonial war begun by this powerful nation, America, unlike the language of other wars known by indigenous peoples, becomes illusive, hidden, ambiguous.

All targets these days are, with malice, indiscriminately called "terrorists," unarmed persons can be called "combatants," dissidents can be arrested while merely walking the streets, innocents can be shot without warning, and loudmouthed radio jocks in favor of a president who obscures the truth and believes in preemptive war sow ruin on Clear Channel and Fox News in the land of the free, the home of the brave.

If anyone who knows the history of the Indian wars of America is not surprised at this turn of events, they nonetheless know that such historical narratives can't help but inspire the memory of colonial wars against the natives of this continent, wars based on genocide and greed.

One of the excessive targets in this war was Ahmed Yassin, an old man and respected spiritual leader of the Muslims in the Arabian Peninsula and since 1987 a founder of an Islamic resistance movement called Hamas. On March 21, 2004, he was assassinated by helicopter gunfire in the Gaza Strip, shot down in cold blood as his family and relatives watched the occupying force of Israelis murder him on his own homeland.

As a student of obscure histories, I am reminded of thousands of such assassinations on the Sioux Homelands a hundred years ago; most particularly, the assassination of a Hunkpapa spiritual leader and resistance fighter of the Oyate murdered by American firepower on a bright, crisp December day in 1890 on his own homeland just a few miles from the Grand River. He was one of many old men of indigenous power who had to be taken out if occupation and colonization was to succeed.

War against enemies is not unknown to the Sioux, about whom it is often said that war was and is what N. Scott Momaday calls "a sacred business." These days, every *wacipi* begins with an honor song to the Indian veterans who have earned the respect and admiration of all the world as hard fighters and defenders of the land. As I listen to the grandfather songs these days, I am worried that the awfulness of this Gulf War, which is a colonial war against an indigenous people in the Middle East, is one that will be remembered by all of us as war by occupiers against the wrong and illusive target.

War was not always like this. In the six months after Pearl Harbor was attacked by the nation of Japan, over 7,500 American Indians entered the military; my only brother, Victor, was one of them and he didn't make it back home. Ninety-nine percent of all eligible Indian men registered for the draft in those days, setting a national standard. The young man who was to become the father of my children, Melvin Paul Traversie Cook from Eagle Butte, was drafted out of Holy Rosary Mission where he was a student to carry a machine gun around Germany, closing out his teenage years as a defender of the country that stole the Black Hills from his people. War is always a complicated business, as we all found out in Vietnam where 42,500 American Indians served this nation proudly. More recently, 3,000 fought in the first Gulf War, which lasted not a dozen years, but only a few days. This latest Gulf War, it is reported, is being fought by thousands of young American Indians. In our confusion and grief, we sing songs to their honor at every tribal gathering.

This war has long tentacles. The pretext that Israel, a USA satellite in the Middle East, uses to kill Palestinians in this war is the same pretext that Americans used to capture and destroy Indians a hundred years ago: well, they killed all those settlers, didn't they? All those innocent women and children who might suffer at the hands of Indians; well, they are dangerous people who refuse to love those who have come to occupy their territories and make them Christians; yes, they have murderous weapons. The pretext to kill Ahmed Yassin as a dangerous religious fanatic is the same pretext they used to kill Sitting Bull: a greasy savage who revered the ghost dance.

Every nation has a right to defend its citizens and its land, but no nation should any longer accept the morality of Western colonialism. All you have to do is look around Indian Country to know that liberation movements, such as the one that Sitting Bull led against the federal policy that was making beggars of his people, will continue even in the face of lies and manipulations, documentaries, and bad reviews. Resistance movements like Hamas and even the mujahedeen are historical, indigenous, and difficult, and they will continue.

This war, led by ahistorical schoolboy cheerleader George W. Bush, is being discredited as a fatal and fraudulent lie because it is directed at wrong targets and shadowy memories. Maybe it is true, what that old dropper of atomic bombs, Harry Truman, once said: *There is nothing new in this world except the history you don't know.*

A CASE IN POINT

It is one of the astonishing realities of contemporary Indian life that there has been almost no organized Indian voice against either of the Gulf Wars fought by this country in the past two decades. Perhaps that has been true of all of the recent contemporary wars fought by the United States against others in which natives in great numbers have participated, with the possible exception of the Vietnam War.

The recent case of Ward Churchill, which is the only example of a voice claiming to be an Indian voice rising up against the current war, seems to be inauthentic and it is nothing if not ironic. In the process of this voicing, it was revealed that Churchill possesses no birthright as an Indian citizen of any Indian nation in the United States and, thus, has been set upon as a fraud by his fellow scholars and students, Indians and non-Indians alike.

One of the most bombastic of ethnic studies professors housed for years at the University of Colorado, Boulder, and a longtime claimant to Indian heritage, Churchill spoke with his usual authority in presenting "the Indian voice" by publishing an essay in which he compared the oppressive nature of U.S. foreign policy in the Middle East to the long-colonized and oppressive behavior of the United States toward Indian nations. His suggestion was that American Indians in the United States may be the only populations in this country who have a parallel history to impart concerning the current Iraq situation of invasion, colonization, and occupation.

Lots of people agree with that assessment; however, in trying to articulate this comparison, he clumsily called the people killed in the World Trade Center attack on September 11 in New York "little Eichmanns," intimating that by going to work every day in the Trade Center, they, like the Nazi bureaucrat Adolf Eichmann who persecuted the Jews in World War II, kept the machinery of war and colonialism and fascism well oiled. His point was that the site of the attack was symbolic and should be taken note of. It was the World Trade Center that was taken down by the terrorists, after all, not the New York Public Library or the high-class homes and apartments in Manhattan's Tribeca neighborhood. In other words, the work done at the World Trade Center, in general terms, Churchill suggested, feeds into and contributes to the worldwide technologies that makes the first-strike war now being waged against Iraq possible. If the United States is going to throw its weight around, he said, people are going to "strike back." This "coming home to roost" essay also referenced the Black Power slogan of several decades ago that was used then as an explanation for the race riots in the large cities of America.

The response to the essay ignited all sorts of dilemmas, all kinds of seeming contradictions. Most poignant, Churchill was outed as a man who had for years desperately wanted to be an Indian, had loudly made the fraudulent claim to be a Cherokee Indian and joined the American Indian Movement of the 1970s, and had very probably gotten the job at the university in the Ethnic Studies Department by claiming that identity criterion for which he could offer no satisfactory proof. Professor Churchill is a man who has spoken out against colonialism all of his professional life and has often attacked traditional modes of history and research in order to achieve what he sees as the new, realistic story of America, a reality that had not made him popular with the academic mainstream even before his latest blast.[5]

After his essay came to light, several Colorado newspapers, right-wing Colorado politicians, and even the state's Republican governor took umbrage at what they saw as Churchill's slander of the innocent victims of the terrorist attack and decided to make an example of what they considered heresy emerging from the intellectual groves of independent thought on the subject of war. Many called for his firing, and a vigorous investigation ensued.

American Indian university faculty members, many of whom may have been in agreement with Churchill on this very subject, had been until this time curiously silent toward the unprovoked invasion of a sovereign country and the newly described first-strike American war policy in the Middle East. There was the notion that the most obvious system where independent thought is said to be the coin of the realm—that is, the university system—found itself under attack by mostly right-wing defenders of the war policy. Stifling mechanisms were suddenly becoming the rule, allowing the attack media and the loudmouthed talk shows, rather than institutions of higher learning, to be constructs of opinion and information.

Amid the Colorado controversy, Columbia University began an investigation of what was being called "anti-Semitism and pro-Palestinian bias" in December 2004, and as it was going forward, several professors there were under scrutiny, if not official investigation. Across the academic landscape, then, professors of Islamic religions were said to be undergoing reevaluation, if not officially, at least privately. Pro-Jewish activists from Columbia and its sister school Barnard publicly claimed they were being "intimidated" and "abused" by faculty members of the Middle East and Asian Languages and Cultures Department (MEALAC).

The takeaway message given by the highly publicized right wing on this controversy was that university faculty members on the public dole are not being paid with taxpayer's money to interrogate the international role of the

United States in Middle Eastern affairs, and especially noticeable are those scholars and professors of "color" or those involved in what may be called "ethnic" studies who are expected to keep silent on such matters. Not since academics first tried to teach evolution as a theory of origin had there been such an attack on the freedom to have an unpopular opinion. Not since Senator Joe McCarthy from Wisconsin ruined the academic, professional, and artistic reputations of hundreds of Americans in the mid-50s had there been such a highly charged public grievance against the freedom to have an offensive opinion put into the public forum.

Ironies abound in this controversy, none more profound than the fact that the academic construct of "ethnic studies" hired Churchill in the first place. This academic construct has always failed to account for the legal and indigenous treaty status of Indians representing the very faulty construct that had allowed Churchill to claim to "be an Indian" for most of his professional life. Universities, never having required tribal citizenship papers to prove that an applicant is a member of a federally recognized, sovereign Indian nation, just requests that a person "check off the ethnic/racial box" on any application form and lets it go at that. No other citizenship identification requirement in any country would pass such a slipshod method.

Most Indians in academia have rejected this "mainstream" perception of their status, adhering to the idea that it is a fact that tribal nations have never given up their right to say who their citizens are in spite of the so-called blood quantum methodology of which Churchill has been particularly contemptuous. In an interview published in the June 10, 2005, issue of the *Rocky Mountain News*, Churchill cited three criteria for his claim to Indianness: (1) self-identification; (2) acceptance within an Indian community; and (3) tribal affiliation, none of which require proof of Indian parentage. The one he didn't cite was the naming of an actual Indian ancestor. Ultimately, in regard to the third criterion, the Keetoowah Cherokees said he was merely an "honorary" member because when he applied for enrollment, he could not prove any Cherokee ancestry.

In other interviews, Churchill traced what has been called "family lore," the story that his mother and his grandmother told him of his Indian heritage when he was ten years old. Lakota activist Russell Means entered the increasingly comical dialogue by saying that "Ward is my brother. Ward has followed the ways of indigenous peoples worldwide."[6] In spite of this ringing endorsement, much of the ensuing investigative activity ended up revealing the clear picture that Churchill has no demonstrable Indian blood.

What does all this have to do with war and the killing of innocents? Well, like I said, ironies abound. Some of us born and raised on Indian reservations in past eras can remember when nobody, not even Indians, wanted to be Indians. Now, in some kind of perverse ironic twist, poststructuralists, postmoderns, intellectual hybrids, postcolonialists, and latent cowboys from Deadwood are claiming their own places on the basis of some kind of universalist articulation of indigenousness. After all, what American (with the possible exception of Dick Cheney) wants to be called an imperialist?

The American Indian Professoriate, an organization formed in the early 1990s and comprised of tribal citizens in academia, published a position paper in an Indian Studies journal, the *Wicazo Sa Review*, on the issue of fraudulent Indian identities, and called for institutions to require documentation of citizenship. It is a move that has gone largely unnoticed by university administrators.

Churchill's claim to Indianness, in spite of the continuing and valiant effort he has made to function as an advocacy historian for the American Indian experience, is the final revelation of his perverse fidelity to an unprovable and very weary identity issue; perverse because stealing tribal identities is every bit as damaging to tribal communities as stealing tribal lands or children or resources. Such theft, indeed, may be the ultimate racist act, an act of invasion and occupation that parallels the very acts of war by the United States that Churchill finds so egregious.

It may be that *identity theft is the crime of significance here,* not an agonizing first-strike war, not plagiarism, not falsifying identity to get cushy university positions, not bad research habits, not even slander. In the end, the whole unfortunate episode may serve only to assist conservatives in their proclaimed efforts at "retaking the university"—and that would be a blow to the fine academic and scholarly work toward decolonization and undoing racism that thoughtful native scholars have done over the past three decades. William F. Buckley Jr., David Horowitz, Saul Bellow, Allan Bloom, and the Collegiate Network may be the winners if this movement to expunge unpopular ideas goes any further.

INTRICATE WAR HISTORIES

Everyone reading this knows that the ghosts of America's racial history are everywhere in academics, art, literature, politics, and law; and I have said it enough times and written it enough times to be able to say that nowhere are these ghosts more visible than in the lives of American Indians, both past and present. I know that, not just because I keep repeating it, but because

I was born a Dakota Sioux Indian on an Indian reservation, one of those places fraught with poverty and challenge, in the twentieth century, born into colonialism without really realizing the condition of colonialism for many decades. I was born and raised just in those few years when the Indian Reorganization Act was being passed and enacted. I was in college when the termination and relocation laws were passed and a young parent when Wounded Knee was revisited in 1973, igniting what amounted to a reassessment of history. But, that being said, the truth is, America knows very little about what it means to be born an Indian in America.

What is accepted by Americans is that it is an anticolonial country going about "freeing" others and promoting democracy around the world, promoting "rescue missions" in other sovereign territories for people "less fortunate." The truth about American history is this: *America is the first settler-colonial country to achieve great power in our time,* its power emerging from its earliest days as it spread political terrorism against the tribal nations; as it stole civilian and tribal property; as it coerced the support of its victims, turning them into proxies for their own agendas; as it eroded citizens' rights in tribal enclaves; as it committed atrocities among civilian populations; and as it claimed its political cover when the places of the victims became the breeding ground for chaos.

All Lakotas and Dakotas know that political and economic terror was a strategy that the United States embraced after the Custer defeat out there on the Powder River and the Little Big Horn, and it has continued that strategy ever since. The first terrorist organization that the Lakotas and Dakotas faced began right here in our midst, in little towns like the Western icon, Deadwood, South Dakota, and the hay camps of the West where terrorists disguised as cowboys and farmers and bankers, ministers and lawyers and politicians managed through the malfeasance of government and the oppression of religious education to overthrow the native and steal his land.

Ever since that time, nonhistorical nations like the Sioux Nation or the Navajo Nation or the other native confederacies of this continent were treated as though they had no citizens' rights, neither in the United States nor in their tribal nations. Their non-Christian religions were thought to be reactionary instead of expressions of culture; so the biggest power in the world became the most brash violator of human rights all the while accusing others of that crime. This strategy for supremacy has been a most successful endeavor and now the United States is the single global power frighteningly disguised as a benign democracy. I write pieces like this and books like this because *I want this power to be held accountable.* I want America to know that there is a difference between human rights and citizens' rights, and that the rights of longtime, ancestral citizens of the sovereign Sioux Nation have been not just eroded, but trampled to death in the past hundred years.

I begin by saying that it is my longtime interest here to explore racial politics, and Indian nationhood, and history. I want to explore the colonization of American Indian tribes as a devastating policy in the United States since its inception. This exploration is related to the present condition of war, this new colonial war in the Middle East, something Indians know something about.

In order to grasp the fundamentals of the position taken here, the condition of indigenous peoples should be clarified. American Indians claim a political status in the United States like no other population in this country. Indians are not "minorities." Indians are not "people of color," neither vanishing nor savage; Indians possess a dual citizenship that they have never given up, tribally specific citizenship as well as U.S. citizenship, ever since the United States conferred its citizenship on Indians in 1924 through legislation. The thing that was remembered in this strategy to make Indians proxies was that Indians had signed treaties as nations of people with the United States and other nations, namely France, England, and Holland, and had fought hard and successful wars in their own defense. Thus, Indians are not immigrants or colonizers or slaves or tourists. And, in the beginning, they were not Christians, either; had never been Christians in the thousands of years of the making of their civilizations before the missionaries came, came as though they were welcome.

Anti-Indianism, in my view, the subject of my latest book and a word that others use as synonymous with "racism," is a concept that has risen out of that status. It is a concept in American Christian life just as anti-Semitism is a concept that rises out of Christian Europe and Islamophobia is a concept that rises out of global Christian nations, and anti-Africanism rises out of the same sources. Practically speaking, however, the dialogue as it concerns indigenous peoples lies somewhere outside of the usual context of racism in America; that is, the black–white dialogue that has been the focus ever since the Civil War, and the "people of color" dialogue that rises out of more recent experience. These misunderstandings allow "wannabes" to emerge and claim Indianness. They encourage the rise of colonial tactics, the recent Middle East adventure the most shocking.

For those who examine history, it seems obvious that colonizing nations have concomitant histories, yet there is often great denial of that reality, which accounts for the erosion of understanding of current events. As early as 1917, during what we students of Indian history in America call the "years of attrition" when hundreds of thousands of American Indians were dying of starvation and disease, the British government in the Balfour Declaration wanted to create a Jewish state in a land occupied by Palestinians (Arabs and non-Christians), forcing an intrusion into a foreign land, very much like the American invasion of the 1800s when white settlers forced their way through government policy to occupy Indian treaty-protected lands in America.

The second World War made this idea of creating a Jewish state palatable because the Germans and the rest of the European world refused to share with the Jewish people their fates and their victories and their failures. The second World War also made it possible to abandon any real discussion of the American Indian's fate. By 1948, the state of Israel was founded and now (after years of missteps of all kinds) can best be described as a non-Arab intrusion, a non-Arab client to its benefactors, Britain and America; a non-Muslim and nonindigenous state deeply despised by its neighbors for its unwelcome intrusion. A decade after the Balfour Declaration, America passed its own law, the Indian Reorganization Act, which created Western-type governments on Indian lands in the United States. In many ways, these governments, if not despised by the people, are notoriously weak and ineffectual, largely bound by colonial intrusion and doing the bidding of the United States on Indian treaty lands.

War with indigenous peoples and its terrible aftermath has been, for America, a most successful phenomenon. That does not mean that they won the wars they fought with tribal peoples, but it means, rather, that they used the chaos of war and its aftermath to do two things: (1) to erode citizens' rights in the tribal nation and (2) to turn victims into proxies to be used by certain power groups with their own agendas. (The so-called tribal police force that killed Sitting Bull in what has been called Dakota Territory comes to mind.) At the turn of the twenty-first century, the indigenous war in Iraq, claimed by the United States to be a defensive war but that was in actuality a preemptive strike, has highlights that remind American Indians of the wars against them a hundred years ago.

One of the highlights of this comparison is the body of law that is being laid down by U.S. forces in Baghdad as I am writing this manuscript. For example, a law passed for Iraq's future in September 2003 by the U.S. powers planning commission in Washington, D.C., opened up Iraq's economy to foreign ownership, one of the first acts initiated even as the bombs were falling. This is an astonishing colonial tactic that has brought about much of the insurgency shown daily on U.S. television. This law in Iraq parallels the

1886 General Allotment Act of the U.S. Congress, which opened up hundreds of thousands of acres of native treaty lands to others, encouraged settlement by non-Indians, and resulted in the loss to Indians of two-thirds of all treaty land title. This act made beggars of every tribe in the country and is the source, today, of endemic poverty. It will do the same in Iraq. These acts, in case anyone wants to give a name to them, are acts of genocide.

Today's war, just like the wars against tribal peoples in America, is brought about by the kind of colonial law that should be seen as criminal acts by the United States, now embedded in the creation of a new constitution being written by and for the Iraqis. It is much like the illegal Indian Reorganization Act (IRA) constitutions that were written by and for American tribal nations a mere eighty years ago. Independent regulators have been put in place in Iraq by U.S. leaders and, more important, fourteen military bases are being built on Iraqi lands housing 110,000 U.S. soldiers (many of them black and native), who will likely be there permanently with more on the way. These bases are called "enduring bases."

This parallels the occupying military force stationed at forts on every Indian reservation in America since 1880. Most of these forts still exist. As previously mentioned, I was born in a public health facility at one of these forts, born into colonialism on an Indian reservation in the 1930s at a place named Fort Thompson, named, in 1863, after an army general who was a military occupier long before I appeared on the scene, a man whose influence has lasted even into present time.

Colonial tactics have remained fairly constant throughout history and they should be recognized today as strategies to diminish freedom for innocent and sovereign peoples. One of the aspects of this history that makes it crucial for all Americans to ponder is that certain political assumptions on the part of the United States reflected during the nineteenth and twentieth centuries are with us today. The foremost of these assumptions on the part of the United States are racial superiority felt by whites, the innocence of colonization felt by all capitalists, and the righteousness felt by all Christians—all assumptions that allow and encourage the United States to use its power to enforce its vision of itself as the indispensable democracy.[7]

THE PITFALLS OF TELLING TRIBAL HISTORIES: LEWIS AND CLARK, COLONIAL DIARIES, AND FOOL SOLDIERS

It is often said by scholars that all histories, even unthinkable and corrupt ones, have the power to symbolize other histories. In American histories, certain conventions concerning individualism, tribalism, community, and nationalism have emerged as methods in modern symbolic historiography, and these conventions are especially vivid now at the dawning of a new millennium; the beginning of a new century.

It would seem that we in the United States are now in the midst of assessing in a variety of ways the commemorative period when Plains Indians and white Americans first met on the upper Missouri River during the 1804 journey of the American colonial investigators Meriwether Lewis and William Clark.

In 2004, the Western "discovery" trail was activated by whites taking part in symposia up and down the Missouri River. So-called reenactments were taking place, sponsored by U.S. government–funded bicentennial commissions in an effort to "celebrate" the "discovery" of the West. Native speakers in the Dakotas had a chance to give their points of view: Alex White Plume told the participants to go home and ignore this whole effort because it was simply propaganda; Bea Medicine said the historical journey marked "the beginning of the racism that we are still living with"; Elaine Quiver said, "I think they taught us how to steal and occupy where we 'are not wanted'"; Vernon Ashley recalled how he testified against the dams that flooded 550 square miles of treaty lands; and others said that the Lewis and Clark "dis-covery" was the beginning of a colonial invasion that brought about racist legislation to steal lands and destroy Indian lives.

For the most part, though, the conventions spoken of in this history still captured the romance, the thrust of adventure, and the clash of cultures that people early on expected would eventually coalesce into a celebration of the making of greater America, a democratic community that would become the envy of other nations throughout the globe. As the bicentenary decade of the Lewis and Clark moment approached, more of this kind of history making emerged, but there was an effort toward a reality check made by the Indian participants as new critics.

Previous historians rarely mentioned in the telling of the Lewis and Clark story that within the short thirty-year span after that fateful journey, Indian nations of the northern Plains and farther west began to experience a series of dramatic and devastating legal and physical upheavals that decimated thousands of individual lives and hundreds of tribal nations. It amounted to a holocaust driven by religion and greed.

As early as 1823, for example, the U.S. Supreme Court incorporated the "doctrine of discovery" theory into federal Indian law, holding to the notion that Indians merely had "occupancy rights" to the land upon which Europe-ans had so recently converged. Indian nations with treaty status were reduced to that of "domestic dependent nationhood under the tutelage of the United States." This diminishment can only be described as the racism in federal law that Indians have faced ever since. As the century progressed, federal officials used their growing military power to colonize the Indians whose lands lay west of the Mississippi River. Instead of talking about aggressive and bloody expansionism by a colonizing force of unequalled magnitude initiated by the Lewis and Clark venture, historians began to write books about the benign investigations of scientists and diarists in the New World. They wrote that the two "adventurers" and members of their party contributed to New World knowledge by documenting thousands of species of plants and animals as they presumed to search for an all-water route to the Pacific. Historians also pejoratively characterized the reluctant Indian participants in the grand scheme of history, giving them nasty traits and unkindly characterizations still evident today in any historical analysis of the period.[1]

Many histories, scholars are likely to admit now, are distorted, self-serving, and fabricated; thus, there is great controversy over where the Lewis and Clark history fits in this description. There seems to be little consensus on any of the matters touched upon by the diaries and this includes the assessments of and about the Indian participants.

In spite of the rise of new critics, native writers often disagree about the efficacy of the Lewis and Clark diaries as historiography, especially those natives in the West and Northwest whose relatives have become part of the cast of characters interpreting the massive drama. Indeed, during the 2004 "corps of discovery" celebrations, Indian participants gave panel presentations that included in their genealogies the possibilities that Lewis and/or Clark may have fathered children among the tribes during their journey.

An excellent example of how to bring up the question of this vague history of miscegenation appeared in the July 8, 2002, issue of *Time* magazine, when it ran a rather extensive piece examining how an amazing adventure 200 years ago continues to shape the way America sees itself. In the process of this recollection, it can be assumed that the same adventure continues to shape how American Indian Country sees itself.

Sherman Alexie, a Spokane Indian poet and novelist whose novel *The Toughest Indian in the World* has achieved some degree of mainstream popularity, had much to say about the grand adventure in an essay entitled "What Sacagawea Means to Me (and Perhaps to You)." "Sacagawea is our mother," he opines. "She is the first gene pair of the American DNA."

> In that sense, *colonization might be a natural process* [my emphasis], tragic and violent to be sure, but predictable and ordinary as well, and possibly necessary for the advance, however constructive and destructive, of all civilizations. After all, Lewis and Clark's story has never been just the triumphant tale of two white men, no matter what the white historians might need to believe. Sacagawea was not the primary hero of this story, either, no matter what the Native American historians and I might want to believe. The Lewis and Clark Expedition was exactly the kind of multicultural, tri-generational, bi-gendered, animal-friendly, government supported, partly French-Canadian project that should rightly be celebrated by liberals and castigated by conservatives. In the end, *I wonder if colonization might somehow be magical* [emphasis added].

He is "stunned," he says, by the contradictions America represents, "by the successive generations of social, political and artistic mutations that can be so beautiful and painful. How did we get from there to here?"

Finally, he rationalizes, again, "Sacagawea is a contradiction. Here in Seattle, I exist, in whole or in part because a half-white man named James Cox fell in love with a Spokane Indian woman named Etta Addams and gave birth to my Mother. I am a contradiction. I am Sacagawea."[2]

While this is a wonderfully written personal story, the work of an anticolonial nationalist it is not, nor, perhaps, should we expect that it should be.

However, the question of how this *Time* essay, by a Native American writer and published at the turn of the century when the Lewis and Clark commemoration is at its zenith as a fabled myth in the American consciousness, can be situated in postcolonial studies, is, perhaps, at the heart of an ongoing controversy about this history. It is inarguable that colonialism happens not just from the outside but it can be accentuated by events and ideas emerging from the inside as well. For those of us who define colonialism as a crime against humanity, it is an indefensible capitulation.

This Alexie essay does little to assist in the decolonization thrust of the discipline of American Indian Studies and other movements referred to as the "new historicism," even though there is an acceptance of the idea that there is a multiplicity of histories to contend with in the new century. In fact, careful analysis of this essay suggests assimilation rather than deconstruction as its intent, but some more-conservative critics might just call Alexie an unintended humanist.[3]

"Deconstruction" is a word coined by French philosopher Jacques Derrida in the early 1960s. It has set in place a discourse concerning the global movements toward national liberations and humanistic thought in all parts of the world. The political restructuring of American Indian tribal nations and the rise of Indian Studies as an academic discipline coincided with the work of theorists like Derrida, but the preoccupation with activist politics by native scholars has always been their focus, unlike the followers of the more mainstream scholars, and no one should think otherwise. One's impression, then, is that this controversial and sociologically oriented commentary by Alexie may be assimilationist in its intent rather than deconstructionist. Others may give it credence as simple humanistic thinking that flourishes as an idea in native enclaves simply because no one wants to argue with a popular writer who may or may not be all that interested in the political thrust of his comments.

The truth is, a journal named *Telos* was founded in 1968 to bring European critical theory to American audiences, and Derrida (the father of deconstructionism) was quite preoccupied with that movement.[4] It has become the core of thinking as it concerns decolonization. The real issue for American Indians is whether writers and critics want to understand history in terms of opposition, which is a political matter, or whether they want to simply cling to cultural and literary theoretical language.

It is worth looking at the public statement on the details of this historical event by a popular American Indian writer like Alexie if for no other reason than to point out the variety of concerns and the ultimate ambiguities in the assessments concerning history by American Indian writers. The question of how the deconstruction of colonialism is to be managed by the storytellers of tribal peoples and whether or not present storytellers have lost touch with their cultural base is crucial. To claim Sacajawea as one's self, as this writer does, is to unaccuse and excuse colonialism, calling it an inevitable phenomenon rather than a deliberate and cruel invasion, giving it the aura of a seal of approval from natives. If one is to think that a writer speaks for broad constituencies (and there is, admittedly, much ambiguity about that), this is even more crucial as an indictment of the colonial conscience. One of the unfortunate outcomes of postcolonial studies in recent decades is the focus on individuals and their subjectivities, rather than keeping the "eye on the prize" as black scholars have attended. That prize, for American Indians, is the sovereign condition of institutions and systems. Alexie's subjectivity can hardly allow him an oppositional position or need or even desire.

The problem of subjectivity is nothing new, of course. Multicultural diasporists, like Alexie, in this instance, have been everywhere. They have been everywhere in indigenous thought ever since Buffalo Bill Cody officially took paroled Sioux prisoners of war like Sitting Bull and the Wounded Knee survival participants around the country in public exhibitions under the banner "Once enemies . . now friends." The oppressive silence of those captive natives, much like the silence notable in the characterization of Sacajawea, now apparently manifests itself in apologia or acceptance of the colonial condition through public statements like Alexie's and in other texts. He speaks and they are silent. Are they saying the same thing? Are they in agreement? Is there some risk for falsification in this collaboration?

In real history, Sitting Bull came back from such controlled adventures to lead his people in war against the Americans and to be shot to death by colonial tribal and federal police not far from his home on the Grand River two weeks before nearly 400 of his relatives were massacred and buried at Wounded Knee, South Dakota. Is the benign plight of Sacajawea, also in real history, a different matter? A matter unconnected to invasion? An event unconnected to genocide? I think not. In light of the differing interpretations of colonial histories, though, what can one say about subjectivity, diaspora, or apologia? As a deconstructionist, one can find no satisfactory response to the humanist issues of benign subjectivity, diaspora, and apologia found in this Alexie commentary, but it has to be denounced because the role of an aggressive power and its devastating consequences in any society should be so much a focus in all theories concerning history and literature. I would venture to say that the sympathies toward such aggressive legacies as described in the events chronicled in the *Time* essay of the Sacajawea tale weaken the decolonization efforts of every tribe in the country, and that is too bad. There is probably no place for such subjugation to the colonial view in the climate of aggressive power that characterizes the twenty-first century. In the teaching of such works, the lack of deconstructionist energy or counterhegemonic dialogue must be at least acknowledged because when it is ignored, there is no alternative for those who continue to regroup and continue their efforts to exercise sovereignty.

Another example of diasporist literature is found in the most recent novel of James Welch, a famed Gros Ventre Indian novelist from Missoula, Montana, who wrote a humanistic story embedded in much of the history of the nineteenth century. Welch offers a fictional account of Buffalo Bill's recruitment of one of the Wounded Knee survivors in his *The Heartsong of Charging Elk*. It is a story that examines the poignant legacy of colonial histories spoken of by Alexie in the *Time* essay and countless others who tread in these historical waters.[5]

Welch's fictional Oglala Sioux character, Charging Elk, is taken to Europe with the Buffalo Bill exhibition along with many other paroled war prisoners, is accidentally abandoned there, and stays in France for the rest of his life, loving his French wife and family and answering forever after to the name Francois. He no longer has to be an Oglala in the modern world. When Francois is given the opportunity to go home, he says, "No. I have a wife. Soon I will have a child, the Moon of Frost in the Tipi. I am not the young man who came to this country long ago. I am a man of thirty-seven winters. I load and unload ships. I speak the language of these people. My wife is one of them and my heart is her heart. She is my life now and soon we will have another life and the same heart will sing in all of us" (437). Isn't this the same sentiment as expressed by Sherman Alexie in his story of the marriage of the white man, James Cox, and the Spokane Indian woman, Etta Addams, his progenitors? Isn't it, after all, just a love story, which means that these characters do not have to tell us what it means to be Indians in the modern world because they are now faced with a compromising ideology. Individual narrating by these characters will no longer have the same social and political function as the tribal voice.

Charging Elk, for some readers, is Caliban of Shakespeare's *The Tempest,* and he is Sherman Alexie's Sacajawea, and he is Powhatan's daughter, Pocahontas, presented to the English court as colonist John Rolfe's Indian wife. The Pocahontas story becomes the American story at the same time it destroys the Powhatans and their story. As a matter of policy, both governmental and literary, the annihilation of the American Indian prevails except in romantic myth making for potential Americanism. It is only in the European supremacy theory that as one nation arises, another must be destroyed, yet that is the message in the newest (and oldest) Indian stories.

One notices this phenomenon in television offerings such as the 2005 miniseries *Into the West,* in which an Indian woman who marries a white man and accompanies him across the prairie in a covered wagon is asked: "Don't you ever miss your family?" and her answer is, "But you are my family now," dismissing thousands of years of survival mechanisms; that is, the clans and *tiospayes* through which tribal societies in the western Plains have survived for generations. Likewise, as Francois says about his wife, "Yes . . . she is my life now," Charging Elk never looks back. In the New World, says critic Stephen Greenblatt, "the European dream, endlessly reiterated in the literature of exploration, is of the grossly unequal gift exchange."[6] There is no "exchange" for Indians, grossly unequal or not in these stories; thus, simplify it and just call it what it is: "the master narrative of Western literature." Whether one agrees with this assessment or not, one must admit that even Indian writers, presently, have reworked history to remark upon how useless it is to resist the imperial dream, and how marvelous it is to belong in the white man's exploration dream.

What about the "exchange"? A precursor to Alexie and Welch in the matter of exchange, perhaps, can be found in the 1920 writings of Mary Austin, who detailed the stories of the promised land and the takeover of the American continent from the Indian, both the story as well as the land. Austin was a romantic who believed in colonization as an inevitability, just as Alexie supposes, but by sheer will she became an Indian thanks to her Uncle Jeff Dugger who discovered that "there was an Indian strain in the Virginia branch of the family," a little like today's black folk who now want to be related to Thomas Jefferson.[7] Legions of Americans after Austin claimed descent from the Indian princess Pocahontas. Oddly, thousands of white Americans of that period acknowledged the possibility of a Cherokee grandmother and still do in spite of the genocidal practices of the period. These claims to an inexplicable and largely fraudulent advocacy with what was perceived as a dying race became the patriotic stories of America, and they are still told by many sympathizers throughout the land.

In the making of these characters and in the reading of these stories, I find that I am not so much interested in discovery issues or stereotype issues as I am in the failure to deconstruct the colonial story. What is unforgivable about all of this literary history is the failure to admit to the doctrinal hatred for Native Americans that was evident in American life then and now, in legislation and modernity. Without that cruel and distasteful, yet real, acknowledgment, there is no explanation for the genocidal treatment of Indians that continues even today—the theft of lands, unjust laws, and enforced subjugation.

I am not concerned that Charging Elk is allowed to marry a white woman while Othello or Caliban cannot, and such freedom of choice suggests that interracial dating and marriage is an acceptable thing in the modern world as it was not in the ancient world, and that we have, therefore, made progress in race relations. I am not concerned that the new Euro-American attitude now decries its former notions of bestiality and savagery in nonwhite peoples, because I recognize them as stemming from the unavoidable patriotic stories of a compassionate Western theme. The readers who want to focus on the matters of these progressions fail to acknowledge them as falsifications that idealize the ideas of Euro-American superiority, the Hobbesian view that the natural man and the natural world were both undesirable conditions to be gotten rid of and changed into something acceptable. Just because we know better now and we've moved on in societal norms, it cannot be understood that such "love stories" represent a new force in the struggle for justice.

What concerns me as a political writer is that characters such as Charging Elk can never tell us anything about what it means to be *an Indian with a future as an Indian* in modern America, an Oglala on his homelands resisting a damaging history, surviving it and moving on toward a tribal inheritance. Neither can Mary Austin, quite obviously, who hoped for the "vanishing" Indian, but that is another story. Charging Elk is a man who is silenced through assimilation and cannot represent his people in the modern world; that is the tragedy of this characterization. What concerns me is that American Indian fiction in the new century is telling the same vanishing Indian story that was told in the 1800s. Charging Elk is the vanishing Indian of that period and his character gives the reader no insight concerning what might be the consequences of his devastating history. Reading this story, today's reader has as little hope for oppositional movements as there was in Charging Elk's unfortunate time on his homelands, a time of massacres, the death of cultures, the oppressiveness of enforced assimilation, war, poverty, and disease.

I am concerned that the need to challenge the literary or historical academy is not felt by native writers, scholars, and historians because the inevitable (and magical?) yet oppressive structures and imaginations of dependence still beckon us. In too many cases, major American Indian fictionists submit to the old fictions, still writing the same story taught by oppressors, stories of intermarriage and concubinage blurring racial and political distinctions to create a population ripe for colonial rule.

Many years after the dark ages of my college days in the fifties and sixties, when the concept of colonization/decolonization was unmentionable, I was reading Octave Mannoni's book *Prospero and Caliban: The Psychology of Colonization*.[8] I was reading it not because it was assigned (it wasn't), but because, as an undergraduate English and journalism major in college, I had read all of Shakespeare's plays, particularly Othello, with no mention of race relations, and I was in the process of expansive self-education. I was reading "the way west" texts that had no mention of Indians; frankly, I was desperate. Mannoni's work was translated and published in 1956 and was interesting to me because, as an Indian in an all-white educational institution that hardly recognized that Indians or any "others" even existed, I simply had a different take on Othello than that of my professor and colleagues, as well as a different take on the Western myth.

Like those who teach *Romeo and Juliet* without sex, my professor taught Othello without race. This was not unusual in those times. Indeed, the History Department offered a course that used the text *The Westward Movement* that had not one mention of the tribes, which was particularly distracting. I knew there was something missing because the conflict between whites and Indians has been deep in my heritage.

This phenomenon of apologia seems to find its practitioners even today. A 2004 example is the creation of the National American Indian Museum, which took its place on the Mall in Washington, D.C., that year. It is directed by those who do not want to dwell on conflict and war, genocide and oppression. Instead, the museum directors desire to examine indigenous cultures and cultural changes as the major focus of the multimillion-dollar project. Director Richard West says that "the message is cultural redemption and reconciliation." The promos boast, "The displays don't wallow in the genocide, broken promises and bloody wars of the 19th century."[9]

This surely must be of interest to the Jewish scholars who have dedicated their entire museum on that same Mall entirely to their own modern holocaust. If they know anything about American history, they must find it an amusing and unfathomable disclaimer that the word "holocaust" was not even mentioned at the September 2004 opening of the native museum, in spite of a history of thousands of massacres on this soil. There was not one photograph of Sitting Bull displayed prominently at the opening; yet he is world famous as the foremost Dakotah Sioux leader of the nineteenth-century resistance. To display his history and to bring up the subjects that made up the events of his life and his generation would be described, apparently, as "wallowing" in victimhood, according to museum curators. Discussion of the near-total decimation of his people is to be silenced through the activities of the NAIM. It would seem that the entire project is complementary to the success of the colonization story of America. So much for authenticity in the museum business. So much for decolonization efforts through the work of mainstream institutions.

It is astonishing that genocide is not a part of the new historiography that is being displayed at this national museum. I am reminded of a comment by Nailton Pataxo (a Brazilian Indian) who visited a former Nazi concentration camp in 2000. He said: "When you say that approximately six million people died in the concentration camps, the names and date of death of many are known. We indigenous peoples of the Americas remember nearly six million brothers and sisters who were exterminated, and in most cases, there is absolutely no information about these massacres. It was a silent and continuous extermination, which carries on even today."[10] This statement is a true history of every Indian tribe in America. How dare the $219 million museum in this nation's capitol create a collection, a clubhouse, and a cathedral for American visitors for "reflection" and "reconciliation" knowing that justice for American Indians is a joke! To consciously avoid a history of disinheritance is hardly the appropriate function of a modern-day museum of such magnificence, yet there it is, an accompaniment to the "master narrative" of literary studies.

When Nelson Mandela, the South African hero of the antiapartheid movement, was asked about the condition of America in its race relations with natives, he said this: "The decimation of the native peoples in the Americas is like a haunting question which floats in the wind: why did we allow this to happen?"[11] Who is to answer this question if museums and other institutions and writers of fiction and novels fail to do so? In the Americas there are monumental issues that must be solved if justice is to prevail. In the United States, native lands are held in bondage (called "trust" by the federal government); Brazilian Indians are considered minors in law: no tribe is allowed to own land. And on it goes: colonization, genocide. Who will work toward clear and present solutions when clear and present dangers still persist in the Indian world?

In the early days of my education, no one assigned works written by scholars like Octave Mannoni and it was years before Frantz Fanon became an essential Third World scholar.[12] The exclusive discoveries of the colonizing Judeo-Christian world had a fascination for me. It was clear that the focus of our study in those early days offered the surgical cleansing of readings in the college curriculum to which I was subjected. My response was to seek out supplemental materials and I discovered, then, that it really is true that if you are an Indian in the Americas, you have to create your own world. There is no place where that is more true than in academia, even today.

These days, though, moral and political conversations and imperatives have attempted to broaden the scope of possibilities, and scholars like Ania Loomba, an East Indian professor at Jawaharlal Nehru University in New Delhi, India, tell us much about postcolonial studies, which can enlighten the issues in the above-mentioned narratives. Loomba says that postcolonial studies that exclude indigenous thought and history are to be challenged at every opportunity. She brings up what she calls the "dependence complex," which gives us reasons for our behavior as colonized peoples and even, perhaps, touches on the behavior of a character like Charging Elk as well as the diaspora comments from Alexie.

"Colonization always requires the existence for the need of dependence," Loomba says. And, she says, "not all people can be colonized, only those who experience this need."[13] This, perhaps, explains Charging Elk's inability to confront the ethical issues of a colonial history, although some readers just think it is a case of an ignorant Oglala who hasn't seen the world. Even ignorant savages, though, even when they are introduced to civilization, say others, have the need to go home. The dependence complex is a major factor in Indian–white relations because when the indigenous economic and religious systems were deliberately destroyed by the colonizers to this country in the nineteenth century, and when war was the only negotiating tool, peace and interdependence quickly turned into white dominance, Indian failure, and Indian dependence. It explains, too, why there are so few anticolonial writer-activists in the new native Renaissance because, in the modern world, as in other worlds and especially in capitalistic democracies, economies rule and acceptance by the literati is crucial.

The colonization stories rising out of the disagreements concerning how American Indians assess the Lewis and Clark story are, perhaps, among the most important popular literary expressions of our day; because of their pervasiveness and popularity, it is difficult to confront the moral or ethical issues they present—that is, how to challenge colonialism, its self-interest, and bias. More salient to literary critical thought, however, may be the notion that any critical analysis of Native American imaginative literature cannot reject politics as a way to explain the reality of everything in which Indians believe; that is, that the invasion of the United States by Europeans exemplified a violent colonial period.

It can be said that the colonial history of Lewis and Clark introduced the war stories that followed, and they took many forms. Many accounts are now often labeled as a "captivity narrative"; certainly the Sacajawea story can be described as such. This subgenre has become controversial, especially to those historians who look critically at the retelling of events of imperialistic eras with the notion that anecdotal information is suspect.

Because of the perennial Indian–white conflict over what happened during those crucial decades of the 1800s and in the real world, tribal nations today regularly find themselves in U.S. courts fighting legal battles over lands, resources, and rights guaranteed in the early treaty-making period. The hope that people of good and free will can make correct and moral determinations is fragile, indeed, as one surveys the history of massive land thefts, genocidal policies, and the diminishment of tribal sovereignty that have followed the Lewis and Clark intrusion into sovereign lands.

Therefore, the actions of Indians and whites in historical events must be investigated and analyzed in the context of struggle and conflict rather than discussed in a cover-up or romantic mode of fiction or presented in a heroic or epic mode that aggrandizes colonization. It was during these periods that the taking over of lands and resources and the removing of Indians, if not killing them, took place—all of which Helen Hunt Jackson carefully documented in *A Century of Dishonor*.[14] Her work suggests that the extermination of the buffalo was a deliberate and direct consequence of the Lewis and Clark journey, as was the development of the subsequent reservation period characterized by death, poverty, disease, and coercive educational systems.

In the founding days of the Republic, the individual white man's voice was forthcoming and ubiquitous but the individual Indian's voice was rare. Even Sacajawea, a central character in the Lewis and Clark saga, had little to say publicly, as far as we know, and what she did say was, at the very least, hearsay—if not contrived propaganda by those who put words in her mouth for their own reasons. Indian history, then, mostly told by the other, is a history of imperial intention, native failure, racial hatred, sorrow, and death. And the truth in this reality stems from the supposed evidence that people of apparent goodwill went ahead with their theft of the continent and the killing of its inhabitants. To avoid thinking about that possibility and in an effort to bring order to this seeming chaos, legends of all manner, such as the following (which appeared decades later), have been told:

> The Legend of the Fool Soldiers:
> the Fool Soldiers, a group of Teton Indians,
> were led by Charger who had a vision in 1862
> and to prove manhood set about rescuing

white captives (mostly women and children)
from the Santees who were at war on the
Minnesota/Dakota Territory border. At
last his vision would be fulfilled, he said,
and he shouts joyfully I will go to rescue the
white captives from our relatives, the
Santees. We are not afraid to die.
—words that appear on the Fool Soldier Band Monument
in Mobridge, South Dakota[15]

LEGEND? OR PROPAGANDA?

This story was told almost a century after the 1804 Lewis and Clark expedition met the Tetons on the Missouri River, and it symbolizes the extent to which those intervening years of propagandizing the Americanization of tribal peoples was successful. The story is an example of the kind of legend that can be found in the historical collections of the South Dakota and Minnesota departments of history archives and texts published by state historical societies and edited by the noted historians of the region; in this case, the notables were Doane and Will Robinson. It is a collection that emerges from the early 1900s and is clearly the result of successful missionizing among the tribes.

This legend is said to have emerged first in anecdotal form as well as in regional print and text during the Indian war period nearly sixty years after the adventurers Lewis and Clark visited the Sioux Indians of Dakota and Minnesota territories. It is clearly a legend meant to characterize the Fool Soldiers, a band of Minneconjou Sioux Indians, spurred by their visionary leader named Charger, as those who aided those whites in invading and settling in Sioux lands. It illustrates the stories about those unfortunate people who were taken as captives during the war period that followed. This legend is generically described in historical texts as a captive narrative, and it has become a staple in the study of personal narrative. It is an example of the kind of narrative that has been sustained in the northern Plains history for decades as a supportive and sustaining story so necessary to the romanticizing of the white man's western journey. Scant critique of the narrative has emerged as its popularity has grown.

This rescue of white captives by a small band of youthful Minneconjou Sioux is an actual event that took place but has been so fictionalized as to be not only unreliable as history but also evasive and corrupt. Seldom is it written that several of the Fool Soldier Indians who performed this rescue were killed by the U.S. military when one of the captives reported an alleged rape to the officers. There was no independent trial. There was no evidence; only white witnesses. An abridged and cleaned-up version of the entire story, then, surfaced in regional history books as early as 1940 without reference to the fate of the rescuers.

Often such narratives as this one date these tellings as occurring during what regional historians call the Santee Breakout of 1862—"breakout" being the synonym for "war," "rebellion," "uprising," or any of the other words used to obscure the importance of an actual war declared by Santee chieftain Little Crow. By avoiding the use of the more appropriate word "war" in connection with these prisoner tales and by continuing to call them captive stories, colonial historians have been able to excuse the colonial presence and blame the Indians who chose to defend themselves and their lands from imperialistic aggression.

During wartime, opposing armies take prisoners, as the Santees had done, usually under a variety of conditions. In colonial history, however, language is manipulated to obscure events and their meaning. Indian wars can be called "uprisings" or "breakouts" or "conflicts," colonial historians tell us, utilizing not the language of warfare but the language of propaganda; thus, "marauding, savage" Indians, unlike real opposing military armies, take captives who can be described in ways useful to the colonizer's story. Isn't it interesting that there are no captive narratives that suggest Indians took male captives? Did Indians only take women captives? Is that a sensible conclusion to come to or is that just a function of the white stereotype concerning Indian–white sexual obsession? It is crucial to analyze the function of language in this colonial historiography because, through even the most cursory analysis, it becomes clear that language has been used in Indian–white histories to develop and sustain an appropriate American ideology that denigrates Indians without questioning U.S. expansionism of the period. The stealing of America, then, and the killing of its indigenous peoples and the eventual enforced assimilation of the survivors becomes an inevitable destiny, as Alexie suggests or as Welch characterizes, not a crime against humanity. The awful result of this kind of history is that historical events, even murderous, genocidal, and criminal ones, are completely without legal significance, if one's interest is to seek justice.

The Little Crow War of 1862, when this Fool Soldier story is supposed to have taken place, resulted from treaty violations in Minnesota, hunger and starvation among the Sioux, and U.S. land theft. In 1837, the Santees had been forced to give up all their lands east of the Mississippi; in the 1851 cession at Traverse des Sioux they lost more; and in 1858, by simple Senate decree, they were deprived of half their remaining land and left with only the portion of it that lay along the south bank of the Minnesota River. Money was appropriated for the loss, but it was never received.

The Little Crow War was openly and publicly declared by the signatories to that treaty led by the Mdewakanton Dakota chieftain Little Crow, whose September 1861 message to General Sibley renders intent with unequivocal clarity: "For what reasons we have commenced this war, I will tell you." He went on to tell of corrupt federal agents, fraud, and the starvation of his people. "I have taken prisoners," he declared. "We treat our prisoners kindly."[16]

It was during this declared war that the young Minneconjou Sioux volunteers, later described as the Fool Soldiers, arrived among their relatives, the Santees, on what has been described as a rescue mission for fourteen white captives. Although there is little corroborating witness to what the actual intent might have been, it could have been done as a way to curry favor with the aggressing, invading whites whose armies and political structures were stationed on every treaty-designed homeland or reservation in the territory, almost always without the permission of tribal peoples and in direct conflict with treaty directive. Governing bodies of the United States held the tribes in the virtual grip of restrictive colonial political condition at the time that the event was supposed to have occurred. Aggressive Christian missions were placed among the natives at government expense and directive and conversion was compulsive. It can be assumed that the Fool Soldiers were not yet Christians; therefore, to attribute their actions to Christian charity is probably not only bad history; it is absurd.

More rationale for this behavior has been given by historians quoted in the South Dakota historical collections: "In 1989 it was called to the attention of the secretary of the Society by Rev. Philip Deloria, a half Dakota minister of the Episcopal church, and a careful investigation of all of the facts made, revealing the circumstances above narrated."[17] It would seem that Deloria, in his accounting, was concerned that the men were not compensated for the horses and other property that they exchanged for the prisoners, which, considering the military and legal tactics being used against the Sioux, might have been the least of the concerns. Settlers being given preference over Indian landowners was a constant reality. Because Deloria was associated with church matters, he may have been an advocate for what was deemed to be a Christian act on the part of the young warriors. The thought of equality and justice was always on the minds of Christians, both then and now, Indian and white, and such thoughts often relegated political tactics to obscurity. Eighteenth-century philosopher Georg Lichtenberg may have said it best when the subject of Christian actions and proselytization are examined: "What makes the prospect of Heaven so pleasing to the poor is the thought of equality." Perhaps that is what made the prospect of Christian charity to appealing to the Indians.[18]

In addition, another French and Indian scout, Louis LaPlant, informed the society much after the event that "Charger's relationship to Captain Meriwether Louis was a matter of common notoriety among the Indians, that when Lewis returned to the river in 1855 there were many Indians living who vividly remembered the visit of Lewis and Clark, and all of the circumstances surrounding the event, that it was well known that Charger's father, who was then living, was said to be Clark's son, and that he was very proud of it."

The writer for the society of this chapter says, "I did not learn this story until after Charger's death, and so lost the opportunity to get from himself his knowledge of his family history"[19] If it is true that the youthful Charger was the grandson of Captain Clark, the standards for behaving as Dakotahs would be expected to behave in this time of war would have been considerably tainted. Thus, the name Fool Soldiers given by the tribe was, in all probability, done in opposition and ridicule, not as a function of honor. The reliability of much of the history of Lewis and Clark, even of the diaries, when seen in the context of Indian lives is, quite obviously, suspect.

It must be noted that the U.S. government was then promoting westward expansion and using various strategies of negotiations to weaken tribal power and to cause intratribal dissention so that the journey could be less risky. Prior to white invasion of the Sioux Nation territories, historians have found little evidence of internecine warfare among the Sioux or even intertribal interventions among the Seven Council Fires of the Nation (Sicangu, Santee, Oglala, Minneconjou, Yankton, Hunkpapa, Sihasapa). This rescue, then, must be examined within the colonial infrastructure imposed by the U.S. government and its military. The telling of the story suggests that, after negotiating the release of the white prisoners, the Fool Soldiers took them during a vicious winter storm to the U.S. military camp, where the federal government was holding several hundred Dakotahs captured during the Little Crow War in a concentration camp prior to the public hanging.

We are told that the grateful repatriated whites narrated their story for the American public, praising the U.S. military, thanking their Indian rescuers and going forward with their lives as settlers and pioneers in the region.

This recitation suggests that the war was inconsequential and all was well between Indians and the invading whites. This fraudulent telling has become accepted as a full and accurate accounting of the incident. An even more egregious manipulation of legendary tellings is obvious when we find that a U.S. military court later convicted and executed several of the Minneconjou rescuers for allegedly raping one of their former prisoners. In addition, as readers of regional history know, this same court sentenced nearly 400 Dakota patriots to death for participating in the 1862 war. Of the condemned, thirty-eight were hanged in the largest public hanging in the history of the United States. It is said that 10,000 whites came to witness and applaud the hanging. Moreover, whites in the Minnesota region immediately embarked on a campaign to vilify the Dakota Nation and to condemn the war and the political leadership of the Santees as savages. The legacy of this racial myth making remains in place to this day in books, texts, and private and public repositories. None of the facts of history is given authority in the legend of the Fool Soldiers Society because they would reflect negatively on the romanticized version of the journey into the unknown by the intrepid explorers and the biased regional remembrances.[20]

This story takes place during a furious genocidal campaign by the U.S. government toward Indians and might more appropriately be analyzed as treasonous actions by young Indians who, perhaps unwittingly, betrayed their nation, the Oceti Shakowan, a tribal confederacy that was in the struggle of its life. Treason seldom has been held as a possible description for these acts simply because U.S. law was at the heart of the transaction rather than tribal law. If history is to be accountable, this event must not be portrayed as heroic or courageous—in spite of the fact that, like the Spokane Indian writer who wants to claim the story of colonization and Sacajawea's fate as magical and inevitable, the descendants in a Santee/Minneconjou tribal history want to revere the acts of their ancestors. To do so, however, transfers a reverence to the colonial masters and in the end serves to break down traditional structures.

Indians and whites alike have become the victims of this kind of historiography because there is little examination of the realities of the many decades of war and white land-grabbing and genocidal activity. Today, a few Minneconjous live on Indian reservations in South Dakota, many of them relatives of the members of the Fool Soldiers group. Although certainly there is no tribal or public consensus implied here, some Minneconjous, along with a few historians and writers, have taken up the story again to tell it as an act of courage on the part of the Fool Soldiers.

As they tell it, it is a heroic tale of helping the Americans take over the land, which is thought to be a good and Christianlike and inevitable thing that can be taught to succeeding generations of schoolchildren. Those who want to defend it as reliable Indian history say these things: first, the story shows the function of visionary thought among the Lakota. Charger had a vision and was, therefore, destined to perform this act. Second, it is thought by some to reveal the common humanity that moves common people (even savage Indians) to do uncommonly heroic deeds. Third, and most important to those who fail to understand the Santee defense of tribal lands and sovereign rights of the time, it underscores the perfidy of warring Indians and the tribal military. Finally, it shows the swift and deserved punishment by the U.S. military of male Indians accused by white women of the crime of rape. It is a story that some educators in South Dakota and Minnesota believe can be used as a "reconciliation" story, useful for education in a century far removed in time and space from the original events. What it is, in truth, is an exhibition of colonial repression directly tied to historical notions of the inferiority of natives and the continued necessity for the subordination of them. What it means, in terms of scholarship, is that natives have no history or that their only history is that of the Euro-American interpretation, which can only be described as contaminated and without interior meaning.

The sources of the captive narrative and the Lewis and Clark journey are journals and diaries, colonial writings, U.S. government documents, anecdotes by captives told in societies or in missionary tracts, personal remembrances by Indian and white descendants, Indian commission reports and records, written and oral recordings of state history groups and other library repositories, immigrant and pioneer anecdotal writings and remembrances saved in regional libraries and museums, army reports, and settler's stories. Occasionally, an Indian voice from the past that was recorded by the white participants in the events is added, especially if it is supportive of major colonial themes.

Whatever the Indian voice in this genre of history may be, it probably should be interpreted as contrived and unreliable. Definitively, however, it is expressed in the mode of what postcolonialist historians now call the "individualized colonized personality," a voice that emerged when armed resistance was no longer deemed possible; when disintegration of the tribal society became evident; and when the United States had made its encroachments, justified its crimes, and legitimized its dominance. This is the Indian voice that stems from the attempted interiorizing of contrived histories of defeat; its usefulness to understanding indigenous history in the United States is undoubtedly compromised.

Placing the story in the context of a wider geography reveals the Indian voice in these stories as lacking relevance to tribal concerns. The Sioux faced a campaign against them that was relentless and vicious, not only on the battlefield but in enclaves throughout the region and in the political arena that follows in all such contacts. A brief and admittedly incomplete look at that genocidal context is this: in 1855, U.S. troops commanded by Colonel William Harney massacred the Sicangu at Blue Water Creek in Nebraska with the intent to drive the Sioux northward. Chief Joseph of the Nez Perce died homeless as the result of the 1877 war, which forced him and his people from the Wallowa Valley homelands, the same year the U.S. Congress in a congressional act confiscated 7.7 million acres of treaty-protected Sioux homelands in the Black Hills. In 1864, U.S. troops slaughtered between 150 and 200 peaceful Cheyennes, Arapahoes, and Kiowas, mostly women and children, at Sand Creek in a campaign to rid Colorado of Indians. In the Southwest during the 1860s, thousands of Dine died during the Long Walk and while held captive at Fort Sumner. In California, white settlers enslaved and slaughtered thousands of unoffending Indians for sport and land. Many Plains tribes signed peace treaties in 1864 and 1868, only to suffer thirty years of war, death, and displacement, which can only be described as decades of the genocidal practice by the federal government. All of the Sioux heroes have been violently killed by U.S. forces.

In any other war theater, the Fool Soldier Society's story would be seen for what it is, a story of treason in defense of colonialism. It would be known as a crime against one's nation (the Oceti Shakowan) brought about by U.S. war and subjugation practices throughout the region. If "treason" is too strong a word, too burdened by Euro-American experience, call it "deceit," "subversion," "breach of faith," or even "sedition"—none of which are traits of valor in the Indian tribal nation world.

The genius of colonial historians is that they have always known what Professor Ania Loomba of Jawaharlal Nehru University in New Delhi, India, points out: that literary texts are crucial to the formulation of colonial discourses.[21] The literary texts of captivity narratives such as the Fool Soldier Society story of heroism, courage, and religion are the perfect theologies for the white American world of colonialism. They do nothing to illuminate indigenous purpose and intention because the white individual and his or her interest is at the center of the story, and the native individual is mere prop.

It is one of the failures of American historians that so few of them are willing to critique the power of literature and storytelling and narrative in devaluing colonial subjects and in turning historical events into propaganda.

And it is one of the tragedies of Indian lives and histories that the oppressed do not recognize the devastating influence of colonial historiography in contemporary life. To accept the Fool Soldier story as heroic history is the final prejudice. To ask natives to reward themselves and their relatives for participation in such treachery is asking everyone to believe in the absurd notion that there is no contradiction between serving the colonial aggressors and remaining loyal to the tribal nation, and no price to pay. Colonialism and imperialism cannot be placed in the past and reconciliation cannot occur through writing and retelling the colonial interpretation of such events as the Fool Soldier Society narrative. Postcolonial interventions in scholarship concerning indigenous peoples must occur. Decolonization will be a lesson in failure unless scholars take a stand about understanding nationalism (i.e., tribal nationhood) as a real thing, as dangerous as it is powerful, and as necessary to a civilized world as the human spirit.

The idea of a racial hierarchy within colonial spaces is probably nothing new. It has been forged mostly by those colonists and settlers who dispossessed and isolated the natives from the land. Dakota and Minnesota history is not only about regional boundaries; it also concerns academic boundaries. The Fool Soldier story came to the attention of schools and teachers and writers several decades ago when it was noted that the relatives of the captive survivors began holding reunions in Minnesota in the region where the rescue had occurred. Several years ago, Jim Ketcham, a descendant of one of the whites freed by the Minneconjous, started to research a novel and his efforts have been instrumental in bringing the story to the public's attention.

Native writer and educator Virginia Driving Hawk Sneve became interested in the story in 1970 as she completed the research for her nonfiction work, *South Dakota Geographic Names,* which was published three years later. In 1974 she also published a novella, *Betrayed,* the betrayal of her story referencing the hanging of thirty-eight Santees following the 1862 war. Her 2000 book *Grandpa Was a Cowboy and an Indian and Other Stories* contains a version of the incident and refers to it as a long-ago story written for children.[22]

Most of the nontribal writings on this story that have appeared over the years, even the Sneve works, have reflected the pietistic style of affected or exaggerated reverence for doing the right thing toward Indians and claiming reasonable race relations between whites and Indians. While telling their church audiences what they most want to hear, they make their remarks seem to be positive and fair concerning a thoroughly hate-filled war period of attrition waged by whites against native populations—no small achievement. In reality, these recent literary and "celebratory" contributions concerning a much-belated dialogue about war and survival do little except rationalize colonial theft and murder as some kind of incomprehensible morality.

In 1973, the white folks of the Klein Museum, a pioneer museum in Mobridge, South Dakota, erected and dedicated a historical monument and marker inscribed to the Fool Soldiers and to the Indian people, briefly described earlier. Mobridge is a small town located on the outskirts of two large Sioux Indian reservations, Standing Rock and Cheyenne River, that are the homelands of the Fool Soldier group and, not incidentally, the site of several violent racial murders that took place during recent decades.

The Fool Soldier Society monument has a State of South Dakota 1889 seal and was erected by the Northern Oahe Historical Society, the South Dakota Department of Highways, and the South Dakota Historical Society almost a hundred years after the event. It is a remarkable example of how a native historical event feeds into the colonial machine. Its narrative in its totality reads as follows:

> In 1862 a dramatic rescue of White captives held by a band of hostile Santee Sioux took place near this spot. A group of eleven young Teton Sioux boys left Fort Pierre on a cold November day determined to overtake and meet with the Santee to negotiate the exchange of nine women and children for food and blankets which they took with them. The Santees had taken these captives on a raid of a settlement near Lake Shetak in Minnesota four months earlier. The boys Martin Charger, Kills Game and Comes Home, Swift Bird, Four Bear, Mad Bear, Pretty Bear, Sitting Bear, One Rib, Strikes Fire, Red Dog and Charging Dog had decided on their own to attempt this dangerous and entirely selfless mission of mercy after hearing of the plight of the Lake Shetak captives. The hostile band of about 180 Santees was led by Chief White Lodge. History states that they came upon the Santee encampment on the east side of the Missouri River at a point opposite the mouth of the Grand River. The Santees drove a hard bargain and the young Tetons had to give all their worldly possessions including their guns and horses to effect the exchange. Only one horse and wagon was left to carry the weak and distraught captives the 100 miles back to the nearest settlement at Fort Pierre. The Tetons walked and gave their clothes to the white women and children. This Christian act of mercy by the Tetons was never rewarded by the U.S. Government and no record can be found of any repayment for the personal possessions in the exchange. Because the Santees had been on the warpath, the odds against success were very high. Thus, the Teton boys were dubbed the Fool Soldier Band.[23]

There is wide consumption of the narratives of captives such as this one in the primary and secondary schools of the West. Accounts of the Lewis and Clark journey are also used as real history in these schools, even though several generic traits (described next) prove them to be heavily involved in stereotyping and filled with historical inaccuracies. These narratives reduce complex historical events to images and ideas of simple and manageable form. This is the trademark strategy of colonial rather than indigenous history and has as its major intent the distortion of an ugly history in an effort to make it acceptable.

It reflects mainstream fantasy very much in the tradition of all of the works produced by "manifest destiny" thinkers. Indeed, almost two decades after the Fool Soldier incident, historian and orator John Fiske delivered what is probably the first articulation of the Manifest Destiny concept in Oregon in 1880, when he said that because of predestination and original sin, the white man, or what he called "Our Puritan forefathers" was required to bring his god-given morality to the whole world. This meant that any critical analysis of the founding of America as criminal behavior and colonial aggression toward natives would not be tolerated. Much of this struggle of oppositional ideas has been recorded in Drinnon's book *Facing West*.[24]

The tellers of the captivity narrative in particular seem interested in Indians only to the extent that they can be cast in specific roles. These roles are many, varied, and recurrent. To suggest only a few: the wild man or savage occupant of a wild and new land, the helper to the whites, the deficient occupant displaying a willingness to sacrifice self for whites, the barbarians who can be redeemed through civilizing and Christianizing strategies, the dark races and uncivilized populations who threatened the morality of whites.

These stereotypes are only a few of those that now reside in myth. The most persistent is the myth of the nomadic, homeless Indian often portrayed by the Lewis and Clark saga, the Indian who willingly gave up his home for whites. This image is discussed by famed law scholar Felix Cohen, who says that it is perpetuated so that the presence of white colonists is not only acceptable, but viewed as appropriate progress as well. It is unfortunate, says Cohen, that these myths play a significant and damaging role in the litigation by the U.S. court system and in the legislative function of the U.S. Congress even in modern times.

Attempting to cast off these myths and systematize federal Indian law so that natives will be able to defend themselves against colonialism in this century, Cohen addresses the place of tribal power within the democratic system by saying that Indians were not and are neither homeless nor nomadic.

They are, instead, the legal landlords of the continent prior to the European invasion. Cohen has written[25] that law must not adhere to myth but to the three basic principles of the substantiality of indigenous presence: (1) prior to European contact, a tribal nation possessed all the powers of a sovereign state; (2) the European colonial process that Cohen labeled "conquest" rendered the tribal nation subject to the legislative powers of the United States a domestic nation; and (3) that the tribal nations retain internal sovereignty subject to the qualification by treaties and by express legislation of Congress. Often it seems that Cohen neither agrees with nor condemns these principles but just describes them as historic and legal principles embedded in Indian–white law. Other writers, including David Wilkins, analyze the many ways that Congress exercises its claimed plenary power over Indians in violation of the U.S. Constitution. Some argue that the U.S. Supreme Court endowed Congress with this right by devising unconstitutional doctrine, and it is Wilkins's view that this doctrine must be overturned if justice is to be achieved.[26]

Naturally, this kind of legal and political critique of Indian–white relations is unavailable in the Lewis and Clark journals as well as in captive narratives such as the Fool Soldier legend, and it is up to subsequent scholarship to supply such information. In fact, colonial works of the storytelling nature of the journals often carry the opposite messages. Implicitly or complicitly, they suggest that white men had the right to invade, possess, and colonize Indian Country. They indicate further that any Indian personage who objected to these actions was, at the very least, hostile and a mean-spirited troublemaker, and, at most, lazy, cruel, warlike, deficient, un-Christian, and an ignorant, violent killer of the innocent. In the Fool Soldier legend, it is clearly the Santees who are recalcitrant and the perpetrators of violence against faultless whites even though historical fact points out that these Indians were being disenfranchised as a treaty tribe and killed and starved by the same government of invading colonists that had signed those treaties, presumably "in good faith." It is this suggestion of the rightness of white intrusion that the journal writer uses to give pejorative labels to those who object to the colonial intrusion. One of the Lewis and Clark labels for the Tetons on the Missouri River was that they were the "vilest miscreants of the human race."

The basic premise of this brand of history comes in four parts: first, that the journey into the undiscovered and unknown parts of the globe is a good and inevitable thing; second, that white America has the duty and obligation to bring its ideas and values into the undiscovered and unknown parts of the world; third, that these ideas and values will be welcomed because they are good; and fourth, that religiosity is to be the guiding force not only to be shared by others, but also to be mandated. If this sounds familiar, it is because this historical interpretation of nationalistic events and behavior seems to mandate present policy in the Middle East and around the globe as far as U.S. foreign policy is concerned. Thus, the tentacles of a profoundly disturbing history continue to spread.

Today, it seems that all of this presumption is undermined by the observable effects described in much scholarship written about the present Indian condition in America. The effects are as follows: severe degradation of the environment, the extinction of numerous species, endemic poverty and indigenous isolation from economic well-being, inequality and injustice in the law, the placement of colonial structures on Indian lands without the consent of the governed—one could go on and on.

If the captive narrative is an excuse for colonial and imperialistic presence, it also provides a rhetoric of blame. It persecutes and demeans Indian leaders and intellectuals who denounce colonial practice. The treatment of Mdewakanton Dakota Santee leader Little Crow and his relative, Inkpaduta, from the Kaposia band are essential examples of outrageous historical and literary persecutions emerging from the Minnesota/Dakota territories narrative history.

These narratives portray Indians as treacherous, violent, bloodthirsty, cruel, and undeserving. Even the Fool Soldiers, themselves relatives of the Dakotahs, if you take the legendary expression of their intent and rationale as real, must have believed in the stereotype of the Santees in order to take it upon themselves to rescue the people they considered to be victims. We are told in this story that when the young Teton men heard about the bloody war being waged by the Santees, they might have been going to help them militarily but when they saw the extent of the maiming, the cruelty, and the bloodletting, they apparently changed their minds. The dedication story, no doubt written in the pioneer historical mode, suggests that Christian righteousness, not Lakota tradition, motivated the young Teton men and this, in itself, suggests that the nineteenth-century pioneer story has changed very little. For the Indians who want to embrace the story and focus on Lakota tradition instead of Christian righteousness as motivation, there is little room for representation.

The rhetoric of blame has been a substantial political strategy used on an unprecedented scale to legitimize U.S. colonization of the so-called New World. For example, when historian Doane Robinson, longtime archivist of the South Dakota Historical Society, asked, "Who is to blame?" for what he calls the "Minnesota Massacre of 1862," he answered his own question. He said, "Little Crow precipitated the trouble." Later, Will Robinson, Doane's son, wrote that Santee chieftain Inkpaduta, an old relative of the Little Crow band, was in charge of the attack on Reno at the Little Big Horn some two decades later, after the assassination of Little Crow.

Regional historians generally ignore the fact that the military engagement on the part of the Sioux at the Little Big Horn was a defensive one. The Sioux did not attack anyone at the Little Big Horn except in defense of themselves. Certainly, the U.S. military, having tracked the Sioux across the prairie for many weeks with annihilation in mind, was the aggressor in that engagement by anyone's reasonable standards of assessment. As an aside, it is important to note (as another example of confusion in telling tribal histories) that the Santee Dakotas were present at the Battle of the Little Big Horn in large numbers, yet the event is usually described by American historians who are enamored of Crazy Horse and the Oglalas as being essentially a Lakota endeavor. Often, even Sitting Bull, the Hunkpapa, is given short shrift in many histories. Surely, the Cheyennes and Arapahoes, significant allies of the Sioux, are often neglected as participants in this major defensive battle on the Plains.

In any case, the function of colonial history obvious in these accounts to even the most careless, cursory readers is to blame Indians for the crimes of the aggressors. Between the 1862 Little Crow War and 1890 when the Wounded Knee killings occurred, literally hundreds of captive narratives and fraudulent historical stories were told. This brief essay looks only at some of the works appearing in the Minnesota and South Dakota Historical Society collections, works that have been kept in print continuously and should not be thought of as a complete historical overview of the literature. There is much work to be done, much research to be called for in assessing the historiography of the period.

The colonial roles assigned to Indians in these histories perpetuate the concept of legitimate white authority and make it impossible for Indian dialogue to be given any kind of legal significance. It is a concept that cannot be defended morally or ethically because it defends the policy of an aggressor nation seeking to extend its authority over tribal nations, a condition that cannot be sanctioned in the twenty-first century if justice to Indians is to be achieved. This is an imperialistic policy that in today's discourse among nations must be criticized and acknowledged, not given mere lip service in the discussion of global affairs in which democratic ideals are said to be foremost considerations.

The consequences of the disempowerment of Indians and Indian nations in America are recrimination, despair, conflict, and the continued abuse of political authority. The long-sought-after ideal of peace and harmony between Indians and whites may be considered a failed ideal in the modern world if we do not grasp what history has wrought in terms of distance and isolation from the cultural language of many diverse groups, including Indians. More devastating to Indian groups has been the construction or affirmation of the notion of the inferiority of native populations, which is responsible for the self-conceptualization of today's multicultural diasporists who are afraid or unwilling to defend themselves in the face of white dominance. They are the inheritors of what is commonly referred to by Third World critics as "settler colonial oppression."

One of the real academic challenges to this history of diverse groups, therefore, is to try to understand that when history about Indians reduces space to time, when history pays attention to an event unfolding in time alone, or in space alone, such history must be regarded as imperialistic history. This is so because the facts of the event become fixed and detachable and can be put into patterns that allow the legitimization of the event within a colonial perspective rather than giving the event a rational analysis or interpretation. It is a fact that the Santees held captives in time, that those same captives were given over by the Fool Soldiers in what some who told the story called an act of compassion. But these are the facts in time of the captive narrative in which the white captive, not the Indian, is the subject, and any accompanying historical context is dismissed as without legal significance. This is bad history because the space in which such a story exists is vast not only in terms of years but also in terms of geography, law, culture, and the historical process, all of which suggest that the story carries with it much complexity in terms of meaning and outcome.

The mutilation of Santee history occurring under the circumstances described encourages colonial America not only to see itself through rose-colored glasses but also, more significantly, to applaud its continuing infringement on its own principles of due process and fairness to Indian nations. This is especially crucial during the current struggle for tribal autonomy in the twenty-first century.

Some time between the Lewis and Clark journey and the events of the captive narratives many decades later, the story of the violent colonizing of the West told by historians and settlers, frightened captives and defeated Indians, and capitalists and politicians took on the veneer of the good struggle for universal humanism instead of being understood for what it really was, a landgrab by colonial invaders motivated by greed and religion that turned into a vision of democracy forever corrupted. All of this matters if the discussion about historiography that began this essay is to be taken seriously: Many histories are distorted, self-serving, and fabricated.

The consequences are not just academic outcomes; they are the dialogues from which solutions to historical crimes are still being sought by the participants. They should be the crucial dialogues of democratic societies everywhere.[27]

5

DEFENSIVE, REGULATORY, AND TRANSFORMATIVE FUNCTIONS OF INDIAN STUDIES

BEYOND THE YEARS OF ATTRITION

American Indians who read and tell history are reminded of the time prior to the Indian Reorganization Act (IRA) of the 1920s and 1930s, when Indians were starving and dying of disease and seemingly trapped in a web of isolation and colonial policy. They were not jumping to their deaths out of high windows on Wall Street as the New York stock market crashed but were instead laboring to find a place in the new world on what was left of their homelands. Their parents and grandparents had no investments in broader America so very few of them were packing their belongings to head west out of the dustbowl to California and the Golden Gate Bridge as their white neighbors were doing.

The ones who stayed on their treaty homelands were among the hungry, undereducated, and unemployed of America; they were among the ill-fated indigenous folks who had to make the best of it, and, for the most part, they continued to live on the lands of their ancestors, lands supposedly protected by treaty, with little thought of leaving. It would have been unthinkable to leave, for where would they go, when the holy persons who told them who they were and where their lands were located still communicated with them? Some historiographers have made much of an "exodus" by all groups during this time but, for the most part, Indians clung to what they knew of their places in the sun.

What they were doing, then, during those awful years, was coming to the quite sober realization that it was their responsibility to learn how to live on their tribal homelands after what they thought was a treaty-based reconciliation and a reorganization of tribal purpose, after the wars and after the colonial intrusions. These were the beginnings of the inevitable Indian reorganization period. Indians were listening to the suggestions of politicians and villagers and the old folks and they were thinking that, perhaps, the days of the vanishing American Indian were done. They were not looking for empire, love, fame, or riches. They were looking for survival and a gateway to consensus on what their survival as indigenous peoples might mean in terms of the future.

Since that crucial time, an educational tradition of tribalism was being converted to modernism. The schools that had captured the parents and placed them in far-off boarding schools for indoctrination were waning in their influence and the imperial Buffalo Bill histories were seen as mocking spectacles, and educated Indians were writing long narratives about how to look into the future as tribal peoples. Few of those documents have survived, but certainly the treaties that they signed in good faith were thought to be a part of that survival.

It is probably true that Dakota Sioux Indians (and the people of all the tribal nations in America during that period) were doubtless among the most restricted people within what we may call American education. Dakotahs were probably the people most isolated from broader American opportunities in this country. Yet it is one of the strange and inexplicable ironies of our time that they were significantly involved in their own literacy, in the major intellectual and political concerns of their own people, and in the reshaping of their lives as Dakota Indians in the context of a smothering and racist white domination.

Because of that early involvement by tribal leaders, many Indian languages have survived and traditional governing and social systems, while horribly mutilated, have not been forgotten and now form the base as new systems emerge for the coming century. Most important of all, it is still a principle of native history that political authority continues to reside in the tribal nation. This survival is one of the miracles of the modern world. This chapter on pedagogy, then, is a scant outline of ideas, which suggests that the knowledge of indigenous populations on this continent can acquire power if it is organized, regulated, and consensually communicated to its participants.

At the time of the IRA, new educational theories and systems were generated by educated and determined natives. The natives who participated in the cultural and intellectual survival of the tribes did not become great public figures in American life seething with ambition or seeking fame, yet the future was in their hands, those who knew that the educational systems to which they had been subjected for over a hundred years were bankrupt and that it was up to the new generation to intervene on behalf of their children. The most astute of these educators knew they had to throw off the shackles of federal and Christian boarding schools directed toward assimilation and repression in order to seek and find an ethno-empowerment model of education for their future lives.

This was the beginning of the academic discipline we now call "Indian Studies." As a cultural strategy for revitalization, some questions concerning pedagogy in Indian Studies have emerged. They are as follows:

What is Indian Studies? Why Indian Studies?

Is there an emergence narrative of Indian Studies as an academic discipline?

What are the principles of the discipline and its methodologies?

What is a tribal nation model of the discipline? A pan-Indian model? A global model?

What are the parameters of the discipline?

What are the three major functions of the parameters and how does the structure distinguish Native American Studies from other disciplines both pedagogically and methodologically?

How is a tribal model of Indian Studies useful as an educational tool for these three major objectives? (1) cultural revitalization; (2) ideology; and (3) definition, unification, and motivation.

PREPARING THE FIELD

It is always important to prepare the field of such a vast inquiry. It is a little like grass dancing at the community *wacipi* in traditional times, the essential preparation of the grounds or fields or arenas or classrooms for the ceremonial expression of history and culture. The preparation in this case requires definitions of many sorts so that the hard work of the classroom can begin. "Indian Studies," as it has developed over the past thirty years, can be defined in academic language in this way:

Indian Studies is an ethno-endogenous epistemological empowerment model of education directed toward and by indigenous populations in America. Yet, presently, there are almost as many definitions and models of Indian Studies as there are academic institutions offering degrees in the subject matter, which means that we are still in the business of charting the dynamic possibilities of the survival mechanism. But for most people involved in its development during the past three decades, Indian Studies as an academic discipline is what Russell Thornton said it was thirty years ago: *the endogenous consideration of indigenous populations on the American continent.*[1]

This description was expressed in Thornton's essay "Institutional and Intellectual Histories of Native American Studies," but this definition, promising though it was at the time and is even now, leaves practitioners with the notion that Indian Studies can be all things to all people. It can be a little bit of anthropology, focusing on Indian behaviors as anomalies, or it can be a bit of social science, pinpointing problems and developing solutions; perhaps it can focus on multiculturalism and diversity and the study of ethnicity, feminism, law, modernism, postmodernism, Third Worldism, crossbreeding, and all manner of politico-religious thought and ideology. When surveying the past thirty years of this kind of curricular development at universities across the country, it surprises no one that these wide-ranging possibilities have falsified the promise of Indian Studies as a survival mechanism for Indian nations. They have cheated Indians out of a system of intellectual and academic legitimacy directed toward their defense as nations-within-a-nation in the most powerful democracy on earth intent on absorption and assimilation.

It seems much more fruitful, then, in defining Indian Studies, to develop First Nations empowerment models of Indian Studies that are based on two principles within parameters meant to defend, regulate, and transform native histories, cultures, and institutions. Those principles are sovereignty and indigenousness. This model serves as an empowerment model for the Indian nations that have survived the genocidal holocaust of the eighteenth and nineteenth centuries and calls forth a new vocabulary resulting in a renewed debate and dialogue. This means that it is not useful to resurrect older disciplinary and academic divisions, although some scholars continue to believe that such intersections must not be abandoned completely.

· · ·

DISCIPLINARY UNDERPINNING OF INDIAN STUDIES

The use of the word "endogenous" in the succinct Thornton definition of Indian Studies is key to understanding its ideological base, its pedagogical approach, and its specific subject matter. "Endogenous" is a term not always included in all editions of *Webster's New World College Dictionary,* nor is it always found in standard reference works such as Roget's twentieth- and twenty-first-century thesauruses, but it is a term not unfamiliar to the disciplines related to Indian Studies, such as anthropology and other scientific studies of culture and history. It means "originating from within."

Since the 1960s, many of the American Indian Studies curricular models have been developed at major U.S. universities from a stance outside of the cultures and populations being studied, *without discipline-specific standards* and a clear focus—even before such disciplines as anthropology and the social sciences staked a claim to these cultures and populations and utilized the notion that "bias" can be avoided in scholarship if such scholarship is conducted from the outside. In recent years, native scholars have developed strategies to define and strengthen American Indian Studies from the inside of cultures and populations; this is a major distinction from other scientific inquiries. Curricular designs for university study that are being developed at state universities, private colleges, and reservation-based community college systems are directed toward the "endogenous" search for new pedagogical models. As this occurs, course work and academic degrees are being directed to reflect the thinking of scholars who understand the emerging ideological basis of the discipline.

This brief section of this collection of essays is directed toward that understanding and away from the so-called imagined Indian as vanishing victim and/or persecuted minority in American society. The strategies for this new approach include working toward diminishing the conflicts between Indians and whites; preparing professionals in the field; creating strategies for the defense of lands and resources, rights, languages, cultures, and the political status of nationhood; and developing appropriate research models. In 2004, the newly formed American Indian Studies Consortium (AISC) met at Arizona State University in Tempe, Arizona, to adopt a constitution for the purpose of organizing a national consortium to bring together the Native American professoriat from all sectors of native education to codify standards for the discipline.

Board members of this consortium are David Wilkins, professor of Indian Studies at the University of Minnesota; Mary Jo Tippiconnic Fox, director and chair of the American Indian Studies program at the University of Arizona; Carol Lujan, director and professor of American Indian Studies at Arizona State University; James Riding In, editor of the *Wicazo Sa Review;* Elizabeth Cook-Lynn, author and professor emerita of Eastern Washington University; Duane Champagne, University of California at Los Angeles; Michael J. Yellow Bird, director and associate professor of Indigenous Nations Studies at the University of Kansas; and Sophia Beym, student representative, Arizona State University.[2]

The AISC board will help define the key concepts of the discipline, intro-duce major works and bibliographies of and by native scholars for course development, and put in place core requirements. Endogenous aspects of this organizational strategy are the focus of planning. The pedagogical models of studying Indians in related disciplines have generally held that "endog-enous considerations" are more unscientific or unreliable or unprovable than "exogenous considerations." Thus, the related disciplines that have studied native populations and their enclaves in America have developed exogenous methods in order to refute the charge of an inherent bias in the curriculum and related research. Because of the rigidity of the methods and the exclusion of natives themselves in the educational models, it has been theorized by Native American Studies scholars in the past thirty years that the subsequent exclusion of "endogenous" methods and principles could no longer be looked upon as primary for the pedagogical concerns that will go forward to serve the needs of modern study.

Therefore, Indian Studies as a discipline has been in the process of emerg-ing, not as a "corrective" or a "replacement" body of work, but rather as an autonomous approach to a vast body of knowledge concerning the cultures and histories of native peoples on this continent and the development of "endogenous" methods.

Further explication of the term "endogenous" can be found in the texts of biological studies, meaning "growing or proceeding from within," and even in physiological and science studies, which refer to the "metabolism of nitrogenous elements of cells and tissues." Thus, theoretical speculation concerning all manner of experience as it applies to native populations can be broadened and researched. In utilizing the term "endogenous," then, in the discipline of Indian Studies, native or indigenous ideas, and principles and theories of origin, after centuries of exclusion on the basis of "exogenous" theories, legitimately becomes the focus of curricular design.

As just one example of the broadening of pedagogy and research, the chal-lenge to origin theories becomes possible and legitimized in Indian Studies as it perhaps cannot be in other scientific models. "We come from the earth," tribal notables have maintained throughout the centuries. This is a widely held theory of origin in native systems available in what is often called the oral traditions and in the concomitant literatures. Some speak of an even earlier stage of origin by saying that "we come from the stars." Yet these theories of origin and theories of evolution are given little standing in European or scientific theories of origin concerning the population of the American continent. Indian Studies, in its disciplinary approach to knowledge and in its use of "endogenous" methodology, can challenge entrenched theories and pedagogical systems in order to broaden what we can know about the earth and its inhabitants. If this theory is given standing, the Bering Strait theory of origin and migration brought about through other sciences can no longer dominate the study and research concerning origin on this continent, but will take its place alongside a myriad of other theories.

Research models can be designed to benefit the work of diverse scholars. This change of methodology, it has been demonstrated in the past several decades, is not without controversy. However, the "endogenous consider-ations" of origin, lifeway, culture, and experience that make up the foci of American Indian Studies serve to expand the methods of formal analyses available in this discipline and differentiate its methods, principles, and con-cepts from scientific, exogenous, legal, and nonnative humanistic approaches to knowledge. In the process, revisions can be developed in successive stages, just as other ideas and theories concerning other bodies of knowledge have been revised throughout academia.

Little evidence of the endogenous type of study as it concerns tribal peo-ples who are indigenous to specific geographies has been brought into the academies of higher learning in the United States, Canada, and Mexico; therefore, the Indian Studies model of introducing students to endogenous interpretations of terms and ideas from a theoretical approach paralleling native experience and culture distinguishes itself from other mainstream disciplinary knowledge bases.

CULTURE AS A BASIS FOR PEDAGOGY AND RESEARCH

Cultural models of research and pedagogy are derived from within specific tribal cultures to demonstrate the origins of a people. Their major contribu-tion to the academic dialogue suggests that empowerment has been inherent in the people's experiences, culture, and land; such empowerment, referred to by the political terms "indigenousness," "sovereignty," or even "national-ism," can become useful to the people who are being studied.

Although culture as the basis for pedagogy and research has always been the focus of the scientific disciplines that have grown up around the study of indigenous populations, two principles of this study have been neglected and are the least understood of all knowledge paradigms concerning native peoples. To challenge this, it is a tenet of Indian Studies that these two ma-jor principles of the discipline, sovereignty and indigenousness (terms that have been declared too "political" through the domestic colonial tactics of American scholarship), reside in cultural knowledge that is thousands of years old and sustained as the basis for a not-yet-realized curricular model. Native culture as the basis for pedagogy means that it is inherent in and indistinguishable from the knowledge bases of specific land and specific geography. This fact is what makes the problem historically concrete to the invaders and colonizers of the land who felt the need to diminish the presence of the Indian in America. The point here is that the academic disciplines that have Europeanized culture and education in America will continue to import ideologies that provide the basis for this continued diminishment.

The most useful definition of "culture," for the purpose of the development of these essential principles in Indian Studies, is based in work such as that of the now-deceased Dr. Alfonso Ortiz, a major Tewa scholar from New Mexico, who has said, "Culture refers to a system of historically derived meanings and conventional understandings embodied in symbols; meanings and understandings which derive from the social order, yet which serve to reinforce and perpetuate that social order; the intellectual aspects of Indian ideas, rules, and principles as they are reflected in mythology, worldview, and ritual."[3]

The term "endogenous," then, originating in "culture," is essential to consider when designing the curricular models of Indian Studies as significant reflections of the life and cultures of the pre- and post-Columbian and pre- and post-American populations of the continent. And the failure to utilize these principles is a failure to understand the ideological base of the discipline. Parameters of the discipline, not to be considered exclusionary but mere guidelines for course development, are suggested in figure 5.1. As course development occurs within the parameters (culture/history), new ideas and research and writing can be implemented. As the dissecting lines suggest, there are points of conflict and it is at those points that real understanding, analysis, and problem solving can occur.

Figure 5.1 Parameters of Indian Studies

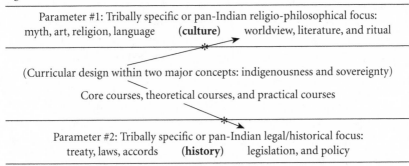

Parameter #1: Tribally specific or pan-Indian religio-philosophical focus: myth, art, religion, language   **(culture)**   worldview, literature, and ritual

(Curricular design within two major concepts: indigenousness and sovereignty)

Core courses, theoretical courses, and practical courses

Parameter #2: Tribally specific or pan-Indian legal/historical focus: treaty, laws, accords   **(history)**   legislation, and policy

For example, if the era when the passage of the termination and relocation laws (in the 1950s) is being studied, the points of conflict (designated by an asterisk showing the intersection of the laws of termination and relocation) require examination. Questions will be revealed and solutions sought. How is this law conflicting with the religion and the worldview of a particular tribe? How would the Hopi, for example, with an extensive clan system, be disrupted by the breaking up of families, and what would be the consequences of that? In this way, specific problem/conflict areas can be addressed in an educational system that will assist both the tribal peoples and the bureaucrats in Washington, D.C., in making a good decision about whether to go ahead with whatever proposal is being considered.

It is within the guidelines below that concepts and knowledge bases are examined in specific curricular design for the purpose of understanding the past and present condition of American Indians in the United States, Canada, and South America, assimilation and resistance conflicts in the present context of Indian–white relations in these geographies, and for the development of future tribal knowledge bases.

In this diagram, the parameters of the discipline are clearly marked. The parameters can be tribally specific, or pan-Indian in scope, depending upon the course intention. Thus, parameter #1 (culture) can be utilizing the knowledge of a Yakima, Hopi, or Lakota worldview and culture, or the Native American perspective in a holistic method called "pan-Indian." Parameter #2 (history) can use, for example, a specific treaty such as the 1868 Treaty of the Dine or the 1868 Fort Laramie Treaty, or it can utilize "treaty" and "legislation" in a broader context.

If it is true that "knowledge has power," as we are often told by educators, American Indians must find a specific model for the symbolic expression of their belief systems as well as an expression of the legal status of native populations in the United States. Scholars must start by forming an academic discipline that develops concepts and principles, describes general knowledge courses (such as history, language, and issues), moves on to specialized courses (such as tribal resource development and tribal government and administration), and then works toward developing applied courses (such as social work and health care). All of this originates in the oral traditions, where there exists tacit theory and implied ideology that is usually tribally specific. If this development occurs with the support and knowledge of the people, change toward written traditions will occur without isolation and failure.

Emphasis for problem solving occurs at the juncture of stress and conflict (see asterisk in figure 5.1) at the point of violation of the parameters. If, for example, a specific treaty of a particular tribe is being studied and at the same time a congressional proposal for the building of a dam comes about and results in the flooding of hundreds of thousands of acres of land, the conflict indicated by an asterisk intersecting parameter #2 is the point of conflict, the point at which the conflict must be examined and analyzed rigorously. It behooves policy makers and Indians to examine and analyze that point of conflict, which may require dialogue, speculation about consequences, environmental research studies and impact statements, findings that suggest whether the legislation should be enacted or whether the dam should be built, and so on. In using an educational model as a means of understanding the conflict in terms of history rather than merely in terms of economic gain or loss or federal legislation, consequences to the tribal future may be processed appropriately.

In this way, the history and the treaty status of Indian nations is respected in the process of economic development and overall institution building on Indian reservation lands because appropriate learning strategies have been set in place. Students who use these parameters and faculty who teach problem-solving methods using this chart can be encouraged that real solutions to long-standing Indian issues can be directed toward appropriate solutions. They don't just have to wring their hands in despair—and neither do they have to ignore the hard questions.

Therefore, any Indian Studies text that sets out to introduce Indian Studies to the academic world as an autonomous academic discipline rather than as an interdisciplinary body of thought will organize the pedagogical and research activities and the learning strategies around these two major concepts of the discipline: indigenousness and sovereignty, concepts that clearly extend the experiences of tribal societies, the interpretation of those experiences, and the evaluation of them.

In studying these two major principles of the discipline as they concern the tribal nation model, we begin by basing our organization of materials in the two parameters indicated in figure 5.1. The terms to be used in the classic examination of the discipline of Indian Studies rise out of culture asserted in mythology and language and experience, as well as the legal and historical events facing native populations after contact with European populations.

It is not only in America that educational models intending toward anti-colonial liberation must be devised. All over the globe, colonizers have been influencing the framework of how we understand the world. In America, however, the rapacious external factors of imperialism and capitalism have stunted the professionalism of the American intellectual and brought about failing institutions of learning. In the process of this failing, American Indians have remained the most poverty-stricken, least well educated, and most socially excluded of any "minority" group in the United States.

• • •

WHY NOT MULTICULTURALISM?

Because America sees itself as a multicultural or diverse population, ethnicity in America is embraced in society and is often the focus of major policy decisions, especially in education. "Ethnicity" is defined as the concept of a social group within a cultural structure deriving its condition based on race or religion. This concept is sometimes used to accord special status to groups. It is an ahistorical concept used, often, to wrongly describe native populations. This definition of the status of indigenous populations is at the heart of the disagreements concerning the treaty status of Indian enclaves and is the major reason that "multiculturalism" is a failed mechanism in the study of indigenous populations in the United States.

Every society has its small ethnic populations within its larger society. In Indian Country, for example, ethnicity is dealt with by talking about clans or societies. This is a very complex matter in a society such as the Dine in Arizona and New Mexico. In another large tribal national group, the Sioux, for example, to say that one is an Oglala or Sicangu is to say that one is ethnically Lakota Sioux. To say that one is Santee or Hunkpapa is to say that one is ethnically Dakota Sioux. To say that one is Yankton is to say that one is Nakota Sioux (Lakota/Dakota/Nakota indicate language groups). These are the cultural groups that distinguish one from another within the larger group; in other words, they describe what may be called "ethnicity" in a tribal organization.

We can thank ethnohistorians and other social scientists who study such groups for directing the polemical, philosophical discourse concerning ethnicity toward assimilation, largely for convenience's sake; however, ethnicity, as America has come to know it in general terms, has to do with outsiders who are becoming insiders through the function of immigration—that is, national origin, race, religion, or some other vaguely symbolic term that directs everyone away from describing difference. Such categorizing fails to take into account the major and essential blood/ancestor connection that is at the heart of tribal identity. To say that indigenous peoples are American ethnic societies is to omit the most important thing about their existence in America: their long-established and historical blood relationships to one another as well as their political status as nations-with-a-nation and signers of treaties with the U.S. government.

Ethnicity performs an important function in native societies, then, but is inappropriate in the broader U.S. description of the term. To say that one is Oglala or Santee or Sicangu is to say that one both belongs to the group called, in the vernacular, the Sioux, yet to use those descriptors is to maintain distinctiveness within the tribal entity. This distinctiveness may have been more significant in traditional native societies than it is in contemporary ones because it originally was geographically centered, yet it is a distinctiveness that is still useful in terms of behavior, politics, custom, and society.

The ambiguity of what is called "multiethnic status" in America is of huge concern to those who are working toward finding a form that describes the American, and there is much emphasis and antagonism these days toward the hyphenated American. For those who are indigenous, it is difficult to participate in these conversations because the fact is, to be indigenous in America is a political/historical category unlike any other and its source is historical in origin and geography, not a comparative racial/color category or an immigrant status or just a need category for the distribution of goods and services.

It is the view of many native scholars that university policy makers should redraft their policies to include native participants in the academy on the basis of their tribal/indigenous/political status rather than on culture or race or color, or a fraudulent "ethnicity." In doing so, tribal communities would be served and their national sovereignty reinforced, rather than just achieving individual assistance toward upward mobility.[4]

ESSENTIAL TASKS AND MYTHS

Many of the models of Indian Studies that have been developed in the past two or three decades do not require an introductory course. Such an omission has led not only to confusion in defining principal categories and major concepts, describing the purpose of pedagogy, and directing research in the field; it is also not helpful when defining the disciplinary nature of the vast indigenous knowledge base of this continent.

It is sometimes suggested that requiring an introductory course is elitist, exclusive, undemocratic, or even prejudiced. This may be a power-based way of looking at the organization of a body of knowledge because it is vital that Indian Studies distinguish itself from other related disciplines such as

American history, cultural anthropology, or sociology—all perfectly legitimate disciplines that organize their outpourings by sharing an exogenous
and nonindigenous overview both in concept and methodology. For some
scholars, this methodology has made serious errors in diagnostic, interpre-
tive, and analytical studies and has been weak in its contributions to cultural
understanding. How else can we explain the perennial nature of Indian–white
conflict in America?

An introductory course in any discipline implies two things: first, that
specific concepts define the direction of the course of study and, secondly,
that the body of knowledge is an autonomous study, organized and taught
in accordance with a particular methodology. This is as true for American
Indian Studies as it is for biology or physics or anthropology or any other
body of knowledge.

Because the major and essential concepts of American Indian Studies as
an academic discipline are sovereignty and indigenousness, a major purpose
of the introductory course is to clarify these concepts in order to promote
understanding of Indian Studies as a fundamental factor in the strategic solution of perennial problems in Indian affairs and public policy in the United
States. These solution mechanisms must not be left up to the endeavors and
research of past disciplines such as social science or other related courses
of study. Nor must they be left up to policy makers and white politicians in
Washington, D.C., because many of those endeavors have been unsuccessful.
The process of identifying and clarifying the ideas that a people have about
the nature of things brings about conceptualization that is connected to
specific experiences.

This can best be done through a focus on tribalism. Otherwise, it is simply
a system of domestic colonization in which scholars and writers and students
never feel any ties with common people. They may, for example, choose race
and ethnicity as major complex issues rather than offering an examination
of the political nation-to-nation (treaty) status of American Indians; thus,
few cultural theories of decolonization will emerge. Linda Tuhiwai Smith,
an indigenous researcher for and the director of the International Research
Institute for Maori and Indigenous Studies at the University of Auckland,
argues forthrightly in her book on decolonization that the exclusion of native
peoples from decision making in education has been the cause of massive
failures in education. The argument in Native Studies, a tenet described in
the introductory course, is that native people themselves must direct the
educational mechanisms of the discipline.[5]

A second major purpose of an introductory course is to assist students in understanding what it means to live in a culturally diverse society and to speculate on the ways that a just society might emerge and develop in the coming decades through a broader definition of cultural difference or political status, one that specifically stems from particular tribal perspectives. Indian Studies must grow out of an indigenous tradition, history, and people, not out of the importation and imitation of others. An introductory course provides students with a thorough knowledge of the bibliographies, the writings of major native scholars, and the publications that have informed the discipline throughout the past decades. This is not just another major task undertaken in this introductory course of study; it is an essential task that informs students on how it is that knowledge may be reconciled with the unique problems posed by interdependence with other cultures and other peoples. As the student progresses through the curriculum, this introductory material advises the research component of student work.

KEEPING IN MIND THE MYTHIC EXPERIENCE

Even before the major concepts of the discipline—indigenousness and sovereignty—are described in historical and legal terms in the readings of Indian Studies scholars such as Deloria and Berkhofer, it is essential to begin the introductory course with a series of lectures outlining the source of both of those terms: mythology.

An essential research text, *The Tewa World* by Dr. Alfonso Ortiz, indicates that the terms "a people," "a nation," or "a tribe," in the indigenous or sovereign lexicon, reside in and can be explored through the study of origin mythology and geography. Other tribally specific texts, such as *Lakota Star Knowledge,* produced by the Indian Studies Department at Sinte Gleska University in Mission, South Dakota, can be utilized in this early course work.[6]

"Mythology" is a term used in a variety of ways. In the most simplistic sense (often used in mainstream literary studies rather than Indian Studies literary study), a "myth" is a story that describes incidents and people from a bygone, imaginative time and is usually described as fantasy. Unfortunately, many of the related disciplines in social sciences argue for this simplistic definition. In Indian Studies, mythology is taken seriously and thought to be the basis for all cultural knowledge. The failure to teach and examine the theories available in native knowledge bases and the failure to give them standing in the development of course work is largely due to the methodology of scientific learning strategies and the lack of appropriate native language study.

In its most complete sense, as used in Indian Studies, "mythology" describes what are called the "oral traditions": or the vast and sophisticated knowledge of indigenous peoples that underlies language, religion, historical events, personal experiences, behavior, custom, literature, and the creative arts. Mythology, in other words, describes all that indigenous peoples know about their origins and their specific human experiences within a specific geography, which can extend over thousands and thousands of years and which are reposited in *Place;* that is, specific place and specific geographic environs. The theories that evolve from this knowledge require study and analysis often regarded as incidental to the work required in related disciplines, but regarded as essential to Indian Studies.

In broad terms, the discipline of Indian Studies defines "indigenous" as aboriginal, inborn, natural, or originating in and characterizing a particular region or country. It defines "sovereignty" as the quality of an independent power or authority. Because these are concepts or principles rather than laws, these definitions are capable of universalization and abstraction. Without understanding that these terms are defined in specific geographies, which is the reason to study what is called the "mythic experience," it is impossible to understand the history of disinheritance and genocide suffered by native peoples and, therefore, impossible to find solutions to past and current events.

What Indian Studies as a discipline has had to contend with in academia since its inception some thirty years ago is a bias against the development of endogenous theory. American educational systems—that is, university faculties, writers, and novelists—have often evaluated the impetus for Indian Studies as "unscientific" and the work of Indian Studies scholars as regressive, irrelevant, political, wrong, denigrating to Western civilizations, or simply unprovable. To counter this perceived problem of unscientific methods and unprovability, related disciplines have focused on methodologies of exogenous facts and observations that suggest, often wrongly, unbiased truth and pure reality.

Because of the perception of unscientific rationale for long-held indigenous theories, early meetings of Indian Studies scholars in the 1960s agreed that Indian Studies "embodied an oppositional character" to American development of the many disciplines that have studied the American Indian.[7] Few texts have been published that chronicle that opposition and the underlying cultural rationale for it, and there are few texts available that have outlined exogenous models of study.

The question, therefore, of what Indian Studies must teach and research and how subject matters must be taught and researched is clouded in ambiguity. The power of ideas resides in faculties in the academic discipline of Indian Studies and must be organized with influential departmental status and tenured professorships. These matters are necessities in providing an academic home for the development of the discipline. It is in pedagogy that scholars reproduce themselves; it is in pedagogy that knowledge becomes empirical; it is in pedagogy and research that the future of any discipline lies.

Because of the two major concepts (indigenousness and sovereignty) that pervade the discipline of Indian Studies, the principle of "nationalism," as it is called in contemporary lexicon, is a style of thought that must be the focus of Indian Studies and upon which the epistemological distinctions of the discipline must rest.

Some argue that this style of thought rose out of the militancy of the sixties rather than from cultural knowledge; thus, critics say that (1) it borrows too much from Euro-American history—that is, "you tribes were not nations until America came along and signed treaties with you and designated you as semidependent"—or (2) this style of thought limits the possibility for transformation—that is, "do you want to go back to living in tipis and wearing hides?" These arguments should be recognized as strategies of cooptation and trivialization made by those who are opponents to indigenous theories. Moreover, taking these arguments seriously results in scholarly damage to Indian populations by catching them up in the flawed "minority rights" dialogue that ordinarily accompanies the building of American public institutions and that ignores the vast history of native occupancy and life on this continent.

In terms of how and what must be taught in Indian Studies, it is important to reconsider historical perspectives and reject theories perpetuated in the courses now offered in historiography. The development of new epistemologies and strategies will be far-reaching, taking up endogenous theories of origin as well as those histories experienced from the moment of colonization to the present day. These epistemologies and strategies will eventually lead to the furtherance of new knowledge bases in the real world.

Strategies for developing the discipline within the guidelines or parameters suggest that pedagogical concerns embody three specific functions: (1) a defensive function, which is the reinforcement and protection of theoretical and experiential knowledge bases of tribal societies; (2) a regulatory function, which is a pedagogical matter outlining what courses will be taught, what degrees will be earned, what works will be utilized, how to assess the building of corresponding bibliographies, and how knowledge will be transmitted; and (3) a transformative function, which directs research, writing, and publishing interests of the discipline in order for tribal societies to assist in institution building and welcoming the target populations—native populations—as participants in American academic life. These functions emerge from appropriate enclaves of tribal repositories as well as from developed faculties and scholars in the field, bringing Indian nations into the present.

In the approach to readings and discussions, careful choices in classic and contemporary selections will reflect the cooperative efforts of many people who have contributed to the dialogues of the past century. Outlining a design for an undergraduate curriculum in a field that has as its purpose the defense and development of native nationhood in a democratic society is a major undertaking, and often finds that other, more established disciplines set in colonial thought patterns and assimilationist beliefs are resistant to change.

The topics in Indian Studies touch on a massive history occurring within the parameters of the discipline. The work of Indian Studies is as challenging as any emerging discipline and requires a focus on what must be done for the future. Some of the topics and obligations of this emerging discipline are as follows: Indian Studies must utilize the work of the major figures of native scholarship, particularly those works that have emerged in the past three decades and the theories that give substance to the defense of sovereignty and the meaning of indigenousness. It needs to review the rise-and-fall nature of sovereignty as it impacts a nation-to-nation status bonded by treaties and to provide various models of educational strategies that clarify the major issue of self-governance and autonomy. In addition, topics in Indian Studies offer the political and intellectual rationale for the development of a disciplinary model based within the parameters of culture and history; provide the research for chapters to be published in textbooks on the major concepts, ideas, and methodologies of the pedagogy that accompanies those concepts; prepare examples of syllabi for undergraduate course development as well as for the development of graduate curricula; create pedagogical techniques, including examples, lectures, and case studies; and assist in the preparation of extensive bibliographies.

While designing an undergraduate course, it must be remembered that mythology (i.e., the bodies of oral knowledge possessed by native peoples) is the basis for historiography and the development of principles and methodologies in Indian Studies. A beginning understanding of mythology as historiography, then, can be useful to scholars who have as a foremost concern the development of curricula in an "ethno-endogenous epistemological empowerment model" of knowledge and pedagogy. This is not an easy task for professors or students and the number of texts available for assisting in such study are few.

An introductory study of mythology is essential, though, not only to show that the First Nations of America are significantly different from other populations in the United States, in social order, worldview, origin, and political status, but also for the development of solution mechanisms that come about later in the course of study. Indigenous mythology as history is a crucial offering in order to understand the origins of nation-to-nation sovereignty for indigenous peoples in this American democracy and it is crucial to understanding the unique political status of native peoples, their governments, and their individual understandings. Mythology in an Indian Studies curricular design should never be taught as incidental to the national status of native populations and their geographical possessions. It must be taught as essential to it.

According to Dr. Alfonso Ortiz, significant differences in human organizational patterns stem from mythology, a major component of culture, worldview, and geography. The mythic experiences of indigenous peoples have served to unite and motivate them as nations of people who have learned to live in the tribal way. Thus, they are sovereign peoples who have created tribally based, oral civilizations and autonomous national enclaves in which they have shared the variety of languages, customs, religions, and specific lands of this continent. The values of tribal societies are necessarily focused on kinship, harmony, and a spirituality that connects them to specific geographies.

Several initial lectures in the introductory course must define culture as illustrative of worldview and social order known to the indigenous peoples on this continent as having derived from and being accessible through geographical origins. One excellent example of a native monomyth that may be utilized in the designing and developing of the Indian Studies courses is the text of the Popul Vuh, which offers a pre-Columbian and pre-Christian worldview emerging in South America from the Quiche peoples of Guatemala and flourishing northward. It is available in several translated texts and assists in binding together what can be called the literary legacy of the entire continent. The spiritual heritage of the Maya and Aztec peoples is part of the spiritual heritage of all native peoples on the continent. These native chronicles always end with the "conquest" and upheaval that followed, a period of literary development that mirrors the experiences of the North American native populations.

It is important to illustrate to mainstream American scholars that in contrast to the male Adam and female Eve of the monomyth of Christianity who occupy an ethereal geography called the Garden of Eden, a substantial tenet in all U.S. and Euro-based scholarship, the native figures of a basic non-Christian and pre-Columbian monomyth known by the peoples of North and South America possess a real geography on this continent that serves as the contrasting tenet for all native scholarship. The connection of myth to specific geographies is essential because it is from these connections that all religious knowledge of the past, as well as contemporary political standing, derive.

The usefulness of such a monomyth in the introductory course of Indian Studies is to illustrate a contrast between native and nonnative worldview in preparation for subsequent course work when, later in the curriculum, it is necessary to understand the philosophical and political conflict between native/colonist viewpoints as it concerns land issues and First Nation possession. Not only is this understanding essential to the examination of the concept of indigenousness, it is also essential to the second concept of the discipline, sovereignty. These terms must be understood as major aspects of culture, defined by Ortiz as geographical as well as philosophical concepts, and refer again to the parameters of the discipline.

The function of cultural belief in the study of these two monomyths (the Christian and the non-Christian) are probably more oppositional than they are similar; because this is so, the cause for much cultural conflict between Indians and non-Indians in America becomes clear. It is necessary to introduce this opposition early in the discussion of the cultural model because it will prove to be inseparable from the historical parameter to be examined in subsequent lectures. It goes without saying that such a monomyth can be the introductory comparison model for the more tribally specific mythologies that will also become part of the curricular offerings in Indian Studies.

RATIONALE

Why use an "ethno-endogenous epistemological empowerment" model? There are many reasons. Certainly one of the foremost is that Indian Studies began in the failure of Euro-based educational systems since 1830 to adequately tell the story of native life and the hopes and dreams of the original participants on the American continent. That failure went on for many decades and is still a force that stigmatizes native life and potential and results in lack of success for the native student in academia. Between 1930 and 1970, the political framework for the development of a tribal intellectual force gradually took shape and an undergraduate curriculum for the disciplinary development of Indian Studies, an introduction to the origins of the discipline, began to emerge. It was not until the 1960s, however, that real self-fulfillment and self-expression of indigenous peoples began to be appreciated by the broader American public and the emergence of native writers and their works began to be available on a grand scale.

While it is often said that the impetus for the development of Native American Studies as an academic discipline grew out of a new sense of social justice and national conscience of the 1960s, its real beginnings go back to one of the most dangerous periods of economic genocide and attrition known to the indigenous populations of America: the period just before and after the Second World War. It may be thought of as a repetitious time, because such periods of genocide and attrition have been a recurring part of the history of natives in this country.

It was during those particular years of attrition, however, that a new federal Indian policy was initiated in accordance with treaty relationships in order to nurture native intellectualism in a defensive model of education. That defensive model eventually became the academic discipline of American Indian Studies and its major constituencies were the tribal nations of America, who came close to the end during that period of enforced assimilation and land loss.

In those crucial decades of the 1920s, 1930s, and 1940s, John Collier, commissioner of Indian affairs in 1933, introduced in the U.S. Congress an Omnibus Bill, which had as its source the treaty relationship between the United States and traditional tribal governments. It was to be the beginning of Indian self-determination and focused on two inchoate areas of development: education and taxation (i.e., economic development). The result of that period of legislative action has been massive change in the way that Indians have looked to their futures. They would no longer be nonparticipants in the development of America, nor would they be forced to vanish as tribal peoples from the American scene through coercive cultural assimilation processes.

In spite of great opposition to the survival strategies envisioned in the Collier plan, a national policy was set in motion "to conserve and develop Indian lands and resources; to extend to Indians the right to form business, educational and other organizations; to establish a credit system for Indians for the support of the rights for home rule." These important policies would be expected to rehabilitate tribal economies; promote self-determination (home rule); end the disastrous allotment period; restore lands; regulate resource development, herding, timber, and soil usage; form governments, courts, and legislative ordinances; and provide funds for educational systems to be removed from church and federal supervision. A seven-member federal court would be established to adjudicate conflicts.

To understand this starting point, which is tied to the inevitability of federal Indian policy and treaty making, is to understand the relevance, the objectives, the principles, and the developmental direction that Native American Studies as a discipline implies. This reorganization period, although weakened by Senate opposition, cannot be separated from the disciplinary approach to course development because when it is, Native American Studies loses its analytical clarity. Fixing this starting point in no way limits the intellectual possibilities for the discipline but it does direct and define the strategies, methodologies, and major principles. It focuses the content of tribal histories and cultures toward revitalization and political/legal clarity.

Since the 1960s, this historical beginning of the discipline has been obfuscated through the intrusion of course development of other major disciplines, mainly literary studies, anthropology, history, multiculturalism, and postcolonial studies. The result has been the diminishment of the defensive aspects of curricular strategies. In other words, in Native American Studies departments and other departments throughout academia, we teach Contemporary American Indian Novels and Creative Writing more often than we teach Tribal Economic Development or Land Restoration or Sovereignty or Tribal Language. In many of the departments in the country, the disciplinary aspects of Native American Studies are not taught in an introductory course, nor are its bibliographies and major interests summarized for its clients in a colloquium requirement, an academic seminar that is used to evaluate a student's grasp of the body of knowledge introduced in a major or minor. These two vital courses (Introduction to the Discipline of Native American Studies and a Native American Studies colloquium requirement) are as essential to the discipline as Introduction to the Genres is to literary studies and Anthropology 101 is to the understandings of human and cultural experience.

A discussion of the parameters of the discipline is useful for analyzing two of the most misunderstood aspects of Indian life: the religio-philosophical truths (culture) and the political-legal experiences (history) accepted as tribal realities by the indigenous populations in the United States. Although these aspects of knowledge began thousands of years ago, they have been reinforced in a treaty, nation-to-nation relationship in the United States that was quickly reconstructed in politics and academics into a colonial relationship.

Because it is the function of Indian Studies as an academic discipline to teach about these things, it is important to see these two parameters as the focus of the discipline. They must not be developed as exclusionary mechanisms but rather, as guidelines. These vital parameters, sometimes tribally specific and at other times pan-Indian, are organizational structures useful in developing course work that will do three things: (1) defend the history and culture of the indigenes; (2) regulate the content and pedagogy of the discipline, that is, what is taught and how it is taught; and (3) transcend through research and writing the narrowly conceptualized approaches to the study of Native America. This puts the burden of new scholarship, texts, and publications on faculty members, who are the repositories of knowledge in any discipline. The transformative function requires that American Indian Studies, as both an investigative and applied discipline, offer theoretical as well as practical approaches to knowledge.

Even though Commissioner Collier in the 1920s and 1930s may have been unschooled in the specifics of the epistemology of native life on this continent, he understood that the nature of knowledge brought about by thousands of years of American Indian life and experience on this continent produced a knowledge base vastly different from Western knowledge. He knew this because he witnessed the failure of the earliest government and church-driven educational systems put in place in the Indian world as the earliest treaties were signed. His political strategies, then, have suggested what many scholars have known for a very long time—that Native American Studies must be seen as a separate branch of knowledge, like biology, botany, or architecture, if we are to seek new ways to knowledge and government and if we are to ultimately produce new solutions to Indian–white conflict.

Though few in Collier's day used what has become now the current vocabulary of Native American scholarship, Collier was struggling through politics to seek what we now call ethno-endogenous epistemological empowerment. This new epistemology organized through the rubric of Native American Studies gives the discipline the three distinctive functions mentioned above and the two major disciplinary concepts that distinguish Native American Studies from related disciplines in the social sciences and humanities.

An analysis of the two major concepts of the discipline is crucial to forming a curricular design that is defensive, regulatory, and transformative. Because the status of American Indian nations has largely been modified through inappropriate political and legal maneuvering, it is essential that Indian Studies be a corrective influence. Its major focus is to find ways to take care of the historical disputes that have been given the colonial interpretation. The only mention of American Indians in the U.S. Constitution is as follows: "The Congress shall have power to regulate commerce with foreign nations, among the several states, and with Indian tribes," and Indians are defined as "Indians. Untaxed." As this history has unfolded, it has meant that Indians claim dual citizenship, one of their own tribal nation and the other of the United States, the only population in the United States with such claims.

These initial descriptions of the colonial/indigenous concept are essential components of how the model of Native American Studies as an academic discipline is structured, and no one, least of all professors of literature or archaeology or humanities or science or government, should take it upon themselves to rewrite this history. There is plenty of evidence that scholars and politicians have meddled in these matters without input from the Indian populations themselves. One remarkable example is the efforts of scholars to accept the self-proclaimed identity of Indian participants in hiring practices at universities while ignoring the historical fact that Indian tribal nations have the right to say who their citizens are and have never given up that right. It has been an enormous struggle for Indian nations to retain this dual-citizenship status for their people.

The distinctiveness of the indigenous populations in American society is a historical fact (they are exempt from the Constitution except for commerce, they are Indians, they are untaxed), and there is no need for the scholarship in any discipline to rescue and reconstruct what many consider to be errors of omission in order to rectify or falsify the ideals of an American democracy. It is not the function of the discipline to rewrite this history, nor has it been useful to forget that the traditional governments of the tribal nations were not formed under the aegis of the U.S. Constitution; this means that there is not much value in asking that Indian nations forego their history and long struggle to maintain their nation-to-nation status in the United States. To ask that Indian nations deny their history is not the thrust of the discipline.

Indians were not made citizens of the United States until 1924, when a congressional act arbitrarily conferred citizenship on them and gave them dual U.S.–tribal nation citizenship. More often than not, the dual-citizenship status of indigenous peoples has been misrepresented in mainstream historical and cultural perspectives and is often described as a recovery strategy rather than as the distinct status of a people, or even as an intrusion into that distinct status.

At the risk of sounding repetitive, it must be emphasized that "indigenousness," as one of the main concepts of the discipline, is ordinarily defined in any dictionary as occurring or living naturally in an area; not introduced; native, intrinsic, innate. This geographical origin is found in all of the mythologies of the native peoples on this continent and should be taught as a theory of origin in conflict with the scientific theory of the Bering Strait theory of origin. The central myth of the continent concerning origins, often referred to as the "Popul Vuh," may be utilized as a basis for origin theory in the same way that the Nile River valley civilizations are used to explore African classical civilizations, or the biblical myths are used to discuss Judeo-Christian civilizations. It is crucial that these mythological origins be taught as the foundations for nationhood that led to the eighteenth- and nineteenth-century treaty-making process and subsequent legislation of the present era.

Curricular design in Native American Studies must have, as a central tenet, the concept of indigenousness because it pervades the historical reality of America and sets the appropriate structure for future research. Following the Omnibus Bill in 1924 (which inspired the citizenship legislation) and the Indian Reorganization Act of 1934, a series of legislative acts substantiated the concept of tribal nation autonomy. Because of these early events, the Economic Opportunity Act of 1964, for example, acted to break the bureaucratic monopoly over funding sources and services to Indians, and the Indian Self-Determination Act of 1973, as another example, provided administrative mechanisms for tribes to contract for and to oversee their own economic lives. While fraught with controversy, the affirmative action policy of the sixties and seventies was another attempt by the federal government to place autonomy in the hands of the people and to reverse the discrimination that had been suffered by all neglected groups in education and economics. Rising out of Title VII of the 1964 Civil Rights Act, this federal policy assisted in the entrance of Native American scholars into the professions, and cannot be overestimated in its influence.

Although much of this federal action might have been interpreted by skeptics as strategies to favor one race against another or as another effort at assimilating native peoples into the mainstream and, thereby, "removing" them from their homelands, in American Indian Studies, the concept of indigenousness must be taught as central to the seemingly contradictory or hostile and inappropriate political and legislative action of the United States if it is to be seen by students as a concept relevant to problem solving. "What is the relationship between indigenousness and sovereignty and federal policy?" is an essential inquiry of Native American Studies. The religio-philosophical parameter requires the introduction of several courses such as Myths of Origin and Historical Native Religion(s).

It is from the teaching and understanding of such tribally specific knowledge bases and experiences that sovereignty can be understood as a concept that derives from within a culture and is not a condition conferred on Indian tribes from the outside, the United States, the Constitution, or the U.S. legislature. Sovereignty is a concept of tribal autonomy that is inherent and cannot be given or taken away. The bases for sovereignty—the myths of origin, derived from within a culture—have always served to unify and motivate tribal people, and their continued and disciplined use by the people in contemporary life reinforces kinship patterns, teaches social and political responsibility to the community, and fosters the acceptance of new customs based on the values accepted from the past. The ability, then, to make radical changes in thinking and the methods of preserving the tribal ways of life, forced on tribal peoples through their association with the United States, are clearly strengthened through the understanding of these major concepts.

In the absence or underdevelopment of educational strategies such as the formation of Native American Studies as a defensive academic discipline, Russel Jim of the Yakima Indian Nation in Washington State had this to say in 1978 about the matter of continued Indian–white conflict and the failure to find solutions through education:

> The formation of the United States more than 200 years ago created new demands on tribal societies to make radical changes in their thinking and their methods for preserving the tribal way of life. Relations between the United States and Indian tribal governments created a new dimension in the concept of balance. The U.S. government's national objectives of growth, progress, and consumption violently conflicted with the relatively stable and more limited objectives of tribal governments. This fundamental divergence of national and tribal strategies for human survival has been at the center of every conflict between the United States and its citizens and Indian tribes and their citizens.[8]

Such brief but succinct discussions of government and politics should clarify the objectives and academic concerns of universities in their development of appropriate curriculum. Public universities must also defend the principles embedded in this unique history. Indian Studies as an academic discipline should have no higher purpose than to put in place the strategies that diminish the conflict between Indians and whites described by Russel Jim, because it is in the appropriate diminishment of this conflict that motivation of tribal society toward unity of purpose and progress occurs. To suggest that there is some kind of social or political cohesion possible between Indians and whites in America without a massive restructuring of educational models is misleading. Just longing for a more benign national attitude does not erase history and culture, and there is a role to be played in education by the federal and tribal governments that is essential.

Sovereignty, the right to home rule in the contemporary Indian world, is the second essential conceptual framework for the discipline. It, like indigenousness, is an intellectual category that finds its source first in tribally specific mythologies and, later, in Western/native legal history. Although sovereignty originates in cosmology, language, and religion, its pragmatic condition was first articulated in the American hemisphere as the Law of the Indies in the 1300s, the so-called right of occupancy laws. These were laws codified from the Western point of view concerning colonizing and how to take over the lands of other nations in ways that could be said to be effective and ethical. It is one of the ironies of history that scholars believed at that time that the major activity of reasonably stable Western nations was to find ways to move out of their long-held aristocracies and into more democratic governments. In the process, the taking of others' lands and the spread of democracy was the dual focus.

In the colonial world and in the modern world that followed, colonialism was always the enemy of indigenous concepts of sovereignty and this antagonism resulted in a pattern of a "rise-and-fall" nature, as historical events reveal. It is upheld in some instances—reluctantly, as some historians would suggest—and, at other times, simply legislated out of existence. As a concept in native life that has survived these vicissitudes of history, however, sovereignty for native nations in the modern world must be looked at as a reality between First Nations and America; to do that, the study of sovereignty can be organized around specific texts and specific dates in history or eras.

In a quick review of what must be done, curriculum developers should begin with a study of the oral traditions of the tribes, teaching myths of origins and historical migrations as essential to an explanatory overview of the indigenous theory of sovereignty. Sovereignty, as we have suggested, resides in myth. Introduction to the function of mythology, then, as a body of knowledge that forms the conceptual basis for social behavior, religion, literature, and language is essential to the concept of sovereignty, identity, and home rule. Culture and the underpinnings of culture are the bases for the theory of sovereignty. Ritual and ceremony express the intellectual aspects of mythology while the ideas, rules, and principles of worldview are expressed in politics and government.

Many themes are taught in the mythology courses: (1) the creation of the cosmos; (2) the ordering of the world of people and of the gods and ancestors of the other world, which parallels current rulers and specific places; (3) the triumph of the ancestral humans over the forces of death and disease; (4) the miracle of true rebirth out of sacrifice and how the forces of evil are kept in check through ritual and ceremony; and (5) the origin of the substances of the earth that sustain the people.

An understanding of the function of mythology as an essential component in analyzing the two major concepts in Indian Studies (indigenousness and sovereignty) is the idea that these two concepts derive from within the culture rather than being conferred on a people from the outside.

Even though it is an accepted tenet that tribal autonomy, clearly a part of a people's history from the beginning of the universe, cannot be given and cannot be taken away, at least in theory, it is true that an aggressive American government has trampled on this theory from the beginning of its occupation of lands on the continent. This aggression has interrupted mythologies of origin that serve to unify, motivate, and reinforce kinship patterns, which confer social and political responsibility to the nation. It is only through an understanding of the function of mythology that people and nations can accept change and new cultures based on what they know to be valuable from past experiences and knowledge.

From this study of origins (the religio-mythic parameter of the discipline), curricular design moves to the study of recent history (the political-legal parameter of the discipline) in order to identify the Law of the Indies of the 1300s and the colonial "right of occupancy" theory as the significant reflection of the newcomers, whose object was to possess by any means native-held lands.

The examination of the following historical events is useful to students, who need to speculate about the modification and adaptation of theories. The 1607 Jamestown Colony and the 1620 Plymouth Colony came to possess indigenous lands based on the theories of what is called the Law of the Indies, a theoretical body of law that has been antagonist to indigenous thought since that time. In 1763, a British proclamation prohibited the purchase of lands from the indigenes in America except through treaty (an effort at ethical law concerning land issues), but in the subsequent years, when the U.S. Congress gave itself the right to regulate commerce with Indian tribes, it meant that all manner of land theft could occur, and did. This is an immediate example of the rise-and-fall nature of the concept of sovereignty.

After the 1789 Northwest Ordinance, which (on paper, at least) asserted that even when Indian nations were "conquered," their tribal nation titles to their own lands were not to be extinguished, there followed a long period of treaty making and treaty breaking. Although few of the tribes in the West were "conquered" on the battlefields (and many of them never even went to war), the theory of "conquest" pervaded all legal and political discussions of the time and still does. Colonizing ideas as they concern the sovereign rights of indigenous peoples began a century of incredible theft and removal and dispossession, crimes of history seldom addressed in the court systems that excluded American Indian nations from judicial participation for over a hundred years.

At this point in course development, an introduction to eras and policies and historical dates enlarges student understanding of the criminal nature of American legislation toward Indians and deepens their appreciation for the lack of justice in the judicial, legislative, and government systems of capitalistic democracy. The following events and dates are among those that can be contextualized by innovative professors and students who may work together toward the conversations of illumination and dialogues of understanding. There will be much disagreement, dialogue, and conflicting assessment of the function of historiography and the role of past events in influencing the present.

The point here is to emphasize that American Indian survival occurred within an atmosphere of imperialistic hegemony almost as vicious as the atmosphere of fascist Italy or the papal authority of the Middle Ages. What is important here in the study of the following events and dates is to challenge the external oppressor in order to give substance to the internal felt cultures and political presence of tribal nationalism. These are some of the topics that will give substance to that challenge, listed at random:

Theory of origin
Theories of treaties
Theory of "Manifest Destiny"
Cherokee cases
The 1830 Indian Removal Act
Marshall Supreme Court decision
"Domestic Dependent Nations"
"Trust" doctrine (tribes east are moved to Indian Territory, west of
    Mississippi River on specific and designated lands)
Gold discoveries
1834—BIA/police/schools
1849—Department of the Interior established to take control of Indians
    from War Department
1850–1890—War and reservation period begins
1862—Homestead Act

1872—Elk and buffalo exterminated as economic base for tribes

1876—Custer battle/defeat by Sioux, Cheyenne, Arapahoe

1877—The Black Hills Act, most important land issue case in the United States

A cornerstone analytical event, the General Allotment Act of 1887, can be used to discuss the theft of treaty land by legislation. This era must be examined as an era of genocide. It should take up considerable time in the analysis of the dispossession and disinheritance of indigenous populations.

The Black Hills land case may be utilized as a major case study but there are many such examples that may be developed according to the interests of specific regions and tribes. Thus, the Black Hills land case, which has generated much research and text that is available to curriculum developers, can be used as just one example of land theft that occurred and made its way through the courts in ways that other thefts during the twentieth century throughout the continent did not. Eleven treaties were hanging fire during those crucial decades of war and land theft, when no appropriation bills were passed and entire populations were starving, a political strategy that became the usual method of coercion toward native populations. In 1871, just prior to the legislative action later called by the Supreme Court a "theft" instead of a "taking," an appropriations bill was passed in Congress and a rider was attached to end treaty making. No longer, this bill said, would the U.S. recognize tribes as independent powers. This kind of treaty making and treaty breaking has been at the heart of the decimation of tribal nations' estates, genocide, and poverty.[9]

In 1887, when the Allotment Act was passed—just before the Teddy Roosevelt "carry a big stick" era was in full swing—lands of the continent were being subsumed in one way or another during this time in what was to become America's first unabashed imperial presidency. The act legalized land theft as follows: (1) the president was authorized by Congress to divide tribal treaty lands and assign 160 acres to individuals; (2) each Indian would select his own from tribal communal holdings; (3) the title of such allotments would be placed in "trust" for twenty-five years; (4) citizenship would be "conferred" on those who would abandon tribes and be civilized; naturally, most Indian tribes objected to this scheme and, in addition, citizenship did not occur in large numbers until a separate citizenship bill was passed in 1924, largely without the consent of many tribal nations; and (5) "surplus" lands remaining were to be sold to whites and two-thirds of treaty lands went out of Indian title within a few decades.

This devastating policy went on for forty-seven years, until the 1924 Collier years mentioned previously. It was long enough for the Dawes Allotment Act, as it was named after the senator who wrote the bill, to diminish 60 percent of all lands held by treaty, and many historians today believe that this was the intent of the act. The stated rationale, however, was that Indians needed to turn away from the past and become farmers, agrarians, use land for profit, join the mainstream, become competitive, and improve themselves. This policy went along with establishment of educational facilities directed toward the enforced conversion to Christianity.

Sometime after this legislation was enacted, scholars in history departments throughout the country weighed in to give credibility to the genocidal tactics of what might be considered a greedy and imperial Congress. One major example was Frederick Jackson Turner, considered by his peers to be a "realistic historian," who in 1893 read a paper to a handful of scholars at the American Historical Association, a paper based on the premise that the Indian, as an obstacle to progress and white settlement, represented a mere nuisance to the progress of an important democracy, and deserved to pass into oblivion. Indians, he said, were to be described as a "stage" in frontier development, a passing phase, a vanishing race.[10]

This historical view coordinated what may be referred to as "historiographic theory" useful for describing a period of outright genocide toward native populations as ethical and rational policies by the U.S. government. The coordinated efforts between government and scholarship, which went on for seventy-five years, brought the Indian nations almost to their knees, teetering at the edge of extinction. The 1850–90 war and reservation period ends when all tribes are no longer able to resist, many driven from their homelands, suffering vast poverty and early death, confined to underdeveloped reservation lands. The role that historians and their theories played in this tragedy has been the subject of great debate and controversy.

Generally, courses in colonial history and American history and frontier/ Western studies are taught in the related disciplines. These courses, which say little or nothing about the controversial establishment of "fiduciary" responsibilities inherent in the treaties between the United States and the Indian nations and the failure of those policies, contribute to much misunderstanding of First Nation status in the United States and Canada.

To counter that deficiency in course development, Indian Studies requires specific analytical courses in Treaties and Law, Federal Indian Policy, Contemporary Indian Problems, The War and Reservation Period, The Removal Era, Legal Theory and Congressional Acts, and courses in tribally specific histories that have been designed as major components of the processes that develop the political-legal parameter of the discipline.

Considerable research and writing has been promulgated as the result of this course development, also essential to an explanatory overview of indigenous theory concerning sovereignty. In the application of the philosophy and the principles of the discipline, two major questions concerning pedagogy emerge. They are: (1) Who are the constituencies of Native American Studies? and (2) What are the objectives of the disciplinary organization of the body of knowledge called Native American Studies?

The answers to these questions inform us about what to teach and what the methodologies should be. The development of curricular design, the development of professionals in the field, research focus, design and publication, and the development of bibliographic support emerge as it is understood that, first, the tribal nations of America are the major constituents of this academic apparatus and, second, the objective of the discipline is to find ways to utilize the body of knowledge called Native American Studies in the contemporary world for decolonization efforts and problem solving and, most important, to prepare professionals in the field.

Radicalization of academic consciences in the 1960s had a huge influence on what Native America Studies has become, what is taught, and how it is taught. While the scholars of this period mounted a significant assault upon the long-held notion in academia that there were fixed, authorial values stemming from a Western worldview, student and faculty interventions and needs became the constituents, replacing the tribal nations of America as the major recipients of academic work. Consequently, axiological interests—the study of "values" and metaphysical interests, the study of being, the study of reality, the nature of the universe—resulted in the rise of the religio-philosophical parameter of the discipline. These interests, while worthy pursuits, contributed to the neglect of the political-legal dimension in undergraduate curricular development.

The tendency of intellectual societies to be affected by the real world is a good thing, but, in the case of what may be called the intellectual interests of minority groups, particularly native groups in a colonial setting, this tendency often urges academic movements into self-interested and irrelevant stances.

Some of these activities are, for example, the work of activist English departments, liberal anthropology departments, and bleeding-heart humanities centers on university campuses. They seemed to be interested, as they had often been, in dictating not only content but also methodology in the study of Indians. Because of intrusive interests, native languages suffered neglect and the burgeoning works in contemporary fiction and poetry written in English flourished. Federal Indian policy was no longer taught but postcolonial multiculturalism became the focus of pedagogy. Indian reservations and tribal nations struggling toward economic sufficiency and political empowerment did not see the benefits of this education. This trend may have contributed to the recent increase in the development of policy centers in academic institutions and the think tanks that have emerged in the political environments of many university settings.

The result, to the dismay of those reservation populations and tribal nations (but not necessarily of the white overseers of this educational activity), has been the education of young people and their disappearance into the American mainstream. Students from Indian reservations now make up a thriving middle class, a professional class of spokespersons who often try to eat, think, and work Indian but, more often than not, "sleep white," to use the slang of the reservation vernacular. This means that intermarriage between Indians and nontribal people results in the assimilation of this class of native professionals and very often eventually takes them out of the communities from which they emerged. Some, of course, believe that this is a good thing. Others disagree.

Today, largely because of educational opportunities, but for other reasons as well, Indians marry out of their tribal and/or racial group in far greater numbers than any other "minority" population in America. This is a real dilemma because relationships based on blood have been a tenet of survival and identity in native enclaves from the beginning and continue to be. If the goals of the discipline in the beginning were to empower Indian populations, revitalize native homelands, and combat assimilation and relocation on the basis that assimilation and relocation should no longer be the overt intent of Indian education, it is difficult to accept the reality that education as it exists in the new models has become just another "assimilation" and "relocation" tool.

One of the defensive measures used in native homelands has been the aggressive move to gain native control over native educational systems. In defense of native languages, ancestral connections, and cultures, the Dine Demonstration School on the Navajo Reservation in Arizona became the impetus for the rise of the reservation-based community college system in the West in the 1970s. The struggle for autonomy and social and political space presented by this Indian college movement was a brilliant move in the face of the subsequent failure of the Supreme Court in the 1978 Bakke case to make a clear, supportive, unambiguous statement for the consideration of race and ethnic origin in academic settings. Such a statement is still sought through legislation.[11]

The reservation-based community colleges, while still struggling and considerably underfunded and often overpoliticized, have flourished on the homelands. The curricular designs of this first demonstration school in Arizona, as well as those to follow, were tribally specific and utilized the three functions (defensive, regulatory, and transformative) of the parameters of Indian Studies. This development has often served as a transitional event for those scholars who want to initiate Native American Studies models at public universities.

As is often the case, federal Indian education policy has been crucial to both the successes and the failures in meeting the intention of Native American Studies as an academic discipline. Key to the skewing of the intention of the discipline at state and public universities was the failure of affirmative action as a policy to achieve the building of large and competent faculties made up of native people in the discipline. It is in stable faculties, after all, that ideas can flourish and become sustained in a changing and fluctuating and defensive academic atmosphere.

If the initial development of Native American Studies is understood as a historical matter rather than a "consciousness-raising" episode from the sixties, it follows that course design must rise out of a reasonably autonomous departmental status. This structure seems crucial to course design and degree programs in Native American Studies. In other words, degrees in Native American Studies should be available only from universities that have departmental status. The reason for this is practical rather than ideological. If the model for the discipline is based on empowerment to tribal nations, departments at state universities have to be willing to concede that as a commitment.

Knowledge bases such at those inherent in Native American Studies have to meet certain conditions in order to develop empowerment. First, they must be systematically organized into a discipline that has its own content and methodology, not just a set of isolated courses from history or literature or social studies. As has been consistently mentioned in previous discussions in this text, the organization of Native American Studies as an academic discipline is structured around the two principles of the discipline, indigenousness and sovereignty. In other words, a Native American Studies course does not take the place of any other in history or anthropology. It is its own branch of that collective knowledge and expresses Indian values in the modern world.

Second, knowledge in order to possess power must be normatively regulated. The parameters of the discipline assist with that. For example, if the parameter of a tribal historical reality is violated, it is at that point that an analysis and a discussion takes place or an analytical course is developed around that violation. When the parameter of tribal history based on treaties and the Constitution was violated in the 1950s with a congressional set of laws and policies called termination and relocation, that violation should have been examined and analyzed through educational systems to see what the consequences would be (see figure 5.1). It is the function of Indian Studies to teach about these things before the U.S. Congress acts arbitrarily in a political and coercive way. This means that the appropriate educational model can act defensively to protect the people and the sovereignty of Indian nationhood. This educational regulatory scheme assists in identifying specific problem issues and is a guide to solution mechanisms.

Third, knowledge must be rationally directed toward a specific purpose or goal. A Native American Studies program at a specific university cannot be all things to all people. It must decide how to direct its focus. If, for example, its interest is in developing the resource base of a tribal community or several tribal communities, it must direct its curricular design toward producing native professionals in the field of resource development, remembering that the major constituencies of Native American Studies and the major recipients of Native American Studies development are Indians and Indian tribal nations. If its goal is to produce professionals who will work in government, it must design its courses to do that. If, on the other hand, its goal is to produce teachers who will teach in reservation-based schools, it will develop the appropriate educational model. Many of these goals can overlap if sufficient faculty is available to teach the courses.

Finally, in order for the knowledge of Native American Studies to be empowered, it must be consensually communicated in a collection of academic courses that make up a major or a minor program of study. This means that a body of scholars, faculties, researchers, native intellectuals, and leaders must have authority and influence to develop and evaluate the curricula in the modern period of Indian life in America. To reiterate, this must be done in a departmental setting through collaborative efforts, with university and tribal input.

Instead of understanding the development of curricula in the context of other disciplines, Indian history, Indian sociology, Indian religion, or Native American literary studies course designs, for example, can best emerge from the impetus and disciplinary structures of the parameters (culture and history) in a broader context. Policy and law must provide the core courses of the discipline, language and literature must provide the reconstruction of history and humanity, and applied courses must offer the framework for responding to the intellectual needs of indigenous societies as they move toward self-sufficiency in the modern world. Each regional university, keeping in mind that it is a *regional* institution, serves its state citizens and tribal citizens toward global understanding of the world. However, many seasoned professors in the discipline have suggested that a good twenty-credit core curriculum for undergraduates in the discipline can be as follows:

> Introduction to the Discipline (4 cr.)
> Federal Indian Policy (4 cr.)
> Contemporary Indian Problems (4 cr.)
> Language Study (4 cr.)
> Law and Society (4 cr.)

The bibliography for these offerings must include the classics written by such notables as Vine Deloria Jr., Robert Berkhofer, Helen Hunt Jackson, Donald Fixico, Russell Thornton, David Wilkins, Felix Cohen, and dozens more. University law journals and publications produced through university presses must be included. So must the work of such groups as the American Association of Colleges for Teacher Education, the American Indian Educational Publishers, and the American Indian Lawyer Training Program, as well as from the reservation-based tribal colleges that often publish the contemporary work and research of native professionals in the field. Professional journals such as the *Wicazo Sa Review,* the *American Indian Quarterly,* the *American Indian Culture and Research Journal,* and *Cultural Survival Quarterly,* to name only a few, are essential to the bibliography.

In follow-up student writing activities, consider the following assignments and topics:

> Demonstrate knowledge of the extensive bibliographies.
> Be familiar with the works of major figures, researchers, and scholars.
> Trace the origins of sovereignty.
> How is sovereignty defined?
> What are sovereignty's powers?
> What have been the major obstacles to the full implementation of sovereignty?
> Discuss the rise-and-fall nature of sovereignty and say what the implications of that rise-and-fall history are.

Essential courses in undergraduate Native American Studies, as outlined above, are (1) Introduction to the Discipline, (2) Federal Indian Policy, (3) Tribal Government and Law, (4) the Study of Native Languages, and (5) Contemporary Indian Issues.

If we are to understand the two major concepts of the discipline, sovereignty and indigenousness, it is essential that we not only move judiciously from the religio-philosophical parameter of the discipline (mythology, where some suggest anthropological studies have been stuck for many decades) to the legal-historical parameter (law), but that we also emphasize the political nature of indigenous populations in the United States and in the world through policy courses. No model of Indian Studies is complete without policy and government studies, just as no model is complete without language studies. After having understood the source of the concepts for indigenous populations on this continent, the next step is to take a hard look at the diminishment of those concepts through the colonial intents, policies, and actions of the past 150 years. Some Indian scholars (and I tend to agree with them) suggest that federal Indian policy must be taught as genocidal policy. This suggestion, quite obviously, is fraught with risk and ambiguity and denial and often results in the condemnation from mainstream history scholars as too radical an interpretation of historical events, giving to Indian Studies in general a pejorative definition of political advocacy rather than scholarship. This idea, however, must be attended to if we wish to contribute to the decolonization efforts of the past decade. Two major scholars, Taiaiake Alfred (Mohawk) and Linda Tuhiwai Smith (Ngati Awa and Ngati Porou from New Zealand), are the contemporary thinkers on this subject and their works are required reading.

It is difficult for many Indian scholars to teach about contemporary tribal governments as a positive development of the twentieth century vis-à-vis the policies of disinheritance and diminishment promulgated by the U.S. Congress through its claimed "plenary power" over these governments since their inception. There is widespread animosity toward these governments in some native enclaves. Even grassroots people call them "token" governments with top-heavy executive bodies, weak and inefficient and corrupt court systems, and nonexistent legislative functions.[12]

Yet many native governmental officials, elected by their people to promote justice and democracy on their homelands (including many of my own relatives who worked on the Crow Creek reservation for decades), ask that tribal government be taught as a positive reaction to modern change. In my discussions with former councilmen and -women, as well as tribal council chairpersons, I have heard heated arguments in favor of giving these inchoate governments (only fifty years in development) a chance to thrive and become efficient forums for justice. Assignments in the works of Deloria and Wilkins are essential when the concept of tribal government and the "plenary power" of the U.S. Congress is discussed in this context; yet the lingering notion that these governments have been imposed on unwilling tribes, that they are not "traditional" systems, and that they are simply "colonizing structures" persists.

In 1831, Indian tribal nations were described in legal terms as "domestic dependent nations" in a Supreme Court decision written by Chief Justice John Marshall who is claimed by apologist historians as a defender of native rights. More insightful scholars, however, say that he must be viewed in history as a federalist and, therefore, as an adamant political foe of the states' righter president Andrew Jackson rather than a defender of Indian rights. His decisions are the very documents through which Americans have sought to dispossess tribal peoples of their autonomy. There is no question that his ambiguity toward the sovereign status of Indian tribes reflects the colonial mentality of that period and has had a lasting influence.

The Marshall decisions were written in response to the federal 1830 Removal Act written by Congress, which would dispossess the Cherokee Nation of its homelands and move all tribal nations from east of the Mississippi River to designated places in "Indian Territory," what is now Oklahoma. These decisions and acts can best be described and understood as state-federal conflict with great impact on tribal nation self-governing efforts. Thousands of Indians died of poverty and disease, their lands were taken over, and a theory of "federal trust" or "fiduciary relationship" between Indian nations and the U.S. federal government was reinforced as the "law of the land."

The treaty period would be disclaimed by Congress in another few decades, the "trust" relationship, which was said to translate into a "preserve and protect" legality, was, for all practical purposes, giving mere lip service to an ethical stance, and Americans behaved as though the idea that treaties with Indian nations were the "law of the land" was an absurd notion. The contempt that U.S. politicians and statesmen had toward native populations in the nineteenth century was documented by writer and reformer Helen Hunt Jackson as late as 1885, yet the powerful adversaries of the tribes went unchecked.

From the standpoint of Indians, the laws of this period ushered in criminal and unethical actions on the part of the powerful colonial and imperialistic impulses of the federal government. Throughout American history, the agonizing discourse concerning this history and Indian–white relations in general is spoken of as "conflict," "enforced assimilation," or "postcolonial" but seldom spoken of as "genocide." As the twentieth century closes, however, it seems obvious that genocide in the matter of Indian–white relations in America has not been just a matter of physical extermination as has been experienced by other populations in other parts of the world.

Today, genocide in the Americas is broadened to include other concepts and acts. For example, federal policy has utilized deicide, the killing of god, as native religious practices were criminalized in federal law. Ecocide is another example best described as the intentional destruction of the physical environment needed to sustain human health and life in a given geographical region occupied by indigenous populations.

In the international arena, there is a dialogue concerning the deliberate destruction by the U.S. government of the buffalo in the northern Plains, the salmon in the Northwest Territories, and the rivers throughout the land as acts of genocide. This deliberate destruction, it is indicated in some international discussions, has been used as a tactic to force submission of tribal peoples during the treaty era and since, and these acts are now debated as a function of genocide. This intentional destruction, ecocide (the killing of the earth) and deicide (the killing of god), is well-documented. In the present light of nationalistic crimes across the globe, this destruction has become a persuasive feature in the classical definition of historical genocide, and it is becoming apparent to all the world that the most powerful democracy on earth, the United States, is not exempt from this historical activity.[13]

The systematic "killing of a people" was said in the old days to exist legally in three contexts: religious, racial, and ethnic. Whatever the label, new definitions have emerged as a direct consequence of our witnessing modern national and human events in Europe, Africa, and Asia in the twentieth century. It should be obvious that all forms of genocide are interrelated, pervasive, and criminal and frequently legitimized in policy, law, and practice in every society known.

Genocide, the world now admits as it views its own history and present condition, is always premeditated, forethought, purposeful, and even designed. Today's scholars say that genocide does not, contrary to public notions, "just happen" as fateful events known only to uncaring gods. Instead, genocidal motives and actions are obvious and fathomable in every instance studied by the world's scholars.

Religious genocide is mistakenly thought to be a feature only of ancient history as exemplified by, for example, genocide in the Middle Ages, when the Crusades and the Spanish Inquisition and other similar atrocities went relentlessly on, even if and when the killing of an entire people ran counter to the specific theology held by the society in general. In spite of theology that may have argued against the mass "killing of others," genocide persisted in religious praxis with religious zeal more than reason or theology supplying the fuel, and it was not just an "ancient" phenomenon as students of recent history in Africa and Europe, the Middle East, and elsewhere around the globe can attest. Laws passed in the U.S. Congress to make illegal the practice of native religions were persistent for most of the eighteenth and nineteenth centuries, causing massive disruption in entire tribes. Even into the twentieth century, certain native religious practices were outlawed, and controversies continue into the present time.

Racial and ethnic genocide, a feature of the more modern histories exemplified by Nazi Germany's killing of the Jews in Europe in the twentieth-century Jewish Holocaust, is still thought of by the average person to be a function of ancient history and old irrational hatreds against "others" and kept alive through a religious intolerance in the mainstream coupled with xenophobic public policy and military zeal. There seems to be little historical sense of the present-day ethnocide in the former Yugoslavia except that it is a function of the persistent and pervasive historical cleavages between the sections that have made up the country for multiple generations. Racial and ethnic genocide is premeditated there and in every other instance known to history. In spite of these new global experiences, the United States continues to hold itself exempt from such crimes toward its own indigenous populations.

The extermination of an entire people, which can occur at any juncture in the relationship between various segments of a national society, are dependent upon certain elements and specific developments. The elements usually have to do with law and the developments usually have to do with economics. Why should historians exempt the United States from such historical imperatives in the face of massive historical evidence? Why should historians exempt the colonizing nations of America (or England, or Spain, or France) from this all-too-human potential? They should not, of course, but they do. A major reason for such exemption is that powerful nations still in the thrall of their own success at colonizing weaker states are rarely challenged and remain in charge of any dialogue concerning the issues that such history poses, should it somehow mysteriously emerge from silenced enclaves.

From the beginning of the settlement of this continent, the systematic killing of the indigenous peoples was a fact of life. It has been relentless and premeditated. Dr. Jack Forbes, a native scholar at the University of California in Davis has suggested that by 1650, about 95 percent of the population of Latin America was wiped out, and by the middle of the 1800s, there were 200,000 Indians left in continental America. Two native demographers, Dr. Forbes and his colleague Dr. Russell Thornton, suggest that 80 million indigenous people were killed through colonization in fewer than a hundred years.

Genocide is not now nor has it ever been just a matter of the physical extermination of a people through mass killings, enslavement, torture, enforced segregation, or colonial apartheid. It is also the denial of basic human rights that impedes the development of a nationalist legal, social, and intellectual system that, in turn, makes it impossible for a domestic people or domestic nation to express itself collectively and historically in terms of continued self-determination and sovereignty.

In spite of the reasonableness of any critique of history, nations that have developed genocidal practices toward others within their own nation or society, or even outside of their province, protest their innocence by bringing up the matter of "intent." The United States as well as countless other colonizers have excused themselves and justified their actions by saying that they never intended to destroy the natives. This is a way to excuse and rationalize a history so ugly it cannot be internally acknowledged, yet recent studies offer ample documentation that native peoples from the Missouri River to the Amazon are being destroyed through scandalous public policies. Indeed, African scholar Nelson Mandela, himself and his nation the recipients of decades of a bloody genocide, expressed his belief that no one could claim innocence of this kind of history and in 1995 he said: "The decimation of the native peoples in the Americas is like a haunting question which floats in the wind: why did we allow this to happen?" The question must haunt the entire world, and someone must be held accountable.[14]

6

THE STRUGGLE FOR
CULTURAL HERITAGE

THE PERENNIAL PROBLEM OF HISTORIOGRAPHY
IN INDIAN STUDIES

Prior to the development of present disciplinary models of American Indian
Studies, Western-based disciplines played varied roles in the study of the
indigenous populations of North and South America. For the most part,
the discipline of history utilized moral evaluations as descriptions of Indians and the basic notion of Indians as the antithesis to non-Indians arose
because native mythologies were not utilized as history. They were thought
to be ahistorical, largely imaginative, and therefore unreliable. The historical
descriptors of Indians as moral and historical outsiders to American ideals
and purpose have persisted even in the related scholarly disciplines of anthropology and sociology and literature until very recent times.

THE ART OF PEDAGOGY: AN ESSENTIAL TEXT

How to handle history is a major dilemma for Indian Studies practitioners because of the entrenchment of these descriptors and the flawed ideas they have
engendered. Many historians (Riding In, Deloria, Deboe, Wilkins, Forbes,
Fixico, Berkhofer, Washburn) during the past few decades have produced
texts that are useful for studying the various roles of historical and academic
inquiry. They cannot be ignored in the early development of course work in
Indian Studies. Although it is usually expected that texts written by American Indian scholars, especially in history, are to be preferred because of the
endogenous nature of them, they are often tribally specific and, therefore,
useful for their specificity rather than for an examination of the overreach-

ing Euro-American critical analysis necessary in an undergraduate course. A general text that has become a classic in the discipline is *The White Man's Indian* by Dr. Robert F. Berkhofer, a longtime historian from Ann Arbor, Michigan, who has underscored the basic racism that is at the heart of Indian–white relations in America. This text has become a classic in the discipline because it provides historical theory concerning the 500-year colonial relationship between Indians and non-Indians in America, a relationship that can be analyzed as either detrimental or useful to the present condition of native populations and enclaves. It can be used as a model when seeking out alternative texts, but whatever tactic one wants to take, it is imperative to find a history text that analyzes the past 500 years of colonialism in the United States.[1]

A theoretical model of cultural conflict like Berkhofer's, surveying five centuries of epistemology since 1680, is an essential work for introductory history lessons in Indian Studies. In Berkhofer's theory, there are four areas of intellectual influence, contributed over many, many years. These areas of influence give rise to flawed ideas about indigenous peoples on this continent, influencing law and pedagogy and resulting in a perennial cause-and-effect model for cultural conflict in America.

Broad areas of influence in Berkhofer's theory are as follows and will be described later more fully: pan-Indianism (the notion that all of the natives of the continent were alike and they could, therefore, be treated similarly); cultural deprivation (the notion that their cultures were deficient and inferior because they were isolated from European ideas); theories of progress (the idea that all cultures of the dark races are "primitive" but through time they can become sophisticated and civilized through European influence); and, finally, something that Berkhofer suggests is the Fusion of Ideologies, the merging of religious, political, racial, and other disciplinary ideas to form a manageable consensus for colonization. Indian Studies utilizes these historical structures in early undergraduate study to introduce a problem-identifying structure, a cause-and-effect structure that can illuminate specific problems.

It is essential that such a cause-and-effect model be introduced to students early on because they must be given the idea that there are solutions to the historical failures that are so much a part of Indian history. Students understand very early that much of the negativity of Indian history has resulted in an obviously unsatisfactory relationship between whites and Indians in America that persists in present-day educational systems, court systems, and society in general.

When students read about the failure and tragedy of boarding schools, the "removal" scenarios, the making and breaking of treaties, the war and reservation period, and the loss of lands and rights and resources by natives—a history experienced by generation after generation resulting in poverty and social chaos—they feel isolated and without hope. In the face of such history, appropriate educational models like the models being developed in Indian Studies can diminish that reaction and assist new learners in the knowledge that it is possible to forge appropriate solutions to the results of historical and political stages of indigenous and colonial interaction.

The first area of intellectual influence according to Berkhofer's historical theory can be labeled the "problem of origin or theology" (broadly suggesting the description of pan-Indianism; i.e., that all Indians are alike) and explained as follows: all of the peoples of the world were created by God, and in the Americas the people are all called Indians. Theories of theology pose the question of where the native populations of the Americas (unknown and undiscovered for centuries after the Bible was written) fit in if all of God's creatures were created at one time and in one place called the Garden of Eden, a Christian concept. This major influence in European and American study tries to explain why native populations are so different from other known populations and, more essentially, why they are all Indians instead of tribally specific populations and nations; it also asks what their origins are as a people or a race. Aren't we all descendants of Adam and Eve? The answers to that are found in indigenous mythologies, languages, and religions.

Berkhofer suggests that the only way early American and European theorists had to try to fit the indigenous populations of the Americas into this long-standing Christian scheme of a common origin was to see the Indian, as he has been called, as some fallen creature or race, some corrupt copy of a lost world that might have risen out of the fall of the Tower of Babel and the confusion of language.

In the Genesis account of origin, says Berkhofer, it has been assumed that God made all people and made them all equal, all brothers, but the account, unfortunately, does not give any information concerning why the indigenous population in the Americas (unknown at the time of Christ) was so different from other populations then known and accounted for. Why did the Indian migrate across the land bridge, to the exclusion of others, and occupy this continent by himself for so many thousands of years, if one is to believe the Bering Strait theory of origin? Although there is no full answer to these queries, it seemed self-evident to those early scholars asking the questions posed by the presence of native occupants of this continent that his degeneration, his fallen race, unredeemed by Christianity, was simply a foregone conclusion. Such a history as Berkhofer's makes a reasonable case for questioning known theories by critically examining the continuity of historical scholarship.

The second area of intellectual influence according to Berkhofer's theory is the "problem of environmentalism"; that is, the theory that the physical environment accounts for racial and cultural diversity. This has led to the conclusion that Indians must be seen as a distinct race of people in terms of their deficiencies and behaviors and lifestyles and what can be termed "cultural deprivation." This leads to further generalizing as to origin, history, and culture, and, although there is much documentation of how Indians all across the continent are notably different from Europeans, there has been little discussion of how they are different from each other. Thus, the term "Indian," the idea that all natives are alike, persists, and the notion that their cultures are "deprived" and that these cultures emerged from specific constriction of environment pervades all scholarship.

Two pedagogical problems arise from these lines of thought. First, the cultural and political development of native peoples is often neglected in course development and, more devastating and dangerous, it is problematic to think that the Indian race (or native nationality) is a culturally deprived form of humanity. Early racial theories, by excluding cultural and political explanations, often had this result.

Common origins were thought to be a fact in theological realms, but, some posited that, because of environment, people changed, lived in uncivilized worlds of race dominance, and were classified as white or black or red or brown or yellow. The Indian, these ideas suggest, is savage because he lived in what was perceived as a savage environment. The idea that all species were immutable troubled scholars for many generations.

Third, according to Berkhofer's examination of history, the "theory of progress" prevailed in academic thought as the result of the fusion of several ideological systems as explanations concerning the indigenous populations of America. This theory of "progress"—that with time all races and cultures will fuse—brought about the mixing of ideology with ethnography, meaning that if all Indians are not at the present moment enlightened, and racial theories could form classifications, the notion of inferior/superior paradigms seemed useful.

Many ideologies, scientific and religious, have developed theories of "progression" as concerns peoples throughout the world, so it is essential that part 1 and part 2 of *The White Man's Indian* or any other such cumulative history text be assigned to students as required reading. In the Berkhofer cause-and-effect model of problem identification, these ideas are gathered and can be labeled the "Fusion of Ideologies," the idea that Indians can be described as deficient and without god, the third cause for perennial cultural conflict.

Europeans, who couldn't help but be self-congratulatory concerning their own outstanding accomplishments in science and art and discovery and conquest and commercial and agrarian success, began to point to the "failures" of other cultures and other peoples, particularly the indigenous peoples of the Americas, as evidence of a natural progression toward enlightenment and civilization. The "primitive" peoples of the North American continent, it was believed, could represent the very early condition of present civilized peoples and they, therefore, could advance as well if given appropriate information and guidance. This set in motion laws and educational systems to assist in the advancement of these inferior and savage peoples.

The failure to see the populations in the Americas as being organized as separate nations of people with separate histories and separate cultural worldviews can be labeled "Pan-Indianism" for the purpose of creating an Indian problem-identifying model for Indian Studies. Furthermore, the notion of the Indian's culture as different, "savage," and un-Christian—that is, "inferior, deprived of goodness and usefulness"—can be given the label "Cultural Deprivation" in the cause-and-effect Indian Studies problem-identifying model. Finally, the mixture of ideological thinking as it arose in Europe and early America to deal with the indigenous populations of the continent can be called the "Fusion of Ideologies," a body of scholarship accumulated over the centuries to pose the questions of diversity and difference. In a nutshell, Pan-Indianism is thinking that all Indians are alike. Cultural Deprivation is thinking that all Indian cultures are lacking the basic necessities of civilization. The Fusion of Ideologies is the consensus of theoretical ideas shared by the social scientists that Indians are the other, un-Christian and godless. These three categories can be examined in a cause-and-effect model that explains the white man's insistence on colonization of Indian nations and the cause for perennial Indian–white conflict that continues even today. Although this may seem simplistic in its concept of history to those who have studied the vast historiographies of the globe, this strategy is useful to introduce the controversies of the native experience to beginning students. For these reasons, the Berkhofer text is most useful in undergraduate studies.

The appropriation of this vast history rendered by a text such as the one Berkhofer has written helps students find answers to and formulate questions concerning what happens in society and law and politics when such inadequate information is perpetuated. The questions they bring to the discussion translates into a problem-identifying model useful to teaching history in Indian Studies; in the following group-work discussion and writing called "consensual problem solving" they may better understand the role of history: using Berkhofer's theoretical model (figure 6.1), the causes for perennial conflict between Indians and whites in America may be articulated and problems may be identified.

Identification of the problem is the first step to seeking solutions. How one defines the problem leads to how one solves it. It maybe helpful for early learners to categorize the problems as (1) individual, (2) societal, (3) institutional, (4) systems, and (5) other. Whether the Berkhofer theoretical model is used or whether the works of other historians are used, it is essential in Indian Studies to introduce a problem-solving/problem-identifying model that illustrates the five centuries of colonial history and ideology and the major historical causes of conflict.

This model is essential in teaching beginning students in the discipline in order to deconstruct colonial history concerning indigenous peoples and give them some tools for understanding that history can be in error and solutions can be found. It is only from a thorough understanding of this colonial history, its effects, and the introduction of terminology and vocabulary that insightful historiographies can be created and emended. This in no way negates the arguments of those who believe that the colonization of American

Figure 6.1

Essential Cause	Problem	Effects
1. Pan-Indianism (all Indians are alike)	?	(unjust laws)
Related causes: racism, suppression, stereotype, assimilation, oppression		
2. Cultural Deprivation (Indian cultures are thought to be deficient)	?	(poverty)
Related causes: paternalism, colonialism, imperialism		
3. Fusion of Ideologies (European/Christian bodies of definition and ideas)	?	(loss of land)
Related causes: primitivism, heathenism, savagism		

Indians has been a good and worthy endeavor of powerful nations in their relationships with weaker ones. It merely suggests an alternative view of colonization as it has been practiced on this continent.

This problem-solving mechanism is useful in pinpointing problems in the perennial Indian–white conflict. Identifying the problem is essential in finding solutions and it is often difficult for students to historicize the problem area because of the glaring omissions in studying American history at the high school and elementary level. In addition, the failure to teach analytical skills in history is a notorious omission because, generally, facts of history are taught without context. I have found that many beginning students will say that racism is a problem, yet as it is introduced in the Berkhofer model, it is a cause that derives from thinking that all Indians are alike. This helps students to discuss the effects of racism in a society in a more relevant way, the results of which are conflict, exclusion, and poverty. Racism is a cause but only if the idea that *all Indians are alike as a race of people is accepted as historical.* This idea is inappropriate because the native populations are made up even today of more than 500 tribal nations with as many different histories, languages, and political statuses. Much time is spent in academia on finding victims and accusers and trying to do away with racism in American society when, in fact, the tribal nation historical and cultural differences are rarely taken into account. The Yakima Nation in Washington State, for example, is far different from the Hopi Nation in Arizona and always has been since time immemorial. Thus, problems are different; solutions are, as well.

If racism is seen as a cause (related to one of the essential causes of history) rather than a problem, one can identify poverty, for example, as a major effect of racism that needs to be taken on in a realistic, problem-solving mode. Something can be done concerning poverty. Actual solution mechanisms can be achieved in poor communities. The problem, then, can be categorized as follows: (1) institutional, (2) individual, (3) societal, or (4) other. Students can understand more fully the immediate solutions. If poverty is eliminated and people are able to take care of their families and acquire decent housing and education, perhaps other issues, such as the irrational hatred of other human beings different from yourself, can find solutions as well. Perhaps other effects such as unjust laws, hatred and conflict, avoidance and isolation, land loss, and diminished sovereignty, just to name a few, can be mediated.

In addition to getting at specific problems, this mechanism assists students in understanding that a society can be effective in dealing with its perennial Indian–white conflicts. Students do not need to just throw up their hands and say it is futile; that there is nothing to be done about racism.

This model proposed here may be implemented with specific case studies modeled from real experiences at the tribal level. Professors are obliged to deliver specific lectures giving facts of history and interpretations of those facts. Students must take lecture notes; engage in classroom discussion; spend time, in class or out, in consensual or group problem-solving episodes; and prepare writing assignments. One-hour in-class writing assignments utilizing texts, readings, and class notes are effective analytical exercises.

Vocabulary study in this history is essential, and much research and writing can be done by both students and professor as this introduction goes forward because the vocabularies of Indian histories are heavily influenced by colonial thought. As just one example of inappropriate colonial vocabulary, "conquest," a word meaning "defeated in war," has been used throughout the historical record to rationalize colonization and describe the native experience. The term "contact," meaning "the coming together" or "the touching of one to another," is another example of bias and misinformation. Neither term is accurate because many tribes won more wars than they ever lost to the invader, and others did not go to war at all against the invaders of their territories and thus were never "conquered in war."

The invasion of lands owned by other nations in any other historical scenario is not called "the touching" or "the coming together" or "contact." It is called what it is, the "invasion" of territory belonging to another. Yet the term "invasion" is rarely used to discuss the "settling of America." The burden of language is to communicate and conceptualize the self, one's entire world, and the tribal view, and it is imperative in the contemporary struggle for decolonization that the language of white superiority be defeated.

What to do about history has been a major concern and reform effort in Indian Studies curricular development for several decades. The tribal models and intratribal models of Indian Studies, based on the functions of its defensive, regulatory, and transformative parameters, have produced revised pedagogical strategies, deconstructive research, and publications by native scholars.

A model of curricular development is a work in progress directed toward a systematic set of rules and methods regulating a branch of knowledge or teaching called "Indian Studies," the discipline of teaching and learning the indigenous knowledge of this continent.

After the introductory course, in which 500 years of colonial history is examined, further courses in history will be charted. There are many approaches to the development of history courses in the discipline. One of the first approaches concerns the development of broad-based courses such as Treaties and Accords of Native Nations, a course that is rarely taught in traditional history courses. Second, a tribally specific course such as The Sioux Nation and the Red Cloud Legacy, as an example, deals with specific historical figures and eras and needs to be taken by history majors. Historical theory courses (for example, the theory of sovereignty as designed in the 1830 Removal Act) are generally referred to as policy courses rather than history. Law courses are an integral part of history and need to be incorporated in any course of study called "history." The dilemma here is that policy rises out of law, but just as often affects law; thus, it is most effective to teach this material in two separate course designs. Dakota Sioux scholar Dr. Angela Cavender Wilson, Kanien ëkehaka scholar Taiaiake Alfred, Cree historian Winona Wheeler, and many others have called for the teaching of the oral traditions as history in traditional history departments as well as Indian Studies, saying that answers to perennial problems in Indian–white relations will never be understood unless a sustained social and political discourse rising out of traditional wisdom is applied.[2]

At issue here is whether Indian Studies at the undergraduate level can come to a consensus about how to teach tribal knowledge with the intention of liberating First Nations from broad colonial oppression. Mature postcolonial education for American Indians can transform powerlessness into authority. The overall goals of teaching, researching, and writing in the discipline of Indian Studies are to formally introduce students to an emerging discipline, to promote public awareness and understanding of Indian Studies as a fundamental factor in solving perennial problems in Indian affairs and public policy in the United States, to train professionals in the field, and to transcend the present condition of colonization through research and writing. At the risk of sounding redundant, it is essential that the major functions of the parameters, defensive, regulatory, and transformative, be the focus.

If we look at Indian Studies as a discipline and if we think of Indian Studies as a strategy in defensive techniques toward tribally specific social, political, and religious systems, then the preservation, protection, and development of those systems is crucial to grasping the power of the future. In 1936, French scholar André Malraux wrote that cultural heritage is created by a civilization out of everything in the past that helps it to surpass itself. He was a participant in an organization called the League of Writers for the Defense of Culture. I'm not sure that such an organization still exists today, and if it doesn't, it is a loss to the modern world.[3]

What that idea means to Indian Studies scholars is that teaching, researching, and writing are the means by which transcendence occurs for natives who are in conflict with colonizers concerning the present condition. The past and cultural heritage are the means by which decolonization and independence occur—as long as the research on a people is done by the people themselves rather than by the colonizers. This endogenous methodology is often referred to pejoratively as essentialism and it is not looked upon in a kindly way in academe, generally speaking. It is, however, a principle embedded in the earliest discussions of the discipline as well as in the works of such scholars as Malraux.

If one looks at the research and writing that has been done to, for, and about indigenous peoples around the world, one recognizes the necessity of self-representation. Much of the research (up until the past few decades when natives themselves began their anthropological careers), has been scandalous, if not criminal.

As a recent explanation of scandal, the book *Darkness in El Dorado* has come to the attention of scholars who are critical of anthropological studies and history.[4] It is a riveting account of the Yanomami Indians and their Amazon homelands in modern times. It exposes the work of non-Yanomami scholars who exploit and corrupt entire peoples and their homelands. It describes the work of those anthropologists as the ugliest affair in the entire history of anthropology, and, as anyone in Indian Country knows, anthropologists have been in charge of this scholarship for generations. It is worth noting that the American Anthropological Association meeting at the time of this revelation from the Tierney research did not take up the scandal and, astonishingly, the story of how scientists and journalists devastated the Amazon has now fallen into almost complete silence. The most important critique is Ron Robin's *Scandals and Scoundrels.* Unfortunately for the Indians, concludes Robin, the whole controversy turns out to be analyzed as just a problem between "warring" scholars, thus addressing "the fate of indigenous persons only in passing."[5]

Tierney calls the book and its revelations "darkness in El Dorado" as a historical reference to how Spanish and English explorers 500 years ago sought cities of gold and destroyed the indigenous world. His thesis is that many present-day anthropologists, scientists, professors, and writers are doing the same thing. As those early prospectors destroyed people and places with their own ignorance and brutality, he says, so are present-day college professors and sociologists (and countless others) continuing a sorrowful colonial history of murder and exploitation. Tierney names names—the famous anthropologist Napoleon Chagnon, whose work is read in every introductory course, and a complicit geneticist, James Neal, among them. The most prominent of Chagnon's work is *Yanomamö, the Fierce People,* and it echoes what Tierney calls a "macho theory" of "primitive peoples." Tierney documents fraudulent methodologies, saying that the native internecine warfare discussed by Chagnon was staged.[6]

The book is an exposé much like *Skull Wars,* a book that tells what went on in the invention of the discipline of scientific archaeology, a travesty of manipulation and exploitation of native peoples.[7] Other works come to mind, many of them initiated by the critical scholarly work done by Professor Vine Deloria Jr., who has called upon scholars of every stripe to keep an open mind and to challenge long-held assumptions about native populations in America. In *Red Earth, White Lies,* Deloria tells us that he "eliminates the Bering Strait theory of origin as a possible explanation" of the origins of native peoples of the Americas, and calls on the next generation of scholars to do away with useless empirical falsehoods that have been masquerading for too long as science.[8] Such challenges function to transcend and transform and remind us that native populations must deal with growth and change and the future in appropriate ways. Too often the stress-and-strain theories of the colonial past have functioned to entrap native scholarship in confines that deal only with the past and never the future.

Speaking of what I call the "stress-and-strain" theories and narratives, the old grief stories, the historical grief experiences engendered by 200 years of oppression, have occupied entirely too much space and time in Indian Studies for two reasons: first, that story has been told, to the exclusion of finding solutions to specific historical and cultural issues; second, those grief stories do not belong to the most recent generations. They are not of the present generation. Instead, they belong to the times of our parents and grandparents. When will we second and third generations tire of the old boarding-school stories and all of the history that narrates the ways that our parents as individuals were disenfranchised in their time? For our own political and social health, our scholarship must move on and we must direct our research and storytelling toward answering the questions posed through postcolonial solution mechanisms.

As colonized populations, it is necessary to absorb ourselves deeply in the contemporary world. We went to boarding schools and still do, but we were not taken by the police from our homes and kept in isolation from our families for years. None of us went there without some understanding of the English language. Few of us have been the captured children of the past boarding-school era in the same way as previous generations. It was our parents and grandparents who suffered that particular practice in genocide.

There is some discussion in the Indian world that suggests we have more crucial work to do than to bemoan cruelty in past educational practices. In many instances, tribes are now in charge of their own educational systems. Perhaps we may work more productively to understand the nature of federal Indian law that underlies our present colonial condition, which takes many different forms and may impact our educational systems in different ways. This effort can be directed toward helping U.S. legal systems repudiate the assumed "plenary power" of the U.S. Congress that holds influence over every facet of our lives, not just education.

In addition, it might be a good idea to limit our arguments with antagonists such as anthropologist-turned-historian Shepard Krech III of Brown University because these arguments are too time-consuming. I call these arguments "stamping out brush fires," and admit that such activity is often useful and important but it should be ancillary to the work in other fields. Krech, author of *The Ecological Indian,*[9] said that Indians destroyed their own habitat and were responsible for Pleistocene extinctions. He was set upon by native scholars rather quickly, who indicated that he must be sent back to Providence, Rhode Island, to illustrate the fact that antagonists are still out there but becoming more irrelevant every day. They suggested that Indian scholarship must get on with important matters like developing efficient tribal governments and economic systems, defending the land in court cases, and providing appropriate educational systems for our children. Krech's mainstream reviewers seem to buy his suggestion that concepts like ecology, waste, preservation, and even the natural world are entirely anachronistic when applied to Indians, but that is taken by many native thinkers to be simply a ludicrous and indefensible stance by which a scholar defends his turf. It cannot be taken as serious scholarship, they say.

I hate to suggest that we ignore these antagonists, because Professor Vine Deloria has taught us how to have a little fun while demolishing their premises. More important, Deloria makes the legitimate point that Krech's book, like so many others, is based on inadequate research, resulting in scholarship that looks like a hatchet job, further eroding the already eroded images of Indians. Deloria's fear is that if people buy the academic lies that are told about indigenous peoples, the tribal nations will not survive this so-called viewpoint of modern scholarship as a group of nations unique to the continent. Deloria is the only scholar on record in Indian Studies and political science who says that much of what is going on as scholarship is a "smear" that will make it much more difficult for tribal groups to thrive. Critics, even native critics, are usually much more benign than Deloria in their assessments of inadequate scholarship and have refrained from the use of the term "smear," but Deloria has proven over the years to be a fearless and adamant foe of dishonest scholarship.

What this might mean in postcolonial terms is that native scholarship could stop being overly curious and polite about degrading Eurocentric Western philosophies that simply distract and waste time. What failing to do this might mean in postcolonial terms is that after Deloria's generation, we could have a generation of Indians who don't know who they are and, therefore, cannot defend themselves and their nations. Perhaps they will be genetic Indians, Deloria intimates, who resemble an ethnic group rather than a tribe or a tribal nation of people. They would have become, then, the colonized "laureates" they have feared.

We all should be worried about things in this modern world of research and writing, and we must try to answer the strange charges put forth by some scholars: that Indians were wasteful, not environmentalists, and that Indians were never sovereign—in one case, five rabid justices voted against the Sioux Nation in the 1970s concerning sovereignty; in another, Justice Clarence Thomas, in a Cheyenne River water case, wrote against sovereign rights. Nothing has changed, except, as some have feared, legal theory has gotten more outlandish and fewer of us zero in on these real issues.

The U.S. Supreme Court has never liked the principle of tribal sovereignty and has always wished that Congress, with its claimed "plenary" power, would do something about it. Anti-Indian, reductive books like *Killing the White Man's Indian* by Fergus M. Bordewich become extremely popular as they urge a change in the Constitution telling Indian tribes once and for all that they are not nations. Even Indians have acclaimed this book as a good and useful one, but they are quite misled by the fast-paced and journalistic tone of the work. In the final pages of his book, Bordewich's scare tactic says: "Real sovereignty would carry grave risks and might lead to the liquidation of the tribes themselves." He says that tribes would have to take responsibility for their own failures. He wants to define Indian tribes as "self-governing entities subject in every respect to the laws of the United States." What's new about that?[10]

If not outright anti-Indian, some issues posed as political rantings of writers like Bordewich, who is neither scholar nor historian but, rather, a former international correspondent for *Reader's Digest* and a journalist, sometimes get center stage in Indian affairs, indicating that effective scholarship in the discipline is meager. Because that is so, all sorts of ideas that are simply wrong or irrelevant arise in the discipline.

An example of irrelevance and how far off these questions can get is as follows: at recent meetings of the Native American professoriat, a not entirely tongue-in-cheek question was posed: Should our native students read Wittgenstein? This is a legitimate academic question, one supposes, but the practical, yet casual, answer must be: How much time do we have? In my view, though, this is not just a rhetorical question and probably deserves to be taken seriously. It does focus our attention on the issue of what we must teach in our newly emerging discipline and how much time we can devote to purely philosophical questions or questions posed by foolish historians. It is probably not a question for undergraduate work.

One supposes this issue concerning Wittgenstein is worth bringing up if only for graduate school practice in learning the rhetorical modes of argument available in European/English language study. Ludwig Wittgenstein was a Viennese philosopher born in 1889, who taught at Cambridge, England, was a member of the Moral Society, and was deeply preoccupied with what we now call "solipsism," the theory that one can have secure knowledge only about oneself. Critics have used the term to delve into what must be done concerning what they call "excessive ego." This important scholar developed a Wittgensteinian arm of philosophy at Cambridge, gave up his inherited wealth, and ended up saying things like, "I know that queer things happen in this world. Its one of the few things I've really learned in my life." This observation seems singularly unprofound, and it is unfair to suggest such flippancy. To be more serious about the influence of such philosophers of that age is to know that they often engaged in competition; Wittgenstein's competition with another Viennese philosopher, Karl Popper, became legendary because they disagreed fundamentally on the function of philosophy. Because they engaged their work in the seedbed for Nazism and fought against that abomination all their lives, their contributions cannot be overlooked.[11]

What philosophy can achieve is undoubtedly a proper inquiry. It is the view of many, however, that Wittgensteinian theory may have been more appropriately studied in the 1940s in Europe than in the 2000s in America. Had Indians been in Europe during that period they probably would have been thinking about the political writings of Camus and Sartre rather than Jewish conversion and identity issues because the attempted conversion of Indians in America at the same moment was not about morality, not about philosophy; it was nothing if not political and economic. The issues facing twenty-first-century Indian historians and thinkers in the United States seem always to have been more political than philosophical in intent.

Indian Studies has come a long way in the creation of a new scholarly field that is, at the heart of it, a mechanism to protect, preserve, and develop tribal systems. Even though it is essential that we move on from a traumatic history, we must be discriminating about how we do that in our work. Many native scholars in Indian Studies have been at the forefront of repatriation studies in the West. This is an example of how scholarship has worked to stand at the side of our tribal nations. The present repatriation studies exemplifying the broadening of the curriculum require knowledge of history and politics and, yes, philosophy too, in a limited way. How native scholarship responds to contemporary issues is at the heart of repatriation work.

Most of this work has to do with identifiable ancestral connections, but there are some notions in native mythologies and philosophies that suggest very broad ideas of ancestral connections. In the Sioux language, for example, the stars are considered *Ikce/wicakpi,* or the first Dakotahs, important relatives of present-day Indians, and *Pte/Tatanka* (the buffalo people) are the first ancestors. These are profound ideas about origin, not fantasies, and they are ordinarily ignored by the nonnative scholarship that characterizes almost any of the established disciplines. I was astonished when the bones of a Tyrannosaurus rex found on tribal lands in South Dakota (the Cheyenne River Sioux Reservation) several years ago were thought to be outside the purview of repatriation studies. Scholars and politicians alike assumed that the repatriation laws written in the past couple of decades were and are unconnected to theories of origin such as those described above.

The reason I concerned myself at all is because I had been told about these creatures by storytellers of my tribe, and how they were ancestral figures. The Dakota/Lakota/Nakota people of the region have recognized the existence of these creatures for thousands of years, have names for them, and claim them not as precursors to the Sioux, but precursors in a universe not unknown nor unacknowledged by the Sioux; yet no one in the dialogue that followed this twentieth-century discovery mentioned this tribal knowledge, nor did anyone bring this scholarship into the discourse.

People dug up the creature, fought over it until it went to the private collectors, then to the feds, and then it went to a museum. The unwitting Indian rancher on whose land it was found was paid a pittance by the bone collectors who knew it was worth a fortune, and then it went to the highest bidder—$836,000 at auction. As this text goes to press, it resides at Chicago's Field Museum, after a furious fight in the courts.

Not a single person in the entire public dialogue said it belonged to the Sioux Nation, the Dakotapi, the people who occupied the land for thousands of years, the natives who refer to the *T. rex* in *ohunkaka* terms in their mythology and tribal emergence narratives. Not a single person brought up the notion that indigenous theory might have contributed to the knowledge surrounding such a find. Not a single voice said that the Sioux have stories as old as the earth about its origin, and that the natives have knowledge of the physical world. Not only is it true that such knowledge is ignored by scientists and colonial scholars, but it is also true that there are no mechanisms to protect these systems of knowledge.

An inadequate treatment, *Tyrannosaurus Sue*,[12] was written by Steve Fiffer, a lawyer, journalist, and author who has coedited three anthologies of original essays on home, family, and body and coauthored two books with civil rights attorney Morris Dees, *A Season for Justice* and *Hate on Trial*. *Tyrannosaurus Sue* chronicles the vicious fight over the bones of this prehistoric monster found on an Indian reservation in South Dakota, and seems to take the side of the bone digger managers of an archaeological institute in Hill City, South Dakota, as original claimants. This may be another example of how civil rights and criminal law co-opts treaty rights for indigenous peoples.

It is probably up to trial lawyers, college professors, and tribal politicians to understand the importance of developing and using appropriate research models for defensive action. Discovering ways to preserve and protect native knowledge bases through policy centers and think tanks is a critical part of decolonization, every bit as effective as coming to know the past through simple history courses.

The issue of intellectual property, which is at the heart of such controversies, is perhaps the most crucial issue facing native populations in this century, yet few mechanisms are in place or even on the drawing board as defensive and regulatory and transformative mechanisms.

A DEGRADED CONTEXT OF LAW: RECENT DISPUTES

If history is culpable in defining the native experience pejoratively, law itself seems to be even more suspect. Indigenous law in America has never followed a sustained, thoughtful body of rules of scholarship. The rise-and-fall nature of sovereignty and the constant attack by state powers on home rule as well as state and federal takeovers of treaty lands in the West is evidence of that reality. Rather than sustained, thoughtful rules of scholarship, Indian law has generally emerged piecemeal and haphazardly from an ever-changing proliferation of ideas that make up a legal doctrine unable to constrain itself from politically loyal partisanships and ideological extremes. It seems to me that most of the degradation of law in Indian Country to come out of the courts in my lifetime has been in response to alcohol-related incidents and this is, perhaps, no accident because the preoccupation with Indian alcohol use has been a major theme in historical narratives concerning Indian–white contact.

There are many examples of the degradation of Indian law, but the disastrous anti-Indian cases in Washington State, *Oliphant v. Schlie* and *Oliphant v. Suquamish Indian Tribe* in 1974 and 1978, respectively, are prime examples of it. They reflect an obsession that had been husbanded through the courts by Slade Gorton, who had previously brought a number of suits concerning jurisdiction against Washington State tribes throughout his early career and finally hit pay dirt when he decided to get tough with Indians who thought they were sovereign peoples. He decided to defend Mark Oliphant, a white man from Seattle who had been arrested by the tribal police on the Suquamish Indian Reservation, and he made that decision deliberately in order to overturn *Oliphant v. Schlie*, which earlier had said that tribes could prosecute non-Indians in tribal court. He was looking for the right case to overturn that decision and he found it.[13]

Mark Oliphant had appealed his conviction of Indian offense to the Ninth Circuit Court of Appeals, and Gorton thought this was the perfect case to demonstrate once and for all that the U.S. Congress had never bestowed upon the tribes that power, that they never, therefore, possessed that power of law and order on their own lands, and that they had *never* been sovereign entities. It was Gorton's belief that this was the perfect case to defend the doctrine of the claimed "plenary power" of the U.S. Congress. His thinking was in direct conflict with history because in the 1787 Northwest Ordinance and in the entire treaty-making era, any rights that tribes did not specifically cede in their treaty agreements were retained by them. This principle of Indian law has always rankled white lawyers and politicians like Gorton, and rarely has it been loved and upheld by the U.S. court systems.

In the Oliphant matter, Gorton judged the ahistorical courts and government lawyers correctly and he won the case, overturning the Indian sovereign rights to Indian law and order on Indian homelands. Since then, the matter of jurisdiction on Indian lands all over the country, not just in Suquamish Country, has been a nightmarish battle that has devastated law and order as a coherent system on Indian reservations.

It is probably appropriate to say at this point that "plenary power" as a doctrine in U.S. law, used often to side with the federal government's position on literally any case at hand, has nothing to do with the U.S. Constitution. There is nothing in the U.S. Constitution that gives Congress unlimited power or absolute power over Indian nations, yet it is one of the Alice-in-Wonderland traits of U.S. law that has produced a number of contemporary decisions that describes and defends this problematic (and unconstitutional) doctrine in all its aggressive glory. This claimed power is the power that Slade Gorton wanted to protect in his handling of the Oliphant case in 1974, and he himself became an example of the kind of Indian antagonists, usually lawyers with great expertise, who populate the U.S. court and political systems. Gorton was a successful trial lawyer in Seattle with considerable political clout and influence before becoming a U.S. senator representing Washington State until 2000, when he was defeated at the polls through the political clout and sustained efforts of the Indian tribes of Washington State.

Indian law has been influenced by U.S. justices who, as Harvard law professor Alan Dershowitz quite rightly says, share several desires: "The longing for national [U.S.] solidarity, the longing for the good old days of empire and their own idealization of the new world." These longings cause various proliferations of ideas, most of them detrimental to the "nations within," the tribal nations, the First Nations of America; thus, the sheer political energy dispensed in favor of these influences puts the notion of justice for Indians at risk. In light of this reality, one wonders about the response to indigenous needs in the face of the September 11 attack on the twin towers in New York and the subsequent flag-waving hysteria that brought about G. W. Bush's panicked response and bombing of the Arab world. It was a function of flag-waving hysteria, as Indian histories have revealed, that brought about a wrong-headed legal response to Indians in the United States.[14]

Dershowitz's assessment of the desires shared by U.S. justices reminds historians and other astute writers that early American theorists have influenced not only the law but also, surely, the entire American populace and all parts of the globe; his assessment of those desires rightly suggests that their theories have never included politically and ethnically distinct Indian tribal nations as ongoing participants in the emerging democracy.

The survival of the First Nations of this continent was never a part of the scheme toward progress as envisioned in historical America. Yet that survival has been nothing if not miraculous in the face of aggressive and persistent destructive policies. Writers who have asked "why?" have come up with a myriad of reasons, but few of them have shown an understanding of the native people themselves and their connection to their lands. Like all native peoples anywhere in the world, American Indian tribal peoples have always inhabited a world permeated with living power that has made invasive colonial thought imposed and ineffectual and unacceptable.

The miracle of the 200 years of recent Indian–white history in this country is that in spite of these U.S. nationalistic longings and the resultant detrimental legal history of the courts, America has not fully decimated the tribal first nations of the American continent. It would seem that the indeterminate history regarding the questions represented in these longings has inadvertently allowed Indian treaty enclaves to continue as "domestic, dependent" nations. The question is, for how long? What will be the long-term consequence of this colonial stance? How many more Gortons will impose the theories of the past and the will of the American courts upon the tribes for the purpose of white/Euro-American supremacy? When will the future for American Indians change from bleak and bare survival to predictable and open participation in the greatest democracy of modern times?

As to the real test of this miracle of survival, modernists can make little of the resultant continuation of Indian nations except that Indian nations, it seems, can be allowed to exist in theory but hardly in practice. If the expectation is that these domestic nations can actually thrive, however, this is a different matter. This expectation, if there is such a thing, will certainly be challenged in the courts and in practice because such nationalistic enclaves are still thought by lawmakers and politicians and the general American public to be dangerous and anti-American. If what has happened in the twentieth century can be used as a test for the resolve of the future, there is little reason to believe that American Indian nations will find a significant place in the American historical perspective in the twenty-first century. The unfortunate reality is that the seeming ambiguity that underlies the treatment of Indian nations in the law, however unintentional or purposeful, has meant devastating poverty and failed justice on most of the homelands of indigenous peoples.

Some scholars and most historians as diverse in their thinking as Raymond Williams, Richard White, Franklin Roosevelt, William Rehnquist, Frank Pommersheim, Michel Foucault, and Abraham Lincoln have suggested that there has been a modicum of safety for Indians and Indian nations in the ambiguous and haphazard thinking that has prevailed for two centuries. No one is sure that this is anything but wishful thinking, but the point in much of the writing done by such scholars and historians is that a certain kind of safety has been managed through public opinion, academic criticism, and Indian resistance. This idea or apologia has little merit when looking at the actual practice of the law in the courts throughout the land.

By and large, Indian scholars believe, as Lumbee scholar Dr. David Wilkins of the University of Minnesota tells us in his book *American Indian Sovereignty and the U.S. Supreme Court,* that there is little hope that the courts and specifically the Supreme Court of the United States will be deterred by any of the usual deterrents embedded in our democratic history, such as the previously mentioned public opinion, academic criticism, Indian resistance, or public charges of partisan and race-based politics. Many scholars now believe that the Court is presently so entrenched as an active right-wing court that it will do as it pleases in spite of those obvious deterrents and that its loyal partisanship will not be deterred in its ideological extremism.[15]

There is an accumulation of documentation, Wilkins implies, that has been gathered in the past twenty years that suggest these safety mechanisms of a democratic society no longer matter, that the recent justices in charge of legal systemic thought are no longer deterred by those safety mechanisms and have turned instead to partisan and race-based politics in ways and means not witnessed for at least a hundred years. "Diminishment" is now the interpreted description of the vast body of treaty law that has sometimes protected Indian nations and "disestablishment" has become the action to be enforced. The law toward Indians now has come full circle, turning from decimation to alienation and back to decimation again—and this recent turn has happened in the past twenty years.

An eruption of blatant and racist anti-Indian law since the U.S. high court decision in Oliphant (*Oliphant v. Suquamish Tribe, 435 U. A. 1978*) almost thirty years ago has resulted in the Court's curtailing of Indian rights in an unprecedented, methodical, and contemptuous strategy to rid America of its grudging legal history vis-à-vis its indigenous peoples and First Nations. Now, it is true that protestations have brought about a leniency in this directive through subsequent litigation such as a 1991 law overturning a major criminal case, *Duro v. Reina* (105 St. 646), but the overall thrust of this curtailment is still the intent of the courts. Not since the anti-Semitism of the 1930s in Germany has a nation's court and legislative system so regulated the lives and rights of its "minority" citizens with the intent to exclude them from citizenship and democratic ideals.

Not since the German anti-Semitic laws of the 1930s—generally referred to as the Nuremberg precedents—which significantly curtailed Jewish rights in that country, has such a body of law (built on the Oliphant precedent) been promulgated to exclude a people from fairness and justice and its own history in this country.

The Oliphant doctrine (stemming from a 1970s case in Washington State that ultimately included all of the states in the West) holds that the "overriding sovereignty" of the United States, which presumably (but unconstitutionally) stems from the nineteenth-century "claimed" power of the U.S. Congress, called "plenary power," bars Indian nations from criminally prosecuting non-Indians on their reserved homelands. This has meant that non-Indians remain free to commit crimes against Indians on those reserved homelands without fear of prosecution from the tribal nations. The court decision in Oliphant states that "the inherent sovereign powers of an Indian tribe do not extend to the activities of nonmembers of the tribe."

Oliphant v. Suquamish Indians can most essentially be described as backlash legislation rising out of a pivotal time in tribal–federal relations; that is, the end of the termination policy (1946–54). In its final form it is the decision in what is often referred to as the Rehnquist-led Supreme Court that overturned a lower court decision in the Ninth Circuit (which had held that the tribe had exclusive jurisdiction), and even such liberal justices as Thurgood Marshall and Harry Blackmun were inclined to go along. Yet, looking at the broader spectrum, this legislation differs not a whit from eighteenth- and nineteenth-century ideas of how to legally treat the indigenous peoples, all the way from the Louisiana Purchase in 1803 to the present. The intent of the law is still the colonial intent to take over the land, no matter how law must be manipulated and justified to achieve that intent.

The decision to appeal the lower court decision favoring the Washington State–based tribe that resulted in this outrageous interpretation was the beginning of a vicious backlash led mostly by two right-wing lawyers, Philip P. Malone and Slade Gorton of Seattle. Their interest in overturning this tribal-favored lower court decision gained momentum when these two lawyers-turned-politicians understood that a congressional policy of terminating the treaty (fiduciary) relationship between the Indian nations and the U.S. government (which they had hoped for) was not going to happen. The reason it wasn't going to happen was because the obvious consequences of poverty-stricken and homeless Indians who had invaded the cities of the West during the disastrous termination era were dealt with by the Nixon doctrine, which had at long last described the policy of termination as a failure. In addition, the organized tribal nation protests were largely successful in describing this latest legislation as an abrogation of treaty responsibility and an unjustified backlash to the survival of the notion of sovereignty. The greatest calamity of the termination policy was witnessed by the terminated Menominee tribe, which quickly became the largest taxpayer in the state of Wisconsin and an unbearable burden on the tax base while losing all of its major assets. The subsequent urbanization, in general, experienced by all tribes was a nightmare without organization and appropriate federal funding. Congress was reluctant to go there again, but individual power enclaves developed by people like Slade Gorton mindlessly proceeded in an effort to diminish law-and-order systems on Indian reserved lands.

It seems obvious that the anti-Indian law of the past twenty years built on the same momentum that gave rise to the Oliphant doctrine, and one wonders where and how it will be stopped. One is reminded that other democracies have been brought down because of the presence of a hated minority and the crimes perpetrated against that minority by a powerful and partisan majority. Starting in 1935, for example, emerging from a very long history of hostility, an eruption of anti-Jewish incidents began to occur in democratic Germany and soon there was public demand that the Jews be excluded from the protection they held as citizens. Laws were promulgated to significantly curtail Jewish rights in that democratic country and the consequences were disastrous to the entire country. This has always been a possibility in the United States as it looks upon its ubiquitous Indian populations.

In the past twenty years, the courts in the United States have consistently undermined tribal sovereignty in its dealings concerning state jurisdiction in Indian Country. They have curtailed the rights of tribal citizens in religion and other social matters; the courts have legitimized massive land and resource thefts (the recent Yankton Sioux land case in South Dakota is a major example) and redefined states' rights vis-à-vis tribal nation rights.

Another outrageous example is the fifteen-year fight of the tiny Lower Brule Sioux tribe to put ninety-one acres of previous treaty lands along the Missouri River back in "trust" for economic development over the objections of the state of South Dakota. The tribe had purchased and reclaimed the former treaty lands and won a ruling from the lower courts in 1990 to return this land to "trust" or tribal status to take it off the state tax rolls in order to participate in the native tourist development along the river. Recently, the Supreme Court refused to hear the state's appeals, so after many years, the tribe can go forward. The Lower Brule tribe, which operates the Golden Buffalo Casino in the little agency village of Fort Thompson as well as their own, is committed to using the reacquired land for tourist and economic development, which probably isn't too much to ask because 550 square miles of Sioux treaty lands up and down the Missouri River were flooded by the U.S. Army Corps of Engineers for hydropower in the 1960s. The tribal losses during that period were devastating and have been documented.

The governor of South Dakota, in astonishing ignorance of the historical rights of American Indian tribes, has said, "The issue in this case is whether or not Congress has the ability to delegate their authority to the executive branch of the government through the Department of Interior to place land anywhere in the United States into trust. We believe this [putting land back into trust status] is an unconstitutional delegation of authority from the legislative branch to the executive branch."[16]

The governor also said, "The issue of which government entity should be able to collect taxes should not be decided by the secretary of the Department of Interior. If the tribe wishes to buy land 'outside of its boundaries' such property should be subject to state collection of taxes and local zoning ordinances." So says the ahistorical governor of the state of South Dakota who has, apparently, never read the constitution and what it says about Indian tribes, nor has he read the treaty dialogues of the past. The lawyers who represent the state of South Dakota appealed the outcome of a fourteen-year old lawsuit because, as the governor says, it is a necessary legal inquiry into the federal government's ability to take land into trust for Indian tribes. In 2006, the Supreme Court refused to hear the appeal. Because the tribal agreements with the federal government (i.e., treaties) precede the organization of state governments in the West, and because tribes and states had virtually no relationship for many decades, the principle of precedence to tribes over states' rights is what is at stake here in this argument, and it is not a new one. There is no assurance that the courts will continue to recognize that precedence as the struggle for economic sufficiency heats up.

Because the U.S. government asserted the "doctrine of discovery" at the beginning of its time on this continent, the "trust" doctrine has meant that the federal government has a special, protective relationship to the Indian nations. That essentially is the meaning of "trust." The "trust" doctrine is explored in Wilkins and Lomawaima's *Uneven Ground: American Indian Sovereignty and Federal Law* and, frankly, it should be read by all lawyers and certainly state politicians, particularly governors of states like South Dakota where large and powerful tribes exist. Indian scholars believe that the contest over the trust doctrine's meaning (which this governor in all of his ignorance is trying to explore) puts tribes at risk. They cannot be assured that their rights will be protected by—or from—their "trustee," the U.S. government. Neither can they be assured always of appropriate court interpretation.[17]

When one looks at the history of the past several decades, it is evident that recent policies and laws, especially those concerning land and economic issues, have been a detriment to native populations and their sovereign rights as nations-within-a-nation.

While wrangling goes on in political enclaves and in the courtrooms of Indian Country, tribes are unable to organize coherent economic policies, develop political strength, claim law-and-order rights to protect their citizens, and develop the tribal nation judiciary. The degradation of justice inherent in legal action and theory for American Indians threatens all of us. If the historical rights of Indian nations cannot be upheld, the rights of any American cannot be held sacred.

THE GHOSTS OF AMERICAN HISTORY
IN ART AND LITERATURE

It is not possible to read Western literature without remembering that imperialism has almost always been the mission of that art, whether by design or by accident; it is, therefore, not possible to study any of the literatures of the world without thinking about the nature of literary expression and its import. I'm not talking Jungian theory or Northrop Frye, Leslie Fiedler or Freud, just pointing out that without recognizing the crucial, systematic necessity to identity, enculturation, resistance, and representation that such artistic endeavors provide, literary studies come to naught. Put simply, the importance of the word, the book, the literature, and the daily news of any society cannot be underestimated as carriers of ideologies.

As the previous chapters have suggested, all of the stories of America contain the ghosts of an imperialistic history, yet readers and critics alike often seem to miss this essential ingredient of historical imperial thought, or perhaps they just ignore it, and that has been my constant lament as an aspiring analyst in Indian Studies.

Sometimes just reading the morning newspaper brings the unwelcome news that America is, more than anything, full of exiles who have no knowledge of indigenous forerunners, full of well-meaning people who come to the land of the free and the home of the brave to define themselves in imagined communities that have no notion of the vast histories that precede them. Every now and then my acknowledgment of all that makes its way into my thinking, just as it did one spring morning when I sat in the Phoenix Sky Harbor Airport, casually reading the letters to the editor of the *New York Times*.[1] I read the following:

As the adoptive parents of a Chinese girl, I was pleased to learn that other parents are grappling with their children's cultural identity. In our American Reform Jewish family, we are teaching our daughter that being an American is a privilege for us, regardless of . . . ethnic and religious heritage. She is learning to read and write English but she also takes Hebrew and Jewish studies and attends a Mandarin language and dance class.

Another letter said:

As parents of two children from Cambodia we agree that parents must teach children about the culture they were born into. But we believe that it does most for the children's sense of self when that culture is embraced by the wider family.

The letter goes on:

In other words, not only are our kids Cambodian American but in some sense our family is, too. As we learn about Buddhism, it enlivens our Judeo-Christian perspective. This year, we are preparing for the Cambodian New Year on the heels of Easter and Passover—it gives us insight on our own lives here in New Jersey.

As I boarded the plane for Seattle, I thought about all of the children who are Indian Americans, born and raised in the homelands, many of whom had been taken away from their parents and homes into adoptive places (forcibly), told not to be Indians and told to never look back. I searched the faces in the seats in front of me, the faces of the world, and thought, "Yes. This is America," and these paragraphs in the newspaper are the conversations of today's global America; the talk of immigrants and children of immigrants, the dilemmas of people who are engaged in colonial practices throughout our part of the world, the consequences of dispersions and war and peace, the conversations of attempts to articulate the perceived morality of an immigrant place in democratic terms. "We teach our children the importance of respect for the difference in others," they say, and "we teach our children pride in citizenship." The letters, celebrating hybridity, celebrating the globalization of new and liberating links to others who are mostly described as the "less fortunate," remind us of the spread of Western-style magnanimity.

This talk of today's global America is, by and large, not the talk of American Indians. The issue of adoption in Indian Country is thought to be a far different matter, often uncaring and cruel. Those of us from indigenous backgrounds because of a history of child theft by colonial bureaucracies do not participate in the banality of these conversations for we are not immigrants or children of immigrants. We are not colonists or children of colonists. For those of us who did not come here as adoptees, displaced persons, slaves, émigrés, or exiles, we find these conversations interesting and pervasive, but they are not ours.

In the midst of the cacophony of voices that make up "ethnic" America, it is the business of American Indian writers to ask: Why is it so hard to explain that as the indigenes we feel unconnected, dispassionate about all of this? Is there anyone who speaks for the indigenous populations of America, the people who were always here? We are still here, you know; we have histories.

Little more than a hundred years ago, our relatives fought bloody wars with immigrants and slaves and colonists and exiles for the right to continue to exist here as we had done for thousands of years. Who speaks for that history? Who knows those stories? Who listens? Who cares? As one of the writers who has asked these questions for the past thirty years, I want to say to the people who write those generous letters to the editor quoted above: "Wait a minute, America, wait . . . before you define and imagine the world for yourself and your children only on your terms. Remember, we are here, we have always been here. We are the Indigenes and we do not share your stories."

The truth is, we have been thought of as a despised "minority" in America because we are not what others are, "ethnic Americans" whose intention is to be absorbed and assimilated, slaves and the children of slaves who ask for a piece of the pie, adoptees who are looking for parents to love us. We have been thought of as a despised people in many parts of the world, in the global universe of émigrés, and, yes, in the immigrant nation of America, among movers and settlers, a despised population that most of America has hoped and believed would go away, disappear, or vanish, or, failing that, would simply become assimilated in the ways that other groups have done.

Because our nations have signed treaties with the United States, because we have not gone away, disappeared, vanished, or become assimilated, our resistances have been denied and ignored by greater America. Most Americans deliberately refuse to understand why we object to stereotypical mascot Chief Illiniwek's outrageous burlesque at football games, why we rage at the celebrations of Columbus Day, and why we don't want the famed Oglala chieftain Crazy Horse to be pictured in an imagined pose on bottles of beer or slashed into a mountain he called sacred. America's vision of itself is embedded in a history of imperialism known throughout the world and it is America's intention to absorb and assimilate. When American Indians do not assimilate and absorb and vanish, the innocence of the colonizer, the innocence of the immigrant, and the innocence of the émigré are called into question. The innocence of teaching our children "pride in citizenship" and the innocence of saying that "being an American is a privilege for us" begin to buckle and tilt when the resistances of indigenous peoples in the face of immigrant takeover have to be acknowledged.

To the Indian in America who knows a conversation and history of war and annihilation by immigrant populations, colonizers, and settlers, the difficulty in teaching our daughters and sons that "being an American is a privilege, regardless of ethnic or religious heritage" cannot be underestimated. When the American Indian Movement in the 1970s marched on Washington, D.C., to protest a devastatingly cruel Indian policy and when they cheered Malcolm X's "the chickens are coming home to roost" speech, global America was astonished and horrified. When we say it is difficult to teach our children to "have pride in citizenship," it is because of a history of dispossession unacknowledged by global America. As "ethnic" America settles itself into democratic, legal enclaves and claims land and resources for itself, it suggests that all is well in America when, in fact, the ghosts of an American imperialism that pervades all of Indian America must still be accounted for.

In spite of the seeming banality of the letters to the editor I mentioned previously, it is my experience that they are not banal, nor are they benign. They are political statements and they have a pervasive effect on what it is that America, the most powerful immigrant nation in the world, wants to think of itself. From the point of view of the indigenes, no one is innocent in America, and we are all responsible to know our concomitant histories.

When I reached Seattle, it was raining. Hailing a cab, I went to a meeting of college professors at the university and talked about the problems involved in "Pedagogy, Praxis, and Politics: Multi-Ethnic Literatures in U.S. Education." I told my audience (made up of whites, many Asians, a few Blacks, and two Indians) that I was the least likely speaker to have something useful to say on this subject and then I plunged ahead.

Indeed, I ranted for most of an hour about how as we go about our teaching we must keep in mind that the great political achievement of America has been that it has put together a body of Indian law that has resulted in what I call "white rightness." America has been enormously successful in falsifying its story, I said to the audience that day, though I'm not sure anyone believed me. Indians continue to resist that false story, I told them, at least insofar as it has denied the native experience. Indians have been in a constant fight to retain their sovereign rights to nationhood. In the twentieth century, Indians have lost two-thirds of their treaty-protected lands. They are poorer than any segment of American society. Thus, Indians conclude that white rightness has been successful. That accounts for my reaction to the letter writers I spoke of at the beginning of this discussion who blithely say, "We teach our children it is a privilege to be an American." Yes. It is a white privilege, an immigrant privilege, given through legal means . . . to be an American.

> Law has produced white rightness.
> And it has produced white innocence.
> And it has produced the innocence of immigration.
> And it has produced the innocence of colonization.
>
> Whiteness, then, becomes a political position.
> Indianness, then, becomes a political position.

I felt sad that rainy day in Seattle, saying to my audience of fellow professors that this country in which they take so much pride does not defend the right to be an Indian and certainly does not defend the rights of Indians as historical landlords. It was unfortunate to have to admit that Indian law defends others in this country but does not defend the right to be an Indian. Law does not reduce Indian–white conflict, just as prison does not reduce crime and tanks and armies do not bring peace. Indian law as it now functions does not function to reduce Indian–white conflict or racism or discrimination. What is manifest here in America is a profound conflict of interests and values, both in spirituality and in politics, and it is reflected in everyday stories.

What we are learning now is that as globalization is celebrated, the distance between cultures does not narrow; it widens. Members of marginalized groups and members of indigenous populations are in fierce struggles at the moment to survive and go on. Justice will require the creation of new scholarly fields in order to lessen the imbalances because it is not just academic and personal boundaries that are widening. What is at stake is the very intimate nature of what it means to be human in the process of interacting with one another.

PEDAGOGY: HOW TO TEACH INDIAN STORIES AND WHY

If the story of America is not told appropriately—that is, with its many omissions—how, then, we may ask, should ethnic, immigrant, colonizing, imperialistic America teach the Indian story? It is possible to argue that narratives about being an American will communicate the rightness of one position or another rather than examine and analyze for the purpose of prov-ing one's position wrong or inadequate. To prove one's point of view to be wrong is often not the purpose of narrative. On the contrary, it has been the observation of such American historians as David McCullough and others of his generation that history, the telling of stories of the past and present, is the "bedrock" of patriotism. It is the nature and function of history that brings about what some American historians call the "bedrock" of love of country, the basis for nationalism.

That is the way of history, most scholars of the old school contend. It is only the new historians and the new storytellers at the turn of the century, and the so-called Third Worldists attempting to throw off centuries of colonialism, who contend that such an idea can no longer be defended in a multicultural, diverse society such as ours because it skews what history might tell us about others with some degree of authenticity.

As I continue to teach Indian Studies, Indian literatures, Indian experi-ence, and Indian law and policy courses, I cannot help but come to some unwelcome conclusions: certain kinds of Indian laws that have been proven to be misguided are apparently nonactionable because of the accepted notion of the nature of history. I conclude that it may take many decades before colonial histories and colonial ideas concerning the indigenous peoples of the United States are discarded. Although we may want to look away and beyond, there is still the troubling history that requires acknowledgment, the same old blank piece of paper. We must write on that paper the real story of the Allotment Act of the late 1880s, which reduced treaty-protected lands by two-thirds and brought poverty and death to thousands of Indians; we must look at the coercive boarding school system that stole Indian children and their young lives, and still does. We must look at state–tribal compacts about economic development, gaming in particular, and know that continu-ing thefts and unequal manipulations stand as the law of the land.

Because we have not been willing to look history in its face, nothing is done to refute the Allotment Act and return lands to the indigenes; nothing is done to honor treaties in state–tribal compacts; instead, state governments become the enemies of Indian hopes and needs. We must conclude, then, that Indian laws made by the colonizer are, so far at least, nonactionable. Furthermore, certain kinds of oppression resulting from these law are non-actionable because even when illegal acts are taken into the courtrooms of America, Indians seldom win.

What this means is that narratives that explore these matters seldom ex-press an Indian point of view, only the ideas of a righteous America. What it means is that Indians have little or no recourse, except to remember and tell and retell their own stories, not to rectify wrongs but, simply, *to keep hope alive.* More significantly, this means that presenting such one-sided narratives as we have been subjected to is not the way to develop democracy in the modern world. It is up to the word, the book, the news, the writer, poet, scholar, storyteller, and teacher to reveal that awful reality.

Writers do what they can and it is often insufficient. As a writer, I have come to the conclusion that it is not necessarily my overriding business to create new ways of looking at the world, not my function to find solutions to every injustice, but simply to remember the old ways and to tell my listeners about them. Literature and myth, the narrative and the news have to do with a people remembering who they are and it is the function of fiction and storytelling, and writing in general, to shape that reality, not make new realities lacking in historical perspective.

It is possible to think, as I do, that narrative follows poetry and poetry precedes history, but that is, perhaps, a matter for theorists to take up. Whatever the case, no poet or storyteller should ever be content to leave the past alone. The following examples are given to illustrate some points about native storytelling in which the comment that "I will tell a story" is a common response to finding meaning in life and events. These two stories that follow are taken from the beginning pages of my early novella *From the River's Edge*[2] as we come upon the protagonist John Tatekeya. He is described as sitting just outside an American courtroom waiting for his trial to resume, thinking about justice. His cattle have been stolen by a white neighbor and John is thinking that if this case goes like all of those historical cases before it, he will not in all likelihood get his cows returned to him; they've never returned the land, why would they return a few cows?

Because in tribal conversations poetry often precedes stories, I begin this discussion with a poem about the function of history. I refer to a poem I wrote a long time ago about storytelling and grandmothers, as a way to connect and fuse the literary genres:

HISTORY OF UNCHI

("Grandchild, I am an old woman but I have
nothing to tell about myself. I will tell a story.")

They say
that storytellers such as she
hold no knives of blood
no torch of truth
no song of death;

that when the old woman's bones
are wrapped and gone to dust
the sky won't talk and roar
and suns won't sear the fish beneath the sea.

they even say
that her love of what is past
is a terrible thing
hun-he-eee-e
what do they know
of glorious songs
and children?[3]

. . .

As for the stories, Story #1 and Story #2 are designated in the longer narrative from which they are derived and are, therefore, stories that may be called the "story-within-the-story." Because Tatekeya is the designated storyteller, and some of the story is told in the third person, this is an uncharacteristic performance design (much like poetry) that gives some flexibility to simple narrative. It is an attempt to clarify the rather complex but tacit historical plot and untold and hidden history with which average American readers are ordinarily unfamiliar, but which even the most obtuse reader can understand as a story that indicates theft and injustice.

The story-within-the-story, told in the third-person omniscient point of view, presents the attempts of oppressed men to carry on normally despite overwhelming negative forces. The powers that are being opposed here are bureaucracy, colonialism, racism, and poverty. It is the gap between these forces and the Indian's survival that give the narrative its subtle impact.

"That was the way of history," Tatekeya muses during the trial while he waits for courtroom activity concerning cattle stolen by his white neighbor.[4] This story-within-a-story reflects Tatekeya's thinking concerning the Allotment Act, legislation passed by the U.S. Congress in the latter part of the nineteenth century without the "consent of the governed," but known as part of the tribal history of the people.

We are told by the omniscient third-person narrator: "Private solutions and individual solutions about matters of this kind, Tatekeya would concede, were not always possible, regrettably, nor were they definitive. This explanation does not, of course, exonerate him, but at the same time, neither does it condemn him."

So, much like the old grandmother in the poem, he would simply tell the story or maybe two, perhaps over and over again, but he does not claim the story. It is not his, so it, too, is implied through the third person as a story beyond him, and he is simply relating it as he knows it.

STORY #1

"To be an allottee and a citizen of the United States," the agent told Benno, who stood before him holding a form letter addressed to him from the Bureau of Indian Affairs, Washington, D.C., "you must do what it tells you in the letter."

"No."

"You must choose your allotment."

Benno took out a huge handkerchief, wiped his face, and paused.

"No. Thanks."

"You must choose your allotment."

"No. Sir."

They stood staring into one another's eyes.

Later, the agent chose the allotment for Benno and registered it in his name. "It is way up the Crow Creek, somewhere on past that little white man store up there. Way on up there," the protesting Benno told everyone, his arm flung out in a wide gesture.

"Taskar and them live up there, but me and my family have never lived there. We don't want to live there; there's too much trees there along the ridge and it gets too dark in the winter."

He got another letter in the mail telling him he was an allottee:

Each and every allottee shall have the benefit and be subject to the laws, both civil and criminal, of the State or Territory in which they reside.

Benno has said no again, and for the last time. He never again spoke a civil word to the agent. And he sent the letter back by his eldest daughter, who lived at the Agency. He continued to live along the *sma sma* creek where he had always lived. And when the agent and his secretary came by to "talk some sense" into the potential but recalcitrant allottee and citizen, Benno took a few warning shots at them with an old 30-30 he kept by the front door. He shouted at them in Indian to go away.

"Han sni! Hanta wo!"

Benno was declared "incompetent" by the Department of the Interior at the request of the agent very shortly after this hair-raising event. The agent was, after all, an ex-schoolteacher from Sioux City, Iowa, who had taken up government service because there was more money in it, and he was not, he would tell you in no uncertain terms, accustomed to taking gunfire from crazy Indians.

The allotment which bore Benno's name, then, was put up for sale eventually by the agent who was acting "in his behalf," and a white man from Pukwana who raised pigs and turkeys purchased it.[5]

The history that underlies this story-within-the-story is crucial to understanding the power of narrative because without it, one is simply overwhelmed by the hopelessness of the negative forces. If the function of storytelling and narrative in Indian life is to give meaning and hope, these techniques of ongoing history parables that are so common to native storytelling present the ongoing-ness of the people themselves. Against all of these obstacles, the story-within-the-story is the only thing that is left, because Benno is slowly losing, is declared "incompetent," and suffers the loss of land in the process of "allotment." To understand the impact of history—that is, the power of legislation by a colonial and oppressive government—Benno must lose, but memorable narrative is what is taken into the future, which means that the strength of his protest and the memory of it emerges as personal affirmation. Plot generally involves the protagonist, Tatekeya in this case, but by the force of memory and story-within-the-story narrative, the set of conflicts suggests that there is more to this than just winning and losing for the moment. Memory will out.

Thus, the thoughtful "that is the way of history" gives Tatekeya the power of the moment. He knows this story about old Benno, his fellow tribesman, and how he is pitted against the power of a racist and oppressive bureaucracy, in which he is neither losing nor winning. Tatekeya's comment is, in the same context, neither an *expression* of victory or loss but of *affirmation*. Of what? Of what? *Of his very presence.*

The Allotment Act, as those who study Indian history know, was passed by the U.S. Congress in 1887 in violation of every treaty ever signed by the U.S. government and native nations and it ultimately divested native nations of two-thirds of their treaty-protected lands all across the country. As this story is examined, the works of Donald Fixico and Vine Deloria Jr. must be assigned readings on this historical period. Certainly, in the case referred to by Tatekeya about the resistance to the Allotment Act by his fellow tribesman, Benno, it was known by almost everyone of that era that this legislation was a violation of the treaty of 1868 and many others. It was resisted by Indian leaders of the time and was a major cause for war. It was cause for the ultimate 1890 assassination of the Hunkpapa leader Sitting Bull, who refused to come to an "agreement" concerning this violation of the rights of indigenous peoples as well as the corruption involved in the treaty process.

Most American Indian historians believe that the many decades of the process of implementation of the Allotment Act (still in effect when the Indian Reorganization Act was passed in 1934) occurred during a policy of genocide. This policy brought about war and the theft of the Black Hills and the Massacre at Wounded Knee and the many murders of tribal leaders. Without a doubt, this policy brought about poverty, loss of land, starvation, death, and disease to thousands of Indians. What can Indians do when all of their heroes have been assassinated? They can construct and defend the story.

Tatekeya's comment "that is the way of history" is, therefore, a recognition of the relentlessness of colonial power and the odds against Indians who resist oppression and seek justice, and he tells the story. It is not a recognition of hopelessness so much as it is a recognition of the conditions under which Indians have survived for over 200 years.

For those who have not lived it, as Tatekeya has and as Benno has, and for those whose history has omitted these events, some review of history here is a good thing. The Allotment Act passed by the U.S. Congress distributed vast holdings of tribal, treaty-protected lands to tribal individuals, doling out 180-acre parcels to individual Indians so that tribal treaty lands could be broken up. As stated by President Theodore Roosevelt, the "Rough Rider," it was an essential colonizing tactic to break up the "tribal mass." The federal policy, then, gave what were called "excess" lands to white settlers through the Homestead Act, which had been passed a year earlier.

Indian history can be taught through stories such as those told by Tatekeya either in a pantribal way, because these events were endemic throughout the West, or in a specific tribal way. The reserved homelands spoken of here in a specifically tribal way by Tatekeya and Benno have been in existence since 1863, one year after the Little Crow Territorial War of the Santees in the place now called western Minnesota and eastern South Dakota. The homeland of these storytellers, the Crow Creek Indian Reservation located on the Missouri River, was designated first as a concentration camp and then, later, as one of the official homelands by treaty of the Santees who had participated in the Little Crow War. It was subjected to the Allotment Act within five years of its treaty, a period of enormous land loss and subsequent poverty and death.

These years are often called the "years of attrition" by native historians. Agency superintendents, white men representing the federal government, had total power over individuals and property and devised a legal, bureaucratic method of declaring resistant Indians "incompetent" to handle their own affairs. Psychological testing was not so much a part of this declaration and definition of "incompetence" as was the swearing of "witnesses" to particular actions. Resistance by Indian landowners (allottees) and other tribal people in accepting and speaking English as the language of usefulness and reason was also designated by the federal authorities as evidence of "incompetency." Many Sioux people who refused give up tribal language were simply declared "incompetent" and lost their rights to protest. Church and government boarding schools were set up and funded by the U.S. Congress during this period as indoctrination centers for native children as young as four years of age, until they were eighteen years of age. These schools attempted to stamp out native language and, in many cases, were successful.

Several of the major courses in Indian Studies explore the history of the congressional power referred to in these stories by Tatekeya (officially called "plenary power" or "absolute power," a power claimed by the U.S. Congress with no constitutional basis). Students should refer to the work of David Wilkins, who states very clearly and gives evidence that this "plenary power" of the Congress in Indian affairs is a mere "claimed" power and is unconstitutional. Wilkins, a Lumbee political science scholar who has taught at major universities, defines "plenary power" as a colonial concept of power of one people over another, usually for the purpose of land claims and economics. This kind of historical overview is required background pedagogical strategy and must not be omitted from classroom explication if the entire implication of a largely ignored history is to be understood.

This story-within-a-story is to be understood as a "resistance" story said to be told by an old man of the tribe, and must not be dismissed merely as a sad story simply because in the long run there seems to be no concrete solution found to such complexities as those presented in the narrative. The negative forces that are described here are not the negative forces of life, such as old age or senility, faced by all old men. These are not, for example, the negative forces faced by the old woman in Eudora Welty's short story "A Worn Path," in which the protagonist faces old age and struggles against the powers and loses. Welty's character is in a hopeless condition because old age simply advances and there is nothing to be done. In old Benno's case, contrarily, he is facing a colonial force, which *can* be overthrown. There are overwhelming odds, to be sure, but change can occur and his situation is not doomed to failure. If this is discussed as a resistance story, these differences must be acknowledged by both readers and teachers, so that the literary voice of the characters is an affirmation in support of the people as has always been the case of the oral traditions.

This story-within-the-story is part of a great body of important oral literature generally kept within families or within the tribe and not often told to outsiders, so it is doubly challenging for nontribal students and nontribal teachers to contextualize meaning. The reading brings up the nature of Tatekeya's and Benno's resistance as well as the function of narrative in the telling of personal experience and tribal history. It also affirms the importance of such stories because in the face of such injustice by powerful adversaries as described in the stories, the people must be assured that the function of narrative continues to be a technique of survival. Against the brutal impact of social and political facts like this story illustrates, we can't help but ask, what can mere narrative do?

Part of the answer to that question is that the narrative position Tatekeya (and the author) takes represents a technical and rhetorical mix that is essential to understanding the survival techniques that bring about a certain well-being to the Dakota Oyate in nationalistic and political terms. To make art of such events (as Benno does and as Tatekeya remembers) is the way the Sioux always managed history, not only to address the presence of outsiders in seeming tacit ways but also, more important, to address themselves. Tatekeya does not keep this information to himself, in all likelihood, because he remembers it and will no doubt share it as he goes on with his life, because in his cultural view and experience, honest and regular self-examination is vital for the people to know themselves as tribal people

Honest self-examination has always stemmed from collaboration, and so the teller of the story collaborates with the hearer of the story and the rememberer. Narrative's partnership with history reaches outward as well as inward. Narrative defines Tatekeya and his people on their own terms and ultimately relies on the usefulness of language and memory as survival mechanisms. These are real events that happened to real people and although realism in literature these days is often replaced by something more "artful," like magic realism and symbolism, for example, these stories in themselves are transformative.

STORY #2 (*this is another Tatekeya story, told over and over again*)

Eddie Big Pipe, Harvey's younger brother, rode over to the "squaw man's" place and shot fifteen head of prime, fat hogs. He did it because the white man, married to a tribal woman and living on her land, would not keep them away from Ed's watering place along the creek.

Big Pipe had paid dearly for the individual action he had taken upon himself. There had been no further dealings between the two antagonists, and the Bureau of Indian Affairs officials at the Agency ever after that looked upon Ed as a troublemaker, one who was unreliable and dangerous.

In defense of this admittedly astonishing behavior, Eddie Big Pipe had later made a joke of it.

"Well," he would say in mock seriousness, "I could'a shot him!" and everybody always roared with laughter.

Some others in the community, however, the "squaw man," his wife and her relatives, and, especially, the Bureau of Indian Affairs officials, were not amused. Seeing no humor in the situation, they avoided Big Pipe, and when they could not avoid him, they glared at him from a distance.

Tatekeya used this story to discuss the ideas of justice as they applied to Indians, and he always gave the impression that shooting the "squaw man" might not have been such a bad idea.[6]

This story-within-the-story, too, is a resistance story. It is a monologue from the protagonist, Tatekeya, as told by the third-person omniscient narrator about Eddie Big Pipe. So, in a way it is removed to the third power in its telling, which is often a method of oral storytelling. It is told in this clumsy way in order to establish the contrast between Tatekeya, the storyteller, and his more "assimilationist" tribal relatives and neighbors. Tatekeya's inference, that "shooting the squaw man might not have been such a bad idea" is the way the story ends in the Tatekeya telling and retelling, and it indicates that he is on Eddie Big Pipe's side. He is, therefore, the persona, the mask for representing the resisters to assimilation and he does it with what he thinks is some humor.

There is some unwritten history in this story as well, which may deserve some explication as prepared for classroom use. "Squaw" is a controversial and offensive term. It is a pejorative term used to describe an Indian woman, a term often thought by modernists to be used only by ignorant whites who, historically, wanted to degrade Indian womanhood. Such information about the word is probably a narrow descriptor, as this story that takes place early in the twentieth century illustrates, because Indians have also used the word.

In the vernacular, a "squaw" is an Indian woman who does not exemplify the tribal values of womanhood expected and honored by the people. In fact, Indians of the Plains tribes used the word just as often as whites did during the early part of the century, although it has fallen into some disuse in recent decades because of a certain kind of "political correctness." Thus, a "squaw man" as the term is used in this story is a man who marries such a woman and, because of his alliance with her, he takes on a quality of dishonor.

One can be confused by the so-called new historians, the "deconstructionists" or the new linguists who want to suggest that this word derives from some obscure language of a now-defunct tribe and that it is, therefore, an acceptable and even benign term for describing Indian womanhood. More confusion arises when it is suggested by linguists that the word describes in pejorative terms the private parts of womanhood.

There is no question that the word has been used in troubling ways, but in this story told by an old man of the Dakotah tribe, it sets aside, in a disparaging way, those Indian women who have married white men without the sanction of the tribe. This is a long-standing and uncomplimentary cultural view held by those traditional Dakotah Santees whose marriage patterns and arranged marriages were, at one time in the past, carefully guarded instruments of survival and virtue. This is what is being expressed by the old traditionalist—and make no mistake about it, his words are meant to disparage.

Culturally, Santees were a polygamous society. They were not Christian societies. Arranged marriages among suitable cultural and tribal allies and friendly nations and tribes were the centerpiece of the *tiospaye* concept of tribal organization. The Santees shared the notion of the *tiospaye* (extended family) with other large groups making up the Seven Council Fires of the Sioux Nation; that is, the Oceti Shakowan made up of Oglala, Sicangu, Ihanktowa, Sihasapa, Minniconjou, Hunkpati, and Santee. Unsanctioned marriage to men outside of the tribe and to white men in particular was one of the first destructive blows to the *tiospaye* concept, and Christian monogamy was the second. The disparaging attitude about all of this is the attitude of Tatekeya and Benno, old Santee patriarchs. Whether it is accepted today is a matter of conjecture, a subject of controversy (as is the use of the word "squaw" itself), but there is no denying that it is an attitude shared by old traditional men of Tatekeya's generation.

Native cultural views, even in the face of enormous destruction brought about by coercive assimilationist and Christian practices experienced by Indians in the past hundred years, are tenacious. Those who study cultural change suggest that cultural values are rarely stamped out by overt or even by covert assimilationists, as long as those cultural values of the people are thought to be honorable and useful and worthy of continuance. Intermarriage between Indians and whites, therefore, is a subject of controversy because it is not only one method of assimilation but it is also a method of land loss and economic/environmental change, as the story-within-a-story suggests.

In this story, the antagonist to Tatekeya's view of the world is the white man who marries the tribal woman and through that marriage not only takes over the land but also introduces new animal husbandry (raising swine) into the community, which seems, in Tatekeya's view at least, to be a pollutant. The discussion of this idea can lead to some fruitful examination of "environmental" views, which are always of interest to today's public.

WHAT ABOUT RESOLUTION?

Fiction in Western literatures, we are told, is made up of event, rising action, climax, falling action, denouement, and resolution. One of the frustrating traits of almost all of my fictional work and the work of many Indian storytellers is that resolutions are rarely forthcoming. Explications and explanations are rarely firm, unwavering, determined explanations, as one has been led to expect in most American fiction. It's a little like reading Russian literatures of a certain Czarist era in which there is little expectancy of the right of the average person to engage in what America calls the "pursuit of happiness," an essential component not only of the American literary tradition, but a component of the very Bill of Rights and Constitution of the United States as well. Read any Russian story and there is quite a deviation from the American expectancy that individuals have the "right" to happiness.

Much of my fiction, in the manner of a lot of the old stories of the Dakotahs, is no exception to the failure of this expectation, as well as to the failure to find resolution in the art of storytelling. I make no excuses for this failure, since this style of writing in English can be reminiscent of the rather long, excursive stories told in the Dakotah language. Story #1 and Story #2 are both stories-within-the-story and they are, therefore, statements of fact and experience more than they are figments of fiction, so the expectation of resolution is perhaps unwarranted in either case. Yet, the reader's expectation of some kind of explanation cannot be turned away completely.

Resolutions in fiction are the function of good storytelling in the Western literary tradition, we are told. Thus, to leave the reader without resolution is a disappointment. In the resistance stories of the colonized, however, conflict is often described in obscure and skimpy ways and there is little hope that resolve is possible because of the bureaucratic nature of colonization, so our satisfaction must come from our understanding of history. Because the function of plot is conflict and the plot, in the case of the story-within-the-story, is without emotional detail, cause and effect does not lend itself to resolve, only understanding. It is history that matters here, not emotion.

Perhaps the reason that these stories-within-the-story are written in a terse, matter-of-fact style is so that the speaker or writer can use words that give meaning to his or her own experiences, but it is not expected that the hearer will interpret the same words with the same meaning. If, for example, such stories are told in the traditional storytelling form, which utilizes repetition, exaggeration, detail, and emotion, the hearer or reader is almost always drawn into it full force to become a believer. This story-within-the-story style presents an existentialist view of language held by some that there is the possibility that language is limited in its ability to really get to the heart of the matter. This is a story, after all, about dispossession, despair, the futility of experience, the loss of meaning, and the shattering of one's ability to have the power to protect one's self and one's property and even one's lifeway. The mask given to Tatekeya in the face of this awful reality is the mask of practicality, humor, and offhandedness.

In terms of the tribal imagination, then, this story provides a strange kind of hope that, in itself, can be considered a form of resolution. In the face of hopelessness, there is hope. Hope for what? For the mere dignity that is the right of any man and his people. These stories are often told as "parables," short allegorical stories designed to convey a truth or a moral lesson. The truth is, the system here is corrupt and the people know it. Because they are not unaware of their situation, their stories given here in shorthand are just as often told in English as they are in Dakotah, the stories themselves challenging the futility inherent in them.

Eddie Big Pipe, a son of a once large and influential family, tells his story to other Dakotahs of the community. John Big Pipe, his brother, repeats the story in order to get across the idea that the "squaw man," although he represents a risk that everyone knows about culturally, is not to be feared. He is a ridiculous figure married to a woman who is an example of failed and dishonored tribal womanhood. They are both, in the view of the storytellers, persona non grata. Irrelevances. They are not Dakotahs. In the tribal imagination, then, Eddie Big Pipe has triumphed over these puny people and he is unabashed in the face of their anger and fear, even though the bureaucracy may be on their side. These people are to be held in contempt in the tribal imagination; so, in willful disobedience or open disrespect both for his white man neighbor and the bureaucracy that brings about such conflicts, Big Pipe is scornful.

In this scene, the writer, without emotion or explanation, gives the reader some food for endless moral and sociological discussion. Can one triumph merely through contempt? Is the destruction of the white man's property a "payback" if, in fact, the destroyer is forced to recompense? Is the action, in either case, futile? Whatever the answers and whatever the questions, the reader is not asked to feel pity or sympathy for these Indian males who are, clearly (and, perhaps, unfortunately) at the mercy of a system of corrupt justice from which there seems to be no relief in terms of conflict resolution. Yet, they are not, in the imagination expressed in the stories, victims. They are part of a long history of resistance. These stories illustrate that historical oppression has marginalized what we think of the colonized but not, necessarily, what they think of themselves.

Pedagogy, then, is not just the profession of teaching characterized by "pedantic formality," as Sinclair Lewis is supposed to have said it was. It is, rather, an art, a specific skill requiring the exercise of intuitive faculties that cannot be learned solely by study. Yet good teaching is not just performance art, and neither is writing. Good teaching and good writing in literary studies is contemplation and intuition and knowing, sometimes without the use of rational processes and, lots of times, it is a matter of good guessing. This means that the artistic development of course content and case studies on the part of faculty members in Indian Studies is essential to successful learning. The subject matters that have interested most good teachers in Indian Studies are, broadly speaking, land issues as well as the function of narrative, which is tied to the land, and, of course, politics, which can best be said to be the conversation we have with one another about how we are governed.

The story-within-a-story technique illustrates that resistance in native literatures and histories requires paying attention to the notion that power to the people can be described through a collaboration that reaches outward as well as inward. Teaching the art of narrative, which has its source in oral knowledge, much of it tacit and unreliable, is acknowledging that processes are at work that mankind can do little to alter. Time is on the side of those whose patience toward that idea or belief is given credence, rather than on the side of those who require immediate resolution.

CONCLUSION

Indian America would be a much poorer place without the storyteller and the poet. But it would not have survived at all were it not for its legendary thinkers, politicians, seers, and teachers. Almost everyone admits that there are two most significant factors in the success for American Indian students in education: home influences and good teachers, neither of which have been much in evidence during the past "boarding school" years.

About teachers, most say that good teachers are born and not made; if that is true, then the granting of permission to teach Indian students and Indian Studies to almost anyone without a criminal record, as was given indiscriminately in the past by the federal government and Christian churches, resulted in what some have described as a sorrowful endeavor through which generations of Indians suffered. These days, Indians are teaching Indians and are trying to interject the notion that teaching is a privilege born of consensus.

Unlike past models, in which civics was taught to tell Indians how to be good Americans and morality was taught to make Indians good Christians, the issue of change and what subjects to teach and how to teach them are the essential provocations of the discipline of Indian Studies. In other words, content and methodology are no longer invested in the notion that basic truths about God and the BIA are inviolate. Rather, content and methodology and good teaching are all based on the idea of developing independent thought and ways of analysis, and the invitation to participate is what we call "pedagogy."

It is crucial, therefore, to develop tribally based materials to be used in the classroom as subject matter and appropriate methods to achieve those goals. It is surprising that there aren't more specific texts concerning what to teach in Indian Studies and how to teach it.

AN ESSENTIAL QUESTION: HOW TO EDUCATE, PROVOKE, AND MOTIVATE IN THE CLASSROOM?

Case studies in Indian Studies models, organized to make up one of the most useful strategies in undergraduate studies, are crucial strategies to encode the cultural and historical information within the essential concepts of the discipline: indigenousness and sovereignty.

The two case studies that I have written about and have found to be most effective are: (1) the Big Pipe case and (2) the Black Hills land case, both readings found in my collections of essays. In Indian Studies, these two cases, one reflecting social issues, the other reflecting land issues, are illustrative of the two parameters of the discipline and can be examined utilizing the Berkhofer history model of perennial cultural conflict. This does not mean, however, that native teachers should not find their own cases with which they are most familiar, write them up, and bring them to the attention of their audiences.

Because most of the perennial conflict analysis in Indian–white relations reveals the pervasiveness of what some call "colonial thinking," but that may also be called, more generally, "egocentric thinking," a regimen of reading, investigation, and research is required in each case. Becoming aware of egocentric thinking on the particularly sensitive matters of Indian–white conflict happens only if we are trained to recognize what egocentric thinking is and how it manifests itself in the processes of reasoning and analyzing. Prereading in the study of 500 years of colonial history in the United States is essential, especially for those teachers and students who are newcomers to Indian Studies.

The false notions about indigenous peoples in this country, the stereotypes, are pervasive and difficult to manage, yet they influence everything that is important to contemporary Indian life: politics, law, culture, religion. Many psychologists say there are several ways certain stereotypes are either accepted or rejected: people think, "It is true because I believe it to be true," which is the first and most pervasive thought pattern; others think, "It is true because we believe it," "it is true because I want to believe it," "it is true because I have always believed it," or "it is true because it is in my self-interest to believe it." Much of the American thinking concerning its own nationalistic history and its own colonial laws made for the subjugation of indigenous tribes is based in stereotype and is not easy to deconstruct accurately into new and more appropriate ways of seeing.

An early discussion with beginning students in Indian Studies can be a simple exercise in asking: What are some of the widely held notions concerning Indians? It is widely believed, for example, that Indians get a payment from the government simply for being Indians. It is believed that Indians love nature and are artistic. It is believed that all Indians suffer from alcoholism because of their biological and racial makeup. It is believed that Indians as a group are artistic and that they are "taken care of" by the federal government. Analysis of these matters by asking students to ask themselves "why I believe these things" or "why I believe others believe these things" is a good starting point for discussion.

The practical outcomes of specific exercises are clarified through writing, which means that accessible writing on the part of the student is, perhaps, the most important pedagogical and learning outcome of all skills. In writing assignments, students are asked to state, articulate, and identify the major problem (i.e., conflict) of the case study. The student is asked to do the following: take lecture and reading notes on the significant historical and cultural background that pervades the case, take notes on the nature of the case and how it has been articulated throughout the period in legal and political terms, write at least two well-developed paragraphs based on these notes that narrowly focus the statement of the problem in terms of the problem-solving model using the materials from the history of 500 years of colonial events, give evidence for reasoning, and write a paragraph that discusses the effect(s) of this conflict. It is not necessary at this point to find solutions to the problems, although that discussion will naturally follow. This beginning exercise is to identify the problem and its effects. That is the first step toward finding solutions. The problem can be stated in many ways: institutional, societal, group, individual, and so on.

IN THE PEDAGOGY OF INDIAN STUDIES, POSTCOLONIALITY MUST ALWAYS START WITH THE LAND

In teaching Indian Studies and other postcolonial subject matters, the issue of land and the law is, perhaps, the quintessential subject matter. Without the possession of land, there are no tribal nations and there is no concomitant relationship between colonials and indigenists. To examine the ongoing and perennial relationship of conflict between Indians and others, then, one must start with the land. It is useful to mark course development in the discipline with land issues and case studies that analyze land issues from the point of view of legal and political rationale, rather than from the point of view of religion, a "sense of place," or green studies. The mythic relationship has been the subject of much study in the past century, but its examination has done little to defend the tribes.

The reason to avoid the mythic and religious issues in beginning courses (and to start with the political) is because of the nature and complexity of religious ideas. It has been the experience of native peoples that the white European invader of this country will never understand the religious stance and the mythic history that natives possess concerning land. An intellectual response can be rendered if the subject matter is taken up in the more advanced courses. Every court case concerning land reiterates a profound lack of understanding of indigenous/religious/homeland issues, and even the Taos Pueblo affair concerning Blue Lake had to be returned to the people by an act of Congress, not the courts. All of this legal history, say some, reveals a political understanding rather than a spiritual one.

It is more effective in the beginning courses to examine the politics and law of history and the political/legal parameters of the discipline prior to the spiritual undertakings. There is the hope that nowadays there can be an understanding of legal and political matters concerning land because of the work of Vine Deloria Jr., who has written extensively on this matter, as has my colleague, attorney Mario Gonzalez, and countless others. In his latest book, Deloria and his coauthor, David E. Wilkins, state: "There is no question that no Indian tribe ever received anything approaching just compensation for its lands from the United States."[1] Compensation, not religion, has become the focus for many land cases, however unfulfilling and unsatisfactory that stance may be.

Deloria and Wilkins say:

> Even the most carefully negotiated treaty only returned to the tribes pennies on the dollar, and some treaties had terms so outrageous as to shock the conscience of even the hardest cynic. Consequently, when the Indian Claims Commission was established in 1946, it was a foregone conclusion that Indian tribes would not receive payment for the real value of their lands.
>
> However, the fact that claims would be heard and efforts would be made to settle long-standing grievances that could not be dealt with in other forums made the commission a positive step forward in Indian/White relations. In the course of settling Indian claims, a strange Doctrine of law involving the Fifth Amendment and the concept of just Compensation evolved. It is in every respect a jerry-rigged apparatus that has no logical consistency and no application outside the field of Indian claims.[2]

By all accounts, almost all of the colonial history of the relationship between the United States and the First Nations can be looked at through the lens of a single event occurring in Sioux Nation tribal history, the 1877 theft of 7.7 million acres of treaty-protected lands in what was then called the Dakota Territories. Grasping the power of what the violation of sovereignty illustrated in this case has meant, is vital if students in Indian Studies and related disciplines are to be able to remove postcoloniality from a dependence upon the colonial condition.

Although compensation has become a significant matter in this case, it is not the essential argument put forth by the Sioux Nation in its struggle to have its holy place, the Black Hills of South Dakota, 7.7 million acres, returned to them in title, nor is it the argument that needs to be put forth if the legacies of colonialism on Indian reservations are to be resisted.

It is not useful, when examining the long discussion on this matter, to start with the killing of Custer, or even with Wounded Knee. The analysis of the matter of land, its possession, its worth, and its compensation must begin with the American colonial history of land theft and its hegemonic actions throughout the decades. The Black Hills case is, therefore, an essential case for historical study.

What attracts scholars to this history are several factors: first, the lack of decent and appropriate dialogue for over a hundred years concerning the theft, which condemned the tribal nation to unremitting poverty for subsequent and ongoing generations; second, the colonial rationale that suggested Manifest Destiny (i.e., the "rightness" of Christian thinking) as the underlying reason for land possession; and, third, the failure of historical examination of state (institutional)-sponsored genocide against all tribal nations in North America during the nineteenth century.

Although this is an introduction to a historical problem for all tribes and a case study in the history of the Sioux tribes, it is also a call for reform concerning the historical view that America is an anticolonial country. Every American who wants to understand the ambiguity concerning indigenous issues that are inherent in a capitalistic democracy of the modern age should analyze this historical case.

Studying the Black Hills land issue, its beginnings and endings, and its journey through the halls of justice of one of the most important democracies of any age is a remarkable way to participate in the language of colonization. This study is not unconnected to the present global actions of the United States. The settling of North America was encumbered with issues of allegiance, power, dependence, being, dying, becoming, and encountering throughout a colonial historical adventure unique to the world—all present in the history of the Black Hills land case. Although the participants in this hundred-year-old case, the colonists and indigenists, sometimes referred to as whites and Indians, are placed in the past, the elements of the case are useful for understanding global relations of the United States with other nations. The relationship between whites and Indians in South Dakota, where this case takes place, and other states like it with large Indian populations has been one of conflict throughout history, but it can also be a microcosm that reflects broader concerns. As America goes forward, now a single global power, it must be held accountable to the history that is illustrated in this case.

On the local level, the struggle for preeminence by the state of South Dakota (since 1889) and survival by the tribal nation of the Dakotapi as this relationship moves into the modern world suggests that political reform is an absolute necessity before any substantive changes, either economic or cultural, can take place. It seems safe to say that the question of Indian self-determination and sovereignty is little understood by state governments and mainstream participants in contemporary society and is the subject of great controversy by scholars and writers. When the major subject is land and estate and treaty, the questions are even more complex.

The office of Senator Daniel Inouye (D-HI) says this about the history of this case:

> Under the Fort Laramie Treaty of April 29, 1868, the United States prom-
> ised to set aside the Great Sioux Reservation which was all of what is now
> the State of South Dakota west of the Missouri River exclusively for the
> Sioux People. The United States agreed to keep all non-Indians out. At
> the same time the Sioux gave up all of the lands that had been recognized
> as belonging to the Sioux Nation under the 1851 treaty of Fort Laramie.
> The Sioux reserved the right to hunt in an area south of the Great Sioux
> Reservation, and they reserved an area under article XVI of the treaty west
> of the Reservation; they reserved the right to use that but not permanently
> to inhabit it. That was the best buffalo hunting ground along the Powder
> River. Finally, under the 1868 Treaty, the United States promised that there
> would be no more cessions of Sioux lands without the consent of three
> quarters of the adult males.[3]

Gold was discovered in the early 1870s in the Black Hills, and the United States Army troops, which were there to protect the Sioux Nation treaty in-terests, were ordered to withdraw by President U. S. Grant in a secret order in violation of the treaty. This executive action opened the way for further settlement without consent of the Sioux. Confronting what some called a fait accompli (and what others simply called an internal coup), Congress, in 1876, passed a law, the Act of August 15, 1876,[4] declaring that no funds would be appropriated for the subsistence of the Sioux unless they gave up their treaty claim over the Black Hills. Although there was no agreement on the part of the Sioux Nation, Congress enacted this claim into law, the Act of February 28, 1877,[5] regularizing a congressional theft of lands belonging to the Sioux Nation. Because the Sioux had no access to U.S. courts, it was only through a political fluke that years later, in 1920, the Sioux claim was filed in the court of claims. They filed under principles that concerned whether the land was paid for, the only legal avenue open to the tribes who until that time had no access to the courts. Never at that time and under the specifications of law was it possible for the Sioux to file a claim that questioned the "taking" by the federal government as a "theft." Thus, compensation became the name of the game played out in the courts for sixty years, even though compensation was not the major issue for the Sioux.

Finally, after decades of court wrangling, the U.S. Supreme Court in 1980 wrote a decision that declared the "taking" of the Black Hills to be a "theft," and compensation was ordered by the courts. To no one's surprise, this order was rejected by the Sioux Nation, which promptly issued a call for land reform and the return of stolen property. The Sioux Nation filed an injunction disallowing the federal treasurer to pay out the money to its advocate, the Bureau of Indian Affairs. Today, there are some, not believing in the resistance tactics of colonized and oppressed peoples, who suggest this case is "done." The Sioux Nation has never agreed and reminds everyone that they filed an immediate injunction to prevent the "payment" authorized by the latest Congress of the United States, saying "the Black Hills are not for sale."

Black Hills/White Justice, by Edward Lazarus, is one of the few historical texts that has been published on this subject.[6] The author, the son of a Washington, D.C., lawyer who settled the case without the consent of his client, urges the Sioux to "take the money." Lazarus's text is largely apologia for legal mistakes and bias but, in all fairness, as a competent if not brilliant lawyer, Lazarus recognizes that the United States is, in all probability, not going to restore its stolen booty unless it is somehow forced to do so, and he thinks there is less and less hope for that as time passes. The Lakotas say that if the law can be made to steal land, the law can be made to return land.

There is little legal history one can point to that suggests the law can be fair to indigenous peoples. Lazarus contends, as do his colleagues and collaborators, that when the Sioux say "the Black Hills are not for sale," this is simply a mantra that has no legal standing. Legal standing, as everyone knows, is rendered by judges and lawyers and courts—none of whom has ever represented indigenous rights with any degree of virtue and integrity.

One of the crucial aspects of this case, which all Americans should ponder and consider while reading the narratives and studying the case itself, is certain political assumptions on the part of the United States during the late 1800s. The foremost of those assumptions is an understanding of the "unilateral" moment in the historical time (1877), the land theft, which allowed the United States to use its power to see itself as the indispensable democracy. It is important to assess what that response in history means to global hegemony in today's world. Indeed, if one were to do that, America would now be defined as the first settler-colonial country to rise to great power in our time, a country that requires the unconditional surrender of any antagonist in its path, and a place where there is no middle ground.

History does repeat itself, and when the Twin Towers in New York and the Pentagon in Washington, D.C., were struck by Al-Qaida in 2001, a defensive and, some say, unnecessary gathering of national power on the part of the United States occurred. War was the result and thousands of young men and women have been sacrificed. There is a connection between this defensive act and the U.S. response to the killing of General G. A. Custer in 1876. In the decade following Custer's defeat and death, Congress passed laws to break treaties, confiscate land, and initiate a genocidal war. Political terror was a strategy used against natives in the same way that military terror is being used in the world today. In 2003, the United States declared war against terror in the Middle East very reminiscent of the war in the northern Plains against the Sioux. That Sioux war lasted from 1876 to 1890, when massacres of innocents occurred everywhere in the northern Plains. At this writing, no one can predict how long the war in Babylon will last, nor who will be buried in the latest mass grave.

The current mission of the United States to become the center of political enlightenment to be taught to the rest of the world began with the Indian wars and has become the dangerous provocation of this nation's historical intent. The historical connection between the Little Big Horn event and the "uprising" in Baghdad must become part of the political dialogue of America if the fiction of decolonization is to happen and the hoped-for deconstruction of the colonial story is to come about. When that historical connection is analyzed, it is possible to understand the consequences of the occupation of the lands of a weak state by a stronger one in the context of modern social and political theory.

Not a lot of the information concerning how the people of the Sioux Nation have felt concerning the Black Hills issue can be read in the documents of the so-called business councils that began forming on the Sioux Reservations after the turn of the century, as early as 1915, but some insight can be gleaned not only from what is recorded but also, often, what is not. It seems clear that even the white superintendents of those agencies who had control over what was published in those documents marked the dialogue, but the Sioux speakers portray in the sense of the times they are describing that the federal government had not dealt with them fairly.

In those documents, the question of whether the U.S. government had the right and the authority to take over the Black Hills was only tacitly a part of the discourse. Manifest Destiny was clearly the theory used by the federal government to bolster their authority, which meant that matters concerning the 1851 and 1868 Sioux treaties were largely ignored by the courts and the battery of lawyers who were on the case for decades. There seemed to be no legal way to address that question even after the case went to court (following a quirky authorization by Congress in 1920). The question of authority could not be posed because of restrictions written into the law; it was not posed then nor since. Indeed, compensation has been the only remedy available in law, a remedy rejected by the entire Sioux Nation for many decades. Part of what is revealed in the documents of the past is the fact that when there seems to be no legal redress, victims lose sight of their goals. Groups and individuals who are victims of colonial practice are turned into proxies for colonial intentions and are used by those in power. There is the fear in the resistance movements at the beginning of the twenty-first century that such proxies will be given authority and support by the adversaries.

Prior to and during the court discussion of the case, two world wars intervened and the Indian Citizenship Act was passed in 1924, making Indians citizens of the United States for the first time, a legal process that had been tried and bungled in legislation for many previous decades. One important consequence of this action that made Indians into Americans was to make sure that Indians did not have to renounce their tribal nation citizenship status; this was done because many tribes were opposed to the act. Thus, native tribal Americans to this day hold dual citizenship in the United States and in their tribal nations.

The best that could be done concerning the theft of their sacred lands in the Black Hills, according to their lawyer, a South Dakota politician named Ralph Case, was to file what has become known as Sioux C-531, in which the tribe asserted that the United States had taken illegally the treaty-protected

Black Hills and failed to fulfill the "trust" responsibility, which was a Fifth Amendment matter. Many unremittingly illegal principles were put into the legislative and legal documents allowing the Sioux to get the case to court. But, most of all, to the Sioux, the entire matter has meant a failure of the "trustee" to protect their treaty lands from seizure, a total of 7.7 million acres, holy and sacred lands essential to their religious interests as a people, and a place of origin.

To the federal government, this has simply meant a failure to pay them for the seizure. The case became a simple claims case (a real estate matter) in which some two dozen petitions were sought, and it was in the courts until 1980 when the Supreme Court called it a "theft" rather than a legal "taking." Because of the limitations placed on how tribal land claims could be brought to the U.S. court system, this matter became only a compensation matter in law. Had the United States paid for it? No. Had it been for sale? No. How, then, could it be a simple real estate matter as the courts have implied? Subsequent discourse has suggested that it was not and is not just a real estate matter. It is a moral, legal, ethical matter of historical significance.

The court actions throughout the litigation process tell us that most of the claims were dismissed by the courts, as was the 1942 *Sioux Tribe of Indians v. United States* case, on the basis that they were, overall, moral claims and outside of the jurisdiction of the Indian land legislation passed in 1920. It was a religious matter, the attorneys deemed, untouchable by the courts, and, according to this interpretation, destined to be dismissed and forgotten. In 1950, the resubmitted claim was dismissed again and during this time, the courts were again assisted by the U.S. Congress in federal efforts to diminish native treaty standings.

In a last-ditch effort to end treaty-protected nationhood for indigenous peoples all over the country, the disastrous termination and relocation laws were passed by the U.S. Congress in that decade. These termination and relocation laws were meant to end treaty responsibilities (such as health and education and, certainly, land claims) and urbanize large reservation populations to be based in cities such as Seattle, Los Angeles, Cleveland, Minneapolis, Chicago, and Oakland.

In that process, two-thirds of the entire Indian population of the United States was relocated to cities in the West in order to separate them from land, family, indigenous rights, and religion. It was an enforced assimilation process put into legal terms affirming the federal government's control and weakening tribal governments' authority over Indian citizens.

These are the matters of "old wars" taken up by "new Indians" who know and remember that thousands have died terrible deaths on this unlucky journey described in these pages. The predictable implication of all of this history can be stated in several ways: to honor agreements that threaten no one concerning the lands and rights of native peoples, yet upholding that honor has been the major resistance of White America; to know that land ownership rights are the crux of moral relationships between indigenous nations and others, yet those rights will not be defended by America; to know that land ownership rights are the key to the survival of tribal peoples everywhere, yet those rights are stolen by America, a powerful nation claiming an honorable place among nations throughout the globe.

The implication of all this history and the reason to write about it is that genocide is a crime against humanity, which means that it is the responsibility of all of us. The facts of this history, stated bluntly, are that the United States has pursued policies throughout the generations that led to the decimation of the first nations on this continent.

America is a new nation. Because of its inexperience and arrogance (as well as its genocidal history toward natives), it is difficult to hold it up as an accomplished beacon of virtue in the world. Because of its intention to be finished with Indians and because of its military and economic power, dangerous contact is still happening to the indigenous peoples of this continent and around the world.

Inquiring about the intention of one people toward another is the challenge that must be met if we are to unravel colonialism in the future. How can we know the future when we know so little of the past? How can we know what the intentions are for the future of Indians in America when we are told by physicists that 96 percent of matter and energy in the entire universe is completely unknown?

One of the ways is to simply take a look at the experience of the past 500 years of American growth and analyze its connection to Indian lives and Indian survival. If what we find is that anti-Indianism is a concept in American Christian life, just as Islamophobia and anti-Semitism are concepts in Christian Europe, and are all derived from specific occurrences and experiences that have matured over the centuries, that is a place to begin.

Practically speaking, the concept of anti-Indianism in the United States can be best understood if it attempts to take the dialogue between indigenous peoples and immigrants outside the usual context of "racism" and to put it into the political discussion of "enforced colonialism." This has been the thrust of Indian Studies for the past three decades.

It is one of the unfortunate realities of race dialogue in the United States that the enslavement of Africans for economic reasons and the effort to overthrow that crime against humanity became the essential focus of contemporary dialogue when, in fact, the black–white dialogue is limiting in terms of the broader, more diverse nature of Americanism. The reason that such racial dialogue can be called unfortunate is because it implies that an end to racism is possible, that an end to blackness is possible, and that white America can overcome its early history simply through law. Instead, a broad intellectual endeavor must be undertaken.

Anti-Indianism is not so easily unclaimed as race dialogue because of its indigenous nature. Anti-Indianism is not only about enslavement, white supremacy, rape, poverty, discrimination, color, busing, whiteness or blackness, guilt, Jim Crow, a piece of the pie, reparations, equality, or even affirmative action. Anti-Indianism is also about the failure of politics, nationhood and sovereignty, possession of land, indigenousness, and self-determination. Anti-Indianism in America is about the failure of the right to nationhood. Because the First Nations of America (i.e., Indians and their nations) possess all of the traits of nationhood—language, land, military, governing forms, religion, citizenship, and ideology—they are considered unassimilable and, therefore, impervious or even dangerous to American ideals. The crimes against humanity set in motion by this reality are a ubiquitous menace still faced by America and its struggle for justice. Because of the possession of the traits of nationhood by American tribal nations, and because of America's narcissism and arrogance concerning its primacy, there exists a political agenda that cannot be propelled into what America wants to see as its rightful place in the world. To deny the indigenous peoples their place as sovereigns in this democracy is an unacknowledged crime against humanity. This is one of America's dilemmas as a world power.

Almost all of the knowledge about the traits of Indianism was dismissed during what is called the "discovery period": when Columbus called the natives of this continent simple and good, Cortez said they were savage and cruel (he was military, after all), priests said they were unknown to god, Christians said they were ignorant and deficient, and the military that faced them for a hundred years said they were not human. These descriptions have pervaded all areas of American life—school, church, government, and community—and has resulted in the concept anti-Indianism.

The kind of colonial law applied on Indian lands for at least 200 years may be seen by some observers as the U.S. government's ongoing criminal activity and may even be viewed by some of its victims as the first nationalist politicization of the cultural identity called "Americanism." If that perception is accurate, we are in a very dangerous time. Now, because of U.S. global influence and because of the comparison that can be made to the illegal Indian Reorganization Act (IRA) constitutions written by and for American Indian tribal nations some eighty years ago, the Islamist terror we are witnessing at the beginning of the twenty-first century suggests constant warfare.

For the victims of the colonial power of the United States, both past and present, the roots of terrorism are vivid and may be the direct consequence of nationalistic Americanism as it is being embedded in the recent behavior of the powerful United States, as it writes a new constitution for the entire Iraqi region. Every nation in the Middle East will reject this constitution because it is much like the illegal, colonial IRA constitutions written for and by American Indian tribal nations eighty years ago, charts for democracy that have, unfortunately, failed to meet the needs of the people. Democracy cannot thrive under such heavy-handed colonial power. Unless America begins to understand that its victims will no longer accept the idea begun 1492 that "inferior" races and civilizations can be wiped off the face of the earth, it will face constant war. A necessary corrective to that threshold for the conquest of the world is overdue. The times they are a-changin', we've been told by everyone from Bob Dylan to Bin Laden.

What gives impetus for such events in the modern world? If, as it has been thought by historians like Robert F. Berkhofer and others in their historical analyses, the Indian of the white imagination and ideology concerning civilization and progress has been the result of early contact and experience, how is it that this same ideology comes to bear on the U.S. relationship to those peoples of a modern nation in the Middle East 200 years later? Is the phrase "history repeats itself" just an unreasoned rhetorical device, self-indulgent and repetitious, or is it a powerful weapon of ideological work that cannot be thrown off without reactionary strategies?

The answer may be that the ideology of civilizing and Christianizing natives so deeply embedded in the Euro-American experience is a consistent body of ideas reflecting the continuing social needs and aspirations of Americans. That is the tragedy of history. The people in the Middle East who have been taken over by the United States in a recent war are not uncivilized, and neither were the indigenous peoples of North America. They are not savage, and neither were the indigenous peoples of America. Iraqis are not without god, language, or culture. Neither were the peoples of the Americas. Yet they have been characterized as that by Western minds. American Indians and other indigenous peoples resist the American threat as they would resist any threat that they see invading and settling in their territory. In the case of the

Iraqis, they are a modern people: lawyers, surgeons, businesspeople, teachers, religious leaders, international athletes, singers, musicians, pilots, and housewives with houses full of all the modern conveniences. And, indeed, since 1970 they have had a working constitution that might be utilized in the modern world if it is cleansed of its Baathist hegemony. Iraq is not a backward country. It is a Muslim country with thousands of years of history, culture, and civilization that has been the pride of the Arab world.[7]

If an ideology about good and/or bad can continue to be presumed even about modern peoples across the globe by the United States, the most militarily powerful nation known to any era (just as was done with the indigenous peoples of this continent 500 years ago), what can scholars and thinkers do to find solutions, a balance of power? What is the goal of any nation if it is not self-determination? How is the self-determination of America or Iraq or the First Nations of this country, the right of all peoples, promoted through the events of the past several decades? How is war an answer to fear and ideological power? These are still the questions that plague us all.

Perhaps it is all too simple: the unfortunate people called the "terrorists" of the twenty-first century in Baghdad have become what the "savages" of the northern Plains were thought to be so long ago; thus, powerful and determined colonizers will out. Yet, who controls the stories and who creates the language by which the stories are told is still the ultimate power. To know that is to know the extent of our loss and to know the possibility of our lives, as indicated by the title of this book: *New Indians, Old Wars*. New Indians must tell the new history about the old wars because they have been witness to savagery and terrorism—and continue to be.

Simply put, the "terrorists" and "savages" (and now "extremists") are called by those names because they resist the colonial effort to seize their lands and resources; make them beggars; convert them to an unknown religion, Christianity; and destroy them economically. Make no mistake: a holocaust happened here in our own lands and it continues here and elsewhere. Long ago, they say, there were bad times. We must tell of them so we can know the future. The Indian wars must be given standing in this ever-growing narrative about America because the terrors the world is now witnessing may be the direct consequence of the events begun in America in the past centuries!

It is essential that educational systems, people of goodwill, writers, and intellectuals of all countries resist the tyranny of failed ideologies and remember to tell our children that, yes, Virginia, history does repeat itself.

NOTES

PREFACE

1. Amos Oz, "Readings," *Harper's Magazine,* November 2003, 16.

2. Carl Schmitt is called a "fascist" philosopher by Alan Wolfe in an issue of the *Chronicle of Higher Education;* Wolfe, "A Fascist Philosopher Helps Us to Understand Contemporary Politics," *Chronicle of Higher Education,* April 21, 2004, B16–B17. It is useful for that, surely, but also it is helpful in understanding the imperialistic thought of America and its historical origins.

3. Elizabeth Cook-Lynn, *"Why I Can't Read Wallace Stegner" and Other Essays: A Tribal Voice* (Madison: University of Wisconsin Press, 1996).

4. The reference to the Badger, a figure in Dakotah traditional literature, comes from a chapbook by Elizabeth Cook-Lynn, *Then Badger Said This* (Fairfield, Wash.: Ye Galleon Press, 1983; ISBN 0–87770–307–8).

INTRODUCTION

1. Edward Valandra, *Not without Our Consent: Lakota Resistance to Termination, 1950–59* (Champaign: University of Illinois Press, 2006). This book began as a doctoral dissertation and discusses the tribal view of resistance of the Sicangu Lakota Sioux to federal power in the mid-1900s; it is the only book of its kind to discuss the state jurisdiction and federal and tribal powers in specific, land-based terms.

2. Helen Hunt Jackson, *A Century of Dishonor: The Early Crusade for Indian Reform,* ed. Andrew F. Rolle (New York: Harper and Brothers, 1881; repr. New York: First Harper Torchbooks, 1965). This is an essential text in Indian Studies.

3. Laura Bush, wife of President George W. Bush, cancelled a poet's gathering in the White House in 2002 (*The Nation,* November 18, 2002, 11). There was a literary program being hosted at this time by Mrs. Bush, who has a master's degree in library science but who remains undistinguished as an important voice in education

or politics. She had invited such luminaries as Patricia Limerick (who claims to be a "new historian"), Justin Kaplan (who wrote a biography of Mark Twain), some photographers, poets, and many other prominent writers and historians. A whole series of writers participated in this activity until there was a cancellation of some of the more obstreperous writers whose work might have been thought critical of contemporary political acts of George W. Bush. When asked by a *New York Times* reporter whether the cancellation might be in response to how some of these writers felt about the Bush foreign policy and Iraq (there was a "poets against the war" movement at the time), Mrs. Bush replied that there is "nothing political" about American literature.

4. *Book TV*, C-SPAN2, December 4, 2004.

CHAPTER 1: TO KEEP THE PLOT MOVING

1. Dinesh D'Souza, *The End of Racism* (New York: Free Press, 1995). The best thing that can be said about this author's work (he also wrote *Illiberal Education: The Politics of Race and Sex on Campus* [New York: Free Press, 1991] after his graduation from Dartmouth College) is its exhaustive bibliography and notes section. D'Souza, a foremost critic of liberalism, was born in Bombay in 1961, became a U.S. citizen in 1991, was educated in elite schools in the East, and became the foremost critic of what is called "liberal" thinking. He said, "I am the best qualified person to address multiculturalism because I am a kind of walking embodiment of it." He is a glib defender of conservative politics in America, is a first-generation immigrant to the United States, and was a John M. Olin Scholar at the American Enterprise Institute, a conservative think tank. He takes issue with "cultural relativism," which he says was introduced to the United States by anthropologists of the Franz Boas school. As with most writers on the subject of race, his discussion has to do with the black–white and "people of color" dimension, but he knows very little about Indian affairs in America.

2. David E. Wilkins, *American Indian Sovereignty and the U.S. Supreme Court: The Masking of Justice* (Austin: University of Texas Press, 1997). This is perhaps one of the most important books on Indian law published in the past decade. Wilkins gives support to the argument that the Supreme Court has used and continues to use what he calls "retrohistory" (303) in order to resurrect repudiated and even demonstrably failed policies of the federal government. Enabling legislation of the courts in general, Wilkins says, is particularly important in structuring state law in its efforts toward primacy over Indian law. He calls for the repudiation of the claimed "plenary power" of the U.S. Congress.

3. Dennis Banks with Richard Erdoes, *Ojibwa Warrior: Dennis Banks and the Rise of the American Indian Movement* (Norman: University of Oklahoma Press, 2004), 54. This is the latest of a series of so-called self-told stories written by Richard Erdoes, a European photographer who got caught up in the Sioux takeover of Wounded Knee in the 1970s. Erdoes's first work was *Lame Deer, Seeker of Visions* (New York:

Simon and Schuster, 1972), a book about the life of John Fire, a Sicangu Lakota Sioux medicine man. Erdoes also wrote the popular book *Lakota Woman* by Mary Moore under the name Mary Crow Dog (New York: HarperPerennial, 1990), which became a classic in feminist literature, as well as several other self-told books.

4. Banks and Erdoes, *Ojibwa Warrior,* 54.

5. Rolland Dewing, *Wounded Knee: The Meaning and Significance of the Second Incident* (New York: Irvington Publishers, 1985; it has become available in other editions since then: e.g., *Wounded Knee II* [Chadron, Neb.: Great Plains Network, 1995]). It is an excellent source for researchers, perhaps one of the best. Yet, ironically, the first chapter, entitled "America's Most Neglected Minority," fails to explore the most fundamental principle underlying the entire American Indian Movement rationale; that is, the historical principle that Indians are not minorities in the United States. They are sovereign nations of people, with signed treaties, who possess lands, have learned to live in the tribal way, and refuse to give up their unique histories and their nation-to-nation political status in the United States.

6. Richard Drinnon, *Facing West: The Metaphysics of Indian-Hating and Empire-Building* (Minneapolis: University of Minnesota Press, 1980). This is an invaluable source for understanding the national will of America (329) and its conduct of the Indian war period. Several chapters are devoted to this period. In 1866, as Drinnon documents, General William Sherman proposed genocidal tactics against the Sioux when he wrote President Ulysses S. Grant on December 28 and said: "We must act with vindictive earnestness against the Sioux, even to their extermination, men, women and children. Nothing else will reach the root of this case." He was probably talking in general terms, but he was specifically referring to the Fort Phil Kearny route in Wyoming. (Because of pressure from these kinds of military leaders, Grant removed U.S. troops from the borders defined by the treaty of 1868 to Sioux lands in a deliberate move to allow untrammeled access by thieves and settlers to the gold fields in the Black Hills of Dakota. The theft of 7.7 million acres of these treaty-protected lands was solidified in 1877 by the U.S. Congress.) What contributions this general's actions made to the discussion of genocide and the rules of war is significant for any historian to take up. Sherman's military position and intention as a colonial raider had started long before he reached Sioux Country and most particularly concerned his actions during the U.S. occupation of the Philippines, but this position remains unnoted by most American historians because of their willing denial of genocide as a national policy. Drinnon tells us that the UN General Assembly in 1946 defined "genocide" in this way: "Genocide is a denial of the right of existence of entire human groups, as homicide is a denial of the right to life of individual human beings. Many instances of such crimes of genocide have occurred when racial, religious, political and other groups have been destroyed, entirely or in part"; *Journal of the United Nations* 58 (Supp. A-A/P,LV.476): 324.

7. Elizabeth Cook-Lynn, "Who Stole Native American Studies," *Wicazo Sa Review* 12, no. 1 (Spring 1997): 9–28.

8. Jack Utter, *American Indians: Answers to Today's Questions,* 2nd ed. (Norman: University of Oklahoma Press, 2001).

9. The Kennewick Man dispute is clarified in a well-organized and brief discussion by Dr. Jace Weaver in his brilliant collection of essays, *Other Words.* He says on page 163, "Having used the Bering Strait theory to make the indigenes not fundamentally different from those who disembarked at Ellis Island, it is now used to make them European as well, the populating of the hemisphere no different from Columbus's (or Viking's) 'discovery' centuries later"; Jace Weaver, "Indian Presence with No Indians Present," in *Other Words: American Indian Literature, Law, and Culture* (Norman: University of Oklahoma Press, 2001), 160–174.

10. *Indian Self-Determination and Education Assistance Act of 1975,* Public Law 93–638 (January 4, 1975), 88 Stat. 2203, can be read in civil rights legislative papers of the federal register.

11. Vine Deloria Jr.'s *The Metaphysics of Modern Existence* (San Francisco: Harper & Row, 1979), *God Is Red* (New York: Dell, 1973), and many occasional papers on origins are the most significant references concerning origins by this major scholar.

12. "The Civil Rights Act required tribal consent before a state could assume jurisdiction" (pp. 228, 236, 243, 283).

13. David E. Wilkins and K. Tsianina Lomawaima, *Uneven Ground: American Indian Sovereignty and Federal Law* (Norman: University of Oklahoma Press, 2001), 213.

14. Linda Chavez, "Remembering the Negative Side of Affirmative Action," *Chronicle of Higher Education,* September 27, 2002.

15. Toni Morrison, *Love, a novel* (New York: Alfred A. Knopf, 2003). A conversation between two important black intellectuals, Toni Morrison and Cornel West, in *The Nation* illustrates how irrelevant much of the so-called black dialogue is to the American Indian. It is a wonderful discussion about what it means to be a black writer in America, about John Kerry and the 2004 presidential election, about books of all kinds, about civil rights and the fiftieth anniversary of *Brown v. Board of Education* and the Supreme Court, but not a word about how the Supreme Court has dealt with Indian cases in the past hundred years. Whether these black scholars have read Wilkins's *American Indian Sovereignty* and Vine Deloria's *Behind the Trail of Broken Treaties: An Indian Declaration of Independence* (Austin: University of Texas Press, 1985) is left to the imagination because there is nothing in their dialogue that suggests the importance of the academic work and writing of these native authors. To listen to most of the "minority" dialogue in the United States, then, is to suggest that the dialogue is too often presented only in black and white. Toni Morrison and Cornel West, "Blues, Love and Politics," *The Nation,* May 24, 2004, 18–28.

16. Similar to most other groups, American Indians registered a decline in the number of professional degrees early in 2000–2001 dropping by 3.7 percent. American Indians also suffered an 11.8 percent decline in doctorates received in these same years, continuing a pattern that began in 1998–99. The American Council on Education's 2003 report shows a loss of Ph.D.'s in education, physical science, social sciences, life

sciences, and engineering when, in fact, for all "minorities" there has been a loss in every category except life sciences and even humanities. American Indians represented the lowest number of doctoral degrees earned among all racial/ethnic groups. Employment in higher education shows that American Indian faculty at universities have more than doubled since 1980 but the number of doctorates has declined, even as overall enrollment in college courses for American Indians increased by 80 percent. This means that successful completion of higher educational degrees will remain a problem for the future. Further information on these statistics can be accessed from the annual report; William B. Harvey, ed., *Minorities in Higher Education Annual Status Report 2002–2003* (Washington, D.C.: American Council on Education, October 2003).

17. Jace Weaver, *Other Words: American Indian Literature, Law, and Culture* (Norman: University of Oklahoma Press, 2001).

18. Linda Tuhiwai Smith, *Decolonizing Methodologies: Research and Indigenous Peoples* (London and New York: Zed Books; Dunedin, New Zealand: University of Otago Press, 1999). Hannah Arendt, the now-deceased German philosopher, is known for exploring the ties between the intellectual production of the colonial world and its growing domination, among other weighty subjects. Scholars Wole Soyinka, Homi K. Bhabha, and Edward Said are sometimes considered controversial, "Third World" intellectuals because they speak for the "secular, liberal and human" strand of information in the academy. Their works not only forced them to flee their homelands but also have often been silenced by regimes not always interested in intellectual pursuits, and their voices have too often been ignored in America. Edward Said, *The Politics of Dispossession: The Struggle for Palestinian Self-Determination, 1969–1994* (New York: Pantheon, 1994); Wole Soyinka, *Art, Dialogue, and Outrage: Essays on Literature and Culture* (New York: Pantheon, 1988); and Homi K. Bhabha, *Nation and Narration* (New York: Routledge, 1990) are among the works of these scholars that should be read by anyone and everyone interested in Native American Studies.

19. Tom Wolfe, *The Bonfires of the Vanities* (New York: Farrar, Straus Giroux, 1987); Richard Wright, *Native Son* (New York: Harper and Row, 1940).

20. Elizabeth Cook-Lynn, *I Remember the Fallen Trees: New and Selected Poems* (Cheney: Eastern Washington University Press, 1998).

21. Elizabeth Cook-Lynn, *From the River's Edge* (New York: Arcade, 1991).

22. Michael L. Lawson, *Dammed Indians: The Pick-Sloan Plan and the Missouri River Sioux, 1944–1980* (Norman: University of Oklahoma Press, 1982). Lawson says that the Pick-Sloan plan in the Missouri River Basin developed by the U.S. Corps of Engineers caused more damage to Indians than any other public works in America. Yet, as in the case of most government projects, Indians from the reservations most devastatingly affected worked on the project in pick-and-shovel jobs for decades: Standing Rock, Lower Brule, Crow Creek, and Yankton, taking home meager paychecks while their lands, resources, and treaty legacies were stolen. Others simply fled to the cities on "termination/relocation" projects. Federal acquisition of "trust" land and the application of Indian/federal policy perpetrated this sad betrayal not

only of loss of land but also of loss of water rights and jurisdiction rights. For first-hand stories concerning this catastrophe, listen to the recordings by Mary Louise Defender Wilson and Francis Cree, *The Elders Speak: Dakotah and Ojibway Stories of the Land,* compact disc, Makoche Recording Company, 1999, and Mary Louise Defender Wilson, *My Relatives Say: Traditional Dakotah Stories,* compact disc, Makoche Music/BMI, 2001.

23. T. S. Eliot, *What Is a Classic? An Address Delivered before the Virgil Society on the 16th of October, 1944* (London: Faber and Faber, 1945; New York: Haskell House, 1974). It perhaps seems odd for a Native American literary critic to use T. S. Eliot's work in defense of anything having to do with an oral and indigenous literature because of the notion that written literature holds primacy over oral literature. Another reason is that Eliot has been accused of everything from elitism to anti-Semitism and is even said to be inclined toward fascism. For example, he was heard to complain that Hitler made intelligent anti-Semitism impossible for a generation—a complaint that was disavowed by his associates—but there is no question that he was the foremost elitist of his generation. His published works from 1917 until 1990 have set standards but not without controversy. This address can also be read in a collection by Eliot called *The Idea of a Christian Society: And Other Writings* (London: Faber, 1982).

24. Adrián Recinos, *Popul Vuh: The Sacred Book of the Ancient Quiche Maya,* trans. Delia Goetz and Sylvanus G. Morley (Norman: University of Oklahoma Press, 1950); taken from Adrián Recinos, *Monografía del departamento de Huehuetenango* (Guatemala: Editorial del Ministerio de Educación Pública, 1913). *Popul Vuh: The Creation Myth of the Maya* (long version, #018), VHS (Berkeley, Calif.: University of California Extension Media Center, 2176 Shattuck Ave., Berkeley, CA 94704; El Teatro Campesino and Berkeley Media LLC, 1989).

25. D'Arcy McNickle, *The Surrounded* (New York: Dodd, Mead, 1936; Albuquerque: University of New Mexico Press, 1978); D'Arcy McNickle, *Wind from an Enemy Sky* (San Francisco: Harper and Row, 1978); D'Arcy McNickle, *The Indian Tribes of the United States: Ethnic and Cultural Survival* (London: Institute of Race Relations, Oxford University Press, 1962).

26. John Joseph Mathews's *Sundown* (New York: Longmans, Green, 1934; repr. Norman: University of Oklahoma Press, 1988) and McNickle's *The Surrounded* are some of the earliest works by writers who were influenced by scholarship in anthropology and ethnology. An excellent reference volume for scholars interested in these works and many others is A. LaVonne Brown Ruoff, ed., *American Indian Literatures: An Introduction, Bibliographic Review, and Selected Bibliography* (New York: Modern Language Association of America, 1990).

27. James Wood, "Human, All Too Human, the Smallness of the Big Novel," *The New Republic,* July 24, 2000.

28. Sherman Alexie, *Reservation Blues* (New York: Atlantic Monthly Press, 1995).

29. Gordon Henry, *The Light People: A Novel* (Norman: University of Oklahoma Press, 1994); Louise Erdrich, *Tracks: A Novel* (New York: Henry Holt, 1988); Gerald

Vizenor, *Bearheart: The Heirship Chronicles* (Minneapolis: University of Minnesota Press, 1978); N. Scott Momaday, *The Ancient Child* (New York: Doubleday, 1989).

30. James Welch, *The Heartsong of Charging Elk: A Novel* (New York: Doubleday, 2000).

31. Soyinka, *Art, Dialogue, and Outrage.*

32. Ray A. Young Bear, *Remnants of the First Earth* (New York: Grove Press, 1996).

33. Lawrence Evers, "Ways of Telling a Historical Event," (paper presented at the thirtieth annual meeting of the Rocky Mountain Modern Language Association, Santa Fe, N.M., 1976; it was also presented at a Modern Language Association seminar on Native American literatures, Flagstaff, Ariz.).

34. N. Scott Momaday, *The Way to Rainy Mountain* (Albuquerque: University of New Mexico Press, 1969).

35. N. Scott Momaday, *House Made of Dawn* (1968; repr. Tucson: University of Arizona Press, 1996).

36. Lawrence Evers, "Words and Place: A Reading of *House Made of Dawn*," was first published in *Western American Literature* 11 (February 1977): 297–320 and, because of its groundbreaking analysis in critique and theory, was republished in 1985 in Andrew Wiget's *Critical Essays on Native American Literatures* (Boston: G. K. Hall, 1985). Evers's critical work has been essential to the study of native literature.

37. Ray A. Young Bear, *Black Eagle Child: The Facepaint Narratives* (Iowa City: University of Iowa Press, 1992).

38. Robert Rebein, *Hicks, Tribes and Dirty Realists: American Fiction after Postmodernism* (Lexington: University Press of Kentucky, 2001).

39. Ibid.

40. Ibid., 7.

41. Ibid., 142.

42. Albert E. Stone, foreword to *Black Eagle Child,* xi, xiv.

43. Craig S. Womack, *Red on Red: Native American Literary Separatism* (Minneapolis: University of Minnesota Press, 1999).

44. Ibid., 301.

CHAPTER 2: AN ASIDE

1. William Jones's *Fox Texts* was published by the American Ethnology Society (Vol. 1; Leyden: E. J. Brill) as early as 1907. Jones went on to write *Kickapoo Tales* (Leyden: E. J. Brill; New York: G. E. Stechert, 1915) and *Ojibwa Texts* (Leyden: E. J. Brill; New York: G. E. Stechert, 1917). *Wolf That I Am: In Search of the Red Earth People* was written by Fred McTaggart in 1976, originally published by Houghton-Mifflin and reprinted in 1984 by the University of Oklahoma Press with a new foreword by William T. Hagan. It had been McTaggart's doctoral dissertation, which was inspired by his reading of *Black Elk Speaks* by Nebraska professor of English and humanities

John Neihardt (*Black Elk Speaks: Being the Life Story of a Holy Man of the Oglala Sioux* (1932; Lincoln: University of Nebraska Press, 1988). McTaggart was said to be half Mesquawkie and a speaker of the tribal language but the work reads like the work of a white scholar's intrusion into a "foreign" land, which is probably what inspired Young Bear's response. It is said that the Mesquawkie didn't tell McTaggart much about oral traditional literature but gave him a sense of himself. R. David Edmunds and Joseph L. Peyser's *The Fox Wars: The Mesquakie Challenge to New France* (Norman: University of Oklahoma Press, 1993) is another scholarly source of history.

2. Frank Cushing, "Outlines of Zuñi Creation Myths," in the *Thirteenth Annual Report, 1891–92* (Washington, D.C.: Smithsonian Institute, American Bureau of Ethnology, 1896), 421.

3. Natalie Curtis Burlin, *The Indians' Book* (New York: Harper and Brothers, 1907).

4. Sophia Alice Callahan, *Wynema: A Child of the Forest* (Chicago. E. A. Weeks, 1891); Simon Pokagon, *Queen of the Woods* (Hartford, Mich.: C. H. Engle, 1899); Christine Quintasket (Mourning Dove), *Cogewea, the Half-Blood: A Depiction of the Great Montana Cattle Range* (Lincoln: University of Nebraska Press, 1927); John Joseph Mathews, *Sundown* (New York: Longmans, Green, 1934); D'Arcy McNickle, *The Surrounded* (New York: Dodd, Mead, 1936).

5. Amos One Road and Alanson Skinner, *Being Dakota: Tales and Traditions of the Sisseton and Wahpeton,* ed. Laura L. Anderson (St. Paul: Minnesota Historical Society Press, 2003).

6. Ella Deloria, *Dakota Texts* (New York: G. E. Stechert, 1932).

7. A. LaVonne Ruoff, ed., *American Indian Literatures: An Introduction, Bibliographic Review, and Selected Bibliography* (New York: Modern Language Association of America, 1990).

8. Robert Rebein, *Hicks, Tribes and Dirty Realists: American Fiction after Postmodernism* (Lexington: University Press of Kentucky, 2001), 136.

9. Ted Solotaroff, "Writing in the Cold," *The New American Review* (1985).

10. Bernd Peyer, *The Tutor'd Mind: Indian Missionary-Writers in Antebellum America* (Amherst: University of Massachusetts Press, 1997), 20, ch. 1.

11. Linda Tuhiwai Smith, *Decolonizing Methodologies,* 20.

12. Richard Rorty, *Philosophy and Social Hope* (New York: Penguin, 1999), 142.

13. Allan Bloom, *The Closing of the American Mind: How Higher Education Has Failed Democracy and Impoverished the Souls of Today's Children* (New York: Simon and Schuster, 1987); Michael S. Moore, "A Natural Law Theory of Interpretation," *Southern California Law Review* 58 (1985): 277–398.

14. Rorty, *Philosophy and Social Hope,* 93.

15. Ray A. Young Bear, *Remnants of the First Earth* (New York: Grove Press, 1996), 241.

16. Ibid., 112.

17. *God Is Red* has been available from Fulcrum Press since 1992.

18. N. Scott Momaday, *The Way to Rainy Mountain* (Albuquerque: University of New Mexico Press, 1969).

19. Ibid., 122.

CHAPTER 3: WARRIORS, STILL?

1. Elizabeth Cook-Lynn, "America's Iraq Attack and Back to the Indian Wars!" *Wicazo Sa Review* 11, no. 1 (Spring 1995).

2. Jean Edward Smith, *John Marshall, Definer of a Nation* (New York: Henry Holt, 1996). Marshall's decisions were never about Indians; rather, they were obsessive about federal power and the power of the Supreme Court, in conflict with states' rights.

3. Richard Drinnon, *Facing West: The Metaphysics of Indian-Hating and Empire-Building* (Minneapolis: University of Minnesota Press, 1980).

4. Elizabeth Cook-Lynn, *I Remember the Fallen Trees: New and Selected Poems* (Cheney: Eastern Washington University Press, 1998), 28–29.

5. For further reading on this fiasco, consult newmedia.colorado.edu or the vast journalistic covering of the story in the *Rocky Mountain News* (Boulder, Colorado). In an example of how hairy citizenship issues concerning American Indians can get, in 2005, longtime University of Colorado professor of ethnic studies and political activist Ward Churchill (under investigation for plagiarism and research misconduct) was called upon to prove that he was an Indian, one of the criteria said to have been used by the university to hire him in the department. His reply to the university was that he met three of the four criteria for determining whether he is an Indian: (1) self-identification; (2) acceptance within the Indian community; and (3) tribal affiliation, none of which require proof of Indian parentage. He didn't say what the fourth criterion was. He also, in news interviews, said that when he was ten years old, his mother and grandmother passed on to him the family "lore" of Indian ancestry in the Cherokee tribe. Despite the mounting evidence that Churchill isn't Indian (according to the *Rocky Mountain News*, June 10, 2005), academic "experts differ on whether it would constitute misconduct for him to pass as one." This whole episode, which quickly became the subject of cartoons in native news organs, clearly illustrates the condition of citizenship rights of American Indians in America, since most agree that one cannot claim to be a citizen of the United States, France, Germany, or any other nation on the globe, without proof. The erosion of tribal nation citizenship rights has become a travesty in the past three or four decades. (It is an outrageous fallacy that family "lore" seems to be acceptable as citizenship criteria in a tribal nation but it comes about because Indians are thought to constitute mere sociological phenomena, not nationhood.) As far as anyone knows, the Cherokee Nation has not given up the indigenous right to say who their "members" or "citizens" are, but "experts," including Churchill, apparently differ on what that means. Universities seem to make no distinction between human rights and citizenship rights, as far

as Indians are concerned. It is one of the tragedies of our times that the essential right of citizenship for American Indians can be hijacked by anyone who grows his hair long and claims "family lore." It is a violation of sovereignty and becomes the breeding ground for other violations.

6. *Rocky Mountain News*, June 10, 2005.

7. This essay is a shortened version of a keynote lecture presented at Michigan State University's fourth annual Race in the Twenty-First Century conference held April 6–8, 2005, in Lansing, Michigan.

CHAPTER 4: THE PITFALLS OF TELLING TRIBAL HISTORIES

1. *Lewis and Clark Diaries.*

2. Sherman Alexie, *The Toughest Indian in the World* (New York: Atlantic Monthly Press, 2000), 21; Sherman Alexie, "What Sacagawea Means to Me (and Perhaps to You)," Viewpoint, *Time*, July 8, 2002, 42. Alexie is to Indian Country what Larry McMurtry is to Texas, perhaps, a figure in a broad landscape, a rare and exceedingly accessible writer who becomes a "tourist" attraction.

3. Gayatri Chakravorty Spivak, *A Critique of Postcolonial Reason: Toward a History of the Vanishing Present* (Cambridge, Mass.: Harvard University Press, 1999), 95. Spivak is the Avalon Foundation Professor in the Humanities at Columbia University and author of many books including *In Other Worlds: Essays in Cultural Politics* (New York: Methuen, 1987), which sheds much light on the works of writers who want to move out of the colonial condition.

4. Alan Wolfe, "A Fascist Philosopher Helps Us Understand Contemporary Politics," *Chronicle of Higher Education*, April 2, 2004, B16.

5. James Welch, *The Heartsong of Charging Elk: A Novel* (New York: Doubleday, 2000).

6. Stephen Greenblatt, *Marvelous Possessions: The Wonder of the New World* (Chicago: University of Chicago Press, 1991), 110.

7. Richard Drinnon, *Facing West: The Metaphysics of Indian-Hating and Empire-Building* (Minneapolis: University of Minnesota Press, 1980), 223.

8. Octave Mannoni, *Prospero and Caliban: The Psychology of Colonization* (London: Methuen, 1956).

9. *Washington Post*, September 20–26, 2004, national weekly edition, 34.

10. Fiona Watson, Stephen Corry, and Caroline Pearce, *Disinherited: Indians in Brazil* (London: Survival International, 2000), 11.

11. Quoted on www.survival-international.org.

12. Frantz Fanon, *The Wretched of the Earth*, trans. Constance Farrington (New York: Grove Press, 1963).

13. Ania Loomba, *Colonialism/Postcolonialism* (New York: Routledge, 1998).

14. Helen Hunt Jackson, *A Century of Dishonor: A Sketch of the United States Gov-*

ernment's Dealings with Some of the Indian Tribes (Williamstown, Mass.: Corner House, 1881); reprinted as *A Century of Dishonor: The Early Crusade for Indian Reform* (New York: Harper and Row, 1965).

15. *The Legends of Fool Soldiers: The Santee War.* These topics can be perused at the Klein Museum in Mobridge, South Dakota. Another reference is the *Chronicles of American Indian Protest* (Greenwich, Conn.: Fawcett, Council on Interracial Books, 1971).

16. Documents of Doane and Will Robinson, 1904–5, Department of History Collections, State Historical Society, Pierre, South Dakota (hereafter SDSHS). There is a rather lengthy discussion of this entire episode in these collections; see vol. 11 (*Sioux Indians*), ch. 25, 253 (Aberdeen, S.D.: News Printing, 1904).

17. Ibid., vol. 11, 313, 323.

18. Georg Lichtenberg (1742–1799) was an eighteenth-century German professor of science. The quote appears in *The Lichtenberg Reader: Selected Writings* (Boston: Beacon Press, 1959); see also Lichtenberg's *The Waste Books* (1990; New York: New York Review Books, 2000). The years of "attrition," when Indians were starving and suffering from constant warfare and attack by the U.S. military, brought about a longing in the hearts of some of the colonizers for some kind of equal treatment for native peoples, but it did not prevent the horrendous theft of land and subsequent poverty in the treaty agreements that were reached. It was said by some treaty commissioners that putting money in the hands of those so unaccustomed to commerce would be a catastrophe. There is much need for research into these ideas of charity toward natives and the treaty process.

19. Robinson documents, 1904–5, SDSHS, vol. 11 (*Sioux Indians*), 305.

20. An earlier version of this critique was published in James Riding In and Elizabeth Cook-Lynn's "Editor's Commentary," *Wicazo Sa Review* 19, no. 1 (Spring 2004): 5–10. This event was also the subject of discussion by the Oak Lake Writers' Society, a Dakota/Lakota writers' group, when a member of the South Dakota Peace and Justice Center in Aberdeen introduced it as a potential curriculum choice and asked the native writers' group its opinion. The group did not give its endorsement, saying that it was not appropriate for a "reconciliation" project. Several writing projects have emerged from this discussion, including an unpublished manuscript edited by Kim Tall Bear and Craig Howe.

21. Loomba, *Colonialism/Postcolonialism*, 76.

22. Virginia Driving Hawk Sneve, *South Dakota Geographic Names* (Sioux Falls, S.D.: Brevet Press, 1973); *Betrayed* (New York: Holiday House, 1974); *Grandpa Was a Cowboy and an Indian and Other Stories* (Lincoln: University of Nebraska Press, 2000).

23. For more information about the story, see the collections at the South Dakota Department of Highways; the South Dakota Historical Society, Pierre; the Northern Oahe Historical Society, Mobridge, South Dakota; and the Klein Museum, Mobridge,

South Dakota. The words on the monument are taken from a printed pamphlet available at the Klein Museum, located next to a Church of God family worship center and three tipis.

24. Drinnon, *Facing West*, 223.

25. Felix S. Cohen, *Handbook of Federal Indian Law* (Washington, D.C.: U.S. Department of the Interior, Office of the Solicitor, 1941). See also Philip P. Frickey's "A Common Law for Our Age of Colonialism: The Judicial Divestiture of Indian Tribal Authority over Nonmembers," *Yale Law Journal* 109, no. 1 (1999): 1–86. Much material surrounding all of this history can be found by reading in the historical archives in the South Dakota State Library in Pierre, although these archives are not critical of the colonial aspects of Indian history.

26. David Wilkins, *American Indian Sovereignty and the U.S. Supreme Court: The Masking of Justice* (Austin: University of Texas Press, 1997).

27. Few studies have been compiled to understand how this kind of history is taught, but Russell Thornton, a professor of anthropology at UCLA and a longtime analyst of Native Studies as an academic discipline, has started the obvious compilation of courses and programs that might be developed. His essay on the development of Native American Studies programs is a review of the works in the field of Native Studies sponsored by universities throughout the United States. It is entitled "Institutional and Intellectual Histories of Native American Studies," in *Studying Native America: Problems and Prospects* (Madison: University of Wisconsin Press, 1998), 79, and it suggests that the critique of history provides a monumental task for future scholars and researchers. Thornton's study is a result of research sponsored by the American Indian Studies Advisory Panel of the Social Science Research Council.

CHAPTER 5: DEFENSIVE, REGULATORY, AND TRANSFORMATIVE FUNCTIONS OF INDIAN STUDIES

1. Russell Thornton, "Institutional and Intellectual Histories of Native American Studies," in *Studying Native America: Problems and Prospects* (Madison: University of Wisconsin Press, 1998).

2. The constitution and bylaws are available through the Indian Studies Department at Arizona State University, Tempe, Arizona. Contact Dr. James Riding In, fax number 480–965–2216.

3. Alfonso Ortiz, *The Tewa World: Space, Time, Being, and Becoming in a Pueblo Society* (1972; Chicago: University of Chicago Press, 1969).

4. Elizabeth Cook-Lynn and Craig Howe, "The Dialectics of Ethnicity in America: A View from American Indian Studies," in *Color-Line to Borderlands: The Matrix of American Ethnic Studies*, ed. Johnnella E. Butler, 150–68 (Seattle: University of Washington Press, 2001).

5. Linda Tuhiwai Smith, *Decolonizing Methodologies: Research and Indigenous Peo-*

ples (London and New York: Zed Books, 1999; Dunedin, New Zealand: University of Otago Press).

6. Ortiz, *Tewa World;* Ronald Goodman, ed., *Lakota Star Knowledge: Studies in Lakota Stellar Theology,* 2nd ed. (Rosebud, S.D.: Sinte Gleska University, 1992).

7. Roxanne Dunbar Ortiz chaired an early disciplinary meeting of Indian Studies at University of California, Los Angeles.

8. This speech is unpublished. My source is notes I took at a speech given by Russel Jim at a 1978 meeting of the Northwest Affiliated Tribes at Lapwai, Idaho.

9. The Black Hills land case can be researched in many sources; one of the most recent is Mario Gonzalez and Elizabeth Cook-Lynn, *The Politics of Hallowed Ground: Wounded Knee and the Struggle for Indian Sovereignty* (Urbana: University of Illinois Press, 1999).

10. Frederick Jackson Turner, a history professor, read this groundbreaking theoretical paper to a national history association in 1893, and it became known as the "Turner Thesis" and was a highly influential discourse. He said that the wars were done (the 1890 massacre at Wounded Knee was already just a memory), the "frontier" was closed forever, the Indian was gone forever, all acting merely as a "stage" in Western history. Now, historians said, America could get on to bigger and better things. The Turner Thesis became set in stone for many American historians for most of the following century; the Indian became the "vanishing" American. Patricia Nelson Limerick, in *The Legacy of Conquest: The Unbroken Past of the American West* (New York: W. W. Norton, 1987) a hundred years later, questioned the theory and asked for a reconsideration of Western history. Classically trained historians have been slow to take on the task.

11. An interesting analysis of the Bakke Case can be read in Howard Ball's *The Bakke Case: Race, Education, and Affirmative Action* (Lawrence: University Press of Kansas, 2000); the author is said to be a veteran of the civil rights movement. He suggests that the legacy of the Bakke case is that "it allows educators to take good-faith measures, without resorting to quotas, to diversify their student, faculty, and staff populations" (206). For someone like me who would *never have had a career* as a college professor or a public voice as a native scholar without legalized affirmative actions on the part of the government and the law that forced the institutions of this country to act affirmatively, Ball's conclusion is not a comforting one.

12. Taiaiake Alfred, *Peace, Power, Righteousness: An Indigenous Manifesto* (New York: Oxford University Press, 1999); Tuhiwai Smith, *Decolonizing Methodologies.*

13. Some of this discussion about how to define genocide is excerpted from Elizabeth Cook-Lynn, *Anti-Indianism in Modern America: A Voice from Tatekeya's Earth* (Urbana: University of Illinois Press, 2001).

14. Survival for Tribal Peoples, www.survival-international.org.

CHAPTER 6: THE STRUGGLE FOR CULTURAL HERITAGE

1. Robert F. Berkhofer Jr., *The White Man's Indian: Images of the American Indians from Columbus to the Present* (New York: Vintage Books, 1978).

2. Angela Cavender Wilson's works are published in tribally specific research; Taiaiake Alfred, *Peace, Power, Righteousness: An Indigenous Manifesto* (Don Mills, Ontario: Oxford University Press).

3. André Malraux, "The Cultural Heritage," *New Republic* 88, no. 21 (October 1936).

4. Patrick Tierney, *Darkness in El Dorado: How Scientists and Journalists Devastated the Amazon* (New York: W. W. Norton, 2000).

5. Ron Robin, *Scandals and Scoundrels: Seven Cases That Shook the Academy* (Berkeley: University of California Press, 2004), 164.

6. Napoleon Chagnon, *Yanomamö, the Fierce People* (New York: Holt, Rinehart, and Winston, 1968).

7. David Hurst Thomas, *Skull Wars: Kennewick Man, Archaeology, and the Battle for Native American Identity* (New York: Basic Books, 2000).

8. Vine Deloria Jr., *Red Earth, White Lies: Native Americans and the Myth of Scientific Fact* (New York: Fulcrum, 1997).

9. Shepard Krech III, *The Ecological Indian: Myth and History* (New York: W. W. Norton, 1999).

10. Fergus M. Bordewich, *Killing the White Man's Indian: Reinventing of Native Americans at the End of the Twentieth Century* (New York: Doubleday, 1996), 339.

11. David Edmonds and John Eidinow, *Wittgenstein's Poker: The Story of a Ten-Minute Argument between Two Great Philosophers* (New York: Ecco, 2001). The charm that Ludwig Wittgenstein has held over contemporary scholarship in philosophy is partly a result, one supposes, of his tortured life as a homosexual in Vienna, but also because he gave authority to the idea that his philosophic ideas could not be separated from his personal life and spirituality. This is often called "solipsism" and is said by some critical scholars to be an examination of excessive ego, among other things that seek out connections to Freudianism. Wittgenstein is considered one of the geniuses of nineteenth-century European philosophic thought. Many of today's American Indian scholars, because of graduate school influence in various disciplines, find the study of Wittgenstein's work useful for the examination of "identity" issues.

12. Steve Fiffer, *Tyrannosaurus Sue: The Extraordinary Saga of the Largest, Most Fought Over T. Rex Ever Found* (New York: W. H. Freeman, 2000). Fiffer is an attorney who was largely taken in by Peter Larson, the self-educated and self-made fossil hunter from the Black Hills Institute, Hill City, South Dakota who found the bones and defended his right to the find because he could see what was there and how valuable it was. He paid Maurice Williams, the Cheyenne River Sioux Indian rancher on whose land it was found a mere $5,000 for bones that he knew were worth millions. The following conversation started the whole ball rolling: Maurice Williams: "You

are going to mount her in Hill City (where Larson had a tourist collection)." Larson answers, "Yeah," and then Williams says, "Good" (pause). "And under that you'll write, stolen from Maurice Williams." They both knew that the real fight for this treasure was just starting. The Fiffer book is an attorney's account of the event.

13. It is probably worth noting that Gorton was considered by many, even his supporters, to be the foremost anti-Indian legislator in the U.S. Senate from Washington State until he was defeated a few years ago. He was a member of the 9/11 Commission in 2003–4, which received universal acclaim for putting out a public report concerning the attack on the Twin Towers in New York and the Pentagon in Washington, D.C., by Middle Eastern terrorists. Some have suggested that the report has ended up defending the questionable actions of the second Bush administration concerning the initial causes and the aftermath of the attack. Later assessment of that report, which appeared in the October 2004 issue of *Harper's Magazine*, called it a "whitewash." Indeed, Benjamin DeMott wrote in that article that the commission report was "a cheat and a fraud" in the name of "patriotic good conscience." No one in Indian Country has been surprised because this latest revelation concerning public policy simply tells us something that we have all known: the Republican Party, and the Republic, must be protected at all cost, and former elected officials like Gorton are often pressed into service to suppress any information that may be damaging to the national ideal. Almost single-handedly, Gorton was responsible for the U.S. government's victory in *Oliphant v. Suquamish Tribe*, the most devastating attack on Indian sovereignty in the twentieth century.

14. Alan M. Dershowitz, *Supreme Injustice: How the High Court Hijacked Election 2000* (New York: Oxford University Press, 2001).

15. David E. Wilkins, *American Indian Sovereignty and the U.S. Supreme Court: The Masking of Justice* (Austin: University of Texas Press, 1997).

16. "State to Appeal Lower Brule Land Decision," *The Native Voice* (Rapid City, S.D.) 3, no. 13 (June 28–July 11, 2004), A102. The South Dakota State attorney general's office (no matter which political party) considers it a sworn duty to appeal every decision and block every move the tribes make toward self-government and economic security. Putting land back in "trust" by the tribes is always considered a violation of states' rights.

17. To read more on this, see in David E. Wilkins and K. Tsianina Lomawaima, *Uneven Ground: American Indian Sovereignty and Federal Law* (Norman: University of Oklahoma Press, 2001), 107.

CHAPTER 7: THE GHOSTS OF AMERICAN HISTORY IN ART AND LITERATURE

1. Letters to the editor, *New York Times*, April 11, 2002, A30.

2. Elizabeth Cook-Lynn, "From the River's Edge," in *Aurelia: A Crow Creek Trilogy* (Boulder: University Press of Colorado, 1999), 7–141.

3. Elizabeth Cook-Lynn, *I Remember the Fallen Trees: New and Selected Poems* (Cheney: Eastern Washington University Press, 1998), 12.

4. Ibid., 35.

5. Ibid., 35–36.

6. Ibid., 36–37.

CONCLUSION

1. Vine Deloria Jr. and David E. Wilkins, *Tribes, Treaties, and Constitutional Tribulations* (Austin: University of Texas Press, 1999), 133.

2. Ibid., 132–33.

3. *The Wicazo Sa Review* 4, no. 1 (Spring 1988): 10. Referenced here are several articles that give points of view concerning the conflict, and they can be accessed and read by scholars and student problem solvers. These articles were first published as a collection in the *Wicazo Sa Review* as a case study to be utilized by native communities to understand the long-standing case law that surrounds this issue. Since then, several collections have appeared and can be accessed at the follow Web site: http://www.lakotaarchives.com.laklandor.html. See also readings from the *Wicazo Sa Review* on the Black Hills case, litigation, and maps; essays by Frank Pommersheim, "On the Cusp of History" and "Brown Hat's Vision," can be found in Mario Gonzalez and Elizabeth Cook-Lynn's *The Politics of Hallowed Ground: Wounded Knee and the Struggle for Indian Sovereignty* (Urbana: University of Illinois Press, 1999), a study that is a good source for facts and interpretations.

4. Act of August 15, 1876, ch. 289, 19 Stat. 176, 192.

5. Act of February 28, 1877, ch. 71, 19 Stat. 254.

6. Edward Lazarus, *Black Hills/White Justice: The Sioux Nation versus the United States, 1775 to the Present* (New York: Harper Collins, 1991).

7. I am grateful to Mahmood Mamdani and his book *Good Muslim, Bad Muslim: America, the Cold War, and the Roots of Terror* (New York: Pantheon, 2004) for some of the final thoughts in this manuscript.

ELIZABETH COOK-LYNN, a member of the Crow Creek
Sioux tribe, is professor emerita of Native American Studies
at Eastern Washington University, a writer, and a poet.
Her books include *Anti-Indianism in Modern America:
A Voice from Tatekeya's Earth, The Politics of Hallowed
Ground: Wounded Knee and the Struggle for Indian Sovereignty*
(with Mario Gonzalez), *Aurelia: A Crow Creek Trilogy,* and
*"Why I Can't Read Wallace Stegner" and Other Essays: A Tribal
Voice,* winner of the Gustavus Myers Center Award for the
Study of Human Rights in North America.

The University of Illinois Press
is a founding member of the
Association of American University Presses.

———————————————

Composed in 10.5/13 Adobe Minion
with Super Duty Heavy display
by Jim Proefrock
at the University of Illinois Press
Designed by Dennis Roberts
Manufactured by Thomson-Shore, Inc.

University of Illinois Press
1325 South Oak Street
Champaign, IL 61820-6903
www.press.uillinois.edu